the Creative Storytelling Guide

for Children's Ministry

Steven James

Standard PUBLISHING

CINCINNATI, OHIO

• Special Thanks •

To Dr. Flora Joy, for her insights into using storytelling in the classroom; to Sir G, Mountain Mike, and Uncle Rich for telling stories to me; to Mark Collins, for his friendship, thoughtful questions, and insightful suggestions; to the children's ministry staff at Grace Fellowship Church, for telling God's story to my daughters; to INCM, for their encouragement and ministry; to Grant Miller, for letting me use his office; and to Miracles Coffee House, for free refills.

• Dedication •

Dedicated to children's ministry directors, pastors, volunteers, and teachers.
Thanks for all you do in sharing God's love with the next generation!

Standard Publishing, Cincinnati 45231
A division of Standex International Corporation
© 2002 by Steven James. All rights reserved.
Printed in the United States of America.

09   08   07   06   05   04   03   02   9   8   7   6   5   4   3   2

ISBN: 0-7847-1374-X

Edited by Theresa Hayes
Cover design by Joel Armstrong
Cover and inside illustrations by Paula Becker
Inside design by Robert Korth

Table of Contents

When All Your Brain Wants to Do Is Fly!

DANNY WAS PRETENDING to be an airplane. He buzzed around the cabin, dive-bombing the other campers. He soared along the camp trails with outstretched arms, shooting down imaginary enemy fighters. Everywhere we went, Danny flew away from the group. At first it was cute, but then it got annoying. I was his counselor, so I was responsible for making sure he didn't crash.

Our group arrived late for every activity. Danny was always absent when we were ready to leave. After searching the area, I'd find him running around the field dodging clouds (which looked an awful lot like trees) sputtering airplane noises.

"Come on Danny, we've gotta get to lunch," I would say, redirecting his flight path toward the dining hall.

"Vroom!" he would say.

Finally, on the fourth day of camp I pulled him aside. "Listen, Danny, you've gotta be more responsible. You need to start listening more carefully. When we're going to an activity you can't run off somewhere to fly around. You have to stay with the group. Do you understand?"

"You mean I can't fly around anymore?" A tremor rose in his voice.

"Well, you can fly around as long as you don't fly away from the group. We have to do things together."

Danny nodded slowly.

By three o'clock that afternoon I'd already reminded him of our conversation five times. Then when we were walking back to the cabin from craft time he roared off again, arms outstretched, across the field. "Come back, Danny!" I called. He turned, saw me, and smiled. Then he began sprinting away from me as fast as he could, laughing with delight.

That was it. The last straw. I was not going to let him manipulate me. I was going to show him who was the boss!

"Danny!" I shouted, "Come back here right now!" When he ignored me, I told Carl, the other counselor, to watch the campers on the way back to the cabin. I was going after Danny.

Danny beat me back to the cabin. I pounded onto the porch, banged open the door, and stomped inside. "Where are you, Danny?" The cabin appeared to be deserted. I scanned the room, pausing to look closely at his bed to see if he'd crawled into the hangar.

"Danny?" Only one place in the cabin had eluded my search—the counselor's closet. I yanked open the door. And there, cowering in the corner of the closet, was Danny.

That's when I lost it. Oh, I didn't physically hurt him, but I said those things we're all tempted to say when we finally reach the end of our ropes. You know the things. You've said them.

I finished by saying, "Danny, I'm upset with you! Why do you keep disobeying me? Why are you always flying away from the group when you know it's naughty? What's going on?"

His eyes glistened as he looked down at the floor. Heavy tears began rolling down his cheeks. "I'm sorry," he said.

At that point, I was sorry, too. I realized I'd been too harsh, lost my temper. I knelt down beside him and said, "Look, I forgive you. I'm not angry. But why do you keep running away from our group?" He looked up and peered into my eyes searching for someone who would understand, who could understand. And then he said the words that took root in my heart. That changed forever the way I would look at education and working with children.

"But Steve," he said, "it's hard for your body to slow down when all your brain wants to do is fly."

Danny's mind wanted to fly and his body couldn't help but follow. And all week I'd been trying to control his body without taking the time to understand his mind. I'd been trying to ground him instead of helping him take off. I finally sputtered something like, "The next time your brain wants to fly, let me know. I'll let you fly out toward the end of the horizon as long as you come back in time for supper."

As I gave him a hug I thought, *He's right. It is hard for your body to slow down when all your brain wants to do is fly . . . but what's the answer?*

> *"Men . . . hardly stir except when jolted by imagination."*
> —Pascal, 17th century philosopher

I think Jesus would have liked teaching Danny. Not only did Jesus love kids, he loved using his imagination!

"Jesus spoke all these things to the crowd in parables; he did not say anything to them without using a parable" (Matthew 13:34).

Jesus would have found a way to let Danny's brain, and his body, fly. And, now, after many years of telling stories and teaching children myself, I'm convinced that we can, too. As Christian educators touching the lives of children, you and I are God's storytellers! Look at our call to teach and tell stories in Psalm 78:

"I will open my mouth in parables, I will utter hidden things, things from of old—what we have heard and known, what our fathers have told us. . . . We will tell the next generation the praiseworthy deeds of the Lord, his power, and the wonders he has done. . . . Then they would put their trust in God and would not forget his deeds but would keep his commands" (Psalm 78:2-4, 7).

- See the creative teaching technique? Parables!
- And where do we get these stories? From what we have heard and known (experience, tradition, and Scripture)!
- To whom do we tell them? The next generation!
- What do we tell stories about? The deeds of the Lord, his power, and the wonders he has done!
- Why do we tell them? So that the next generation can trust in God and keep his commands!

You've been chosen to pass on God's story to the next generation. What an amazing honor, privilege and responsibility! This book will equip you to tell stories in a way that will help your students' brains (and bodies) fly!

How to Use This Book

This book has something I've never seen in any other book—a complete workshop on each chapter that *you can use* to share this information with other teachers or educators. Each workshop includes helpful leader's notes for you, activities, discussion points, and—best of all—copyright permission so you can photocopy handouts for your participants! *That's fifteen ready-made educational workshops in one book!*

Although you may wish to read this book from cover to cover, I suggest that you begin by reading through the first section (chapters one through five). Then choose chapters from the rest of the book that apply to you and read them in any order you wish. You may also flip to the back of the book and read the workshop material for each chapter for more information.

If you're anything like me, you don't want to be overwhelmed by theories that have never been tested. And you don't want to be spoon-fed precisely what to say. I just want you to grow into being a better storyteller, communicator, and teacher. So, in this book, you won't find a hundred paraphrased Bible stories to read aloud, cut out, make into crafts, or eat. On the other hand, you won't need a seminary degree or a Ph.D. to decipher the concepts. And you won't continually be told things you already know. Instead, you'll learn how to become a better storyteller. A better speaker. A better teacher. Period.

Some educators want things made as easy as possible (the practical people), others want to be taught the principles of effective education so they can apply them their own way (the theoretical people). Whichever kind of educator you are, you'll find something specifically for you in this book.

- Section one contains theory and application mixed together to give you a good foundation for creating and telling your stories.
- Section two contains dozens of examples of creative storytelling techniques you can implement in your classroom, today (more practical stuff).
- Section three contains in-depth coverage and explanations of advanced storytelling skills (more theoretical stuff).

This book was born of experience. The examples, illustrations, and techniques are plucked from thousands of hours of actual storytelling and teaching. They weren't just made up to fill pages. They were included because they work. And they will make you a better storyteller. So, if you're ready to be inspired and challenged to become the best storyteller you can be, read on and let's get started!

And may God bless your efforts as you (and your brain) fly to new heights!

> "All you have made will praise you, O Lord; your saints will extol you.
> They will tell of the glory of your kingdom and speak of your might,
> so that all men may know of your mighty acts and the glorious splendor
> of your kingdom" (Psalm 145:10-12).

Preflight: Preparing for Takeoff

Just as a pilot looks over the controls and safety checklists before taxiing down the runway, a storyteller also prepares before launching into a story. Every orally told story has four ingredients: the storyteller, the story, the audience, and the setting in which the storytelling occurs. So in this first section you'll discover ways to prepare yourself, your story, your listeners, and the teaching (or performance) space. You'll also learn how to begin practicing the stories you want to tell.

In this section you'll find helpful hints on
- overcoming stage fright;
- gaining confidence in your ability as a storyteller;
- connecting with your audience;
- matching your story expectations with those of your audience;
- understanding what makes a good story;
- drawing the truth out of Bible stories you wish to tell;
- remembering and rehearsing stories;
- removing distractions from the storytelling event;
- finding the best place to stand or sit as you tell stories;
- making the most of rehearsal time.

If you're ready, let's take off!

Chapter 1

Preparing Yourself

Overcoming Five Myths About Becoming a Storyteller

YOU'RE IN THE MIDDLE of your lesson when all of a sudden you realize it's that time again—time for the Bible story. You sigh, thinking, *If only I were a better storyteller! Then I could really keep the kids' attention.* But, since you don't really feel like a natural storyteller, you decide to just read the story as it appears in your curriculum. You paste a smile on your face and plow forward. But deep down, you really wish you could put the book aside and tell the story yourself.

Well, you can!

As a Christian educator, God has entrusted you with the message of Christ's love and sacrifice. It's your privilege and responsibility to share that message, to plant seeds of the Good News in the hearts of the children you teach. It's the Holy Spirit's job to make those seeds grow. We don't have to be brilliant scholars or master storytellers. We simply need to be faithful and humble messengers!

In this chapter, we will examine five myths about storytelling that many educators believe. You'll also discover practical steps you can take to better prepare yourself to learn and to tell the stories of God. You'll improve your storytelling, gain confidence, and prepare stories in less time.

Myth One: "I'm not a storyteller!"

You may not get paid to write novels, perform one-person plays, direct movies, or preach sermons, but if you're a member of the human race, you're already a storyteller! Human beings communicate and think in stories. We understand our lives by seeing the way our story connects with the stories of others and the stories of God. We remember in stories. Pastors and great teachers know this, that's why they pepper their messages with stories to illustrate their points!

Try this. Try to remember a place you've lived, a person you've worked for, a vacation you've been on, or the loss of something you cared about without remembering a story. It's almost impossible! Researchers who study intelligence are discovering what most of us already know; we don't remember things very well unless they're connected to other things within the structure of—you guessed it—a story.

Everyone is a storyteller. From the way we think to the way we communicate, our lives are saturated with stories. And every time you tell your spouse about your day, pass on a joke, reminisce about the good old days, or rehash the game, you're telling a story. Don't be afraid or ashamed to think of yourself as a storyteller! Admitting that you're already a storyteller is a big step toward feeling comfortable sharing stories with your students.

Myth Two:
"I'm not a good enough speaker to be a storyteller!"

God doesn't rely on eloquence to get his message across. When God called Moses to speak before Pharaoh, Moses complained that he wasn't a gifted communicator. Eventually, God allowed Aaron to be Moses' spokesperson, but God's desire was for Moses to rely on God's Spirit rather than on himself, or his brother! When Jesus chose his disciples, did he choose the most gifted speakers of his day? No! He chose people with very little expertise and experience in public speaking, and look at what they did with God's help!

When Paul went to preach to the people in Corinth, he was completely focused. He wasn't interested in impressing them with his wisdom or wowing them with his eloquence. Instead, he wrote, "I came to you in weakness and fear, and with much trembling. My message and my preaching were not with wise and persuasive words, but with a demonstration of the Spirit's power, so that your faith might not rest on men's wisdom, but on God's power" (1 Corinthians 2:3-5). Weak. Fearful. Trembling. Without wisdom or eloquence. But *with* a reliance on God and his power to change lives. That was Paul's storytelling technique!

Start the process of preparing yourself to tell stories by remembering that you're not here to impress people, or even to simply entertain them. Your goal is to humbly and faithfully share with them the message of hope found in Jesus Christ. And if you're fearful or lack wisdom or eloquence (but are ready to rely on and demonstrate the Spirit's power in your life) then you're perfectly qualified to be one of God's storytellers.

Start by relying on the Spirit's power rather than your own. Then turn to God in prayer. God has promised to hear and answer all prayers that are prayed according to his will. And since we know that sharing his story is his will, he will answer your humble requests for help in story preparation! Then trust that God will use you when you submit yourself to him. Just like he used Paul. And the disciples. And Moses.

And many, many others.

Myth Three: "I'm too nervous speaking in front of people!"

Paul, referring to the confidence believers had in sharing the gospel story, wrote, "Such confidence as this is ours through Christ before God. Not that we are competent in ourselves to claim anything for ourselves, but our competence comes from God" (2 Corinthians 3:4, 5). God doesn't want you to rely on yourself, but on his power working through you when you tell his story. Many times I've found that when I rely on myself, I get "Steve-sized" results, but when I rely on God, I get supernatural, "Spirit-sized" results!

Our confidence comes from God's power, purpose, and promises. Yet, reliance on the Spirit is no excuse for lack of preparation. God has given us an important responsibility as educators. Look at what James wrote, "Not many of you should presume to be teachers, my brothers, because you know that we who teach will be judged more strictly" (James 3:1). So take your job as a teacher seriously and prepare for your lessons accordingly.

One way to do this is through *thorough* preparation. It's tough to be confident doing anything if you know you weren't faithful in preparing it.

Here are a few ways to focus your preparation time and gain more confidence in the storytelling abilities God has already given you:

• **Remind** yourself that God created you as an individual with a unique spectrum of gifts, interests, and life experiences. God designed you in a specific way. He made some people soft-spoken and shy. He made others dramatic and outgoing. Your storytelling style should reflect the personality God has given you. Some people like jumping around and becoming all the characters in the story. That's great! Others are gifted at simply sharing the story in their own words. That's just as great! The most effective storytellers and teachers are always those who bring the story out of who they are, instead of pretending to be someone they're not.

• **Rehearse** your story. First, practice talking about the story and retelling it in your own words. Then tell your story whenever you can, over and over. By hearing your voice and moving your body through the story you'll learn what needs to change to improve the way you tell it. Just thinking about how you might tell the story won't do the job. Words speak louder than thoughts. Also, if you include audience participation in your story, practice making the transition into and out of those story sections.

• **Review** your story. Practice walking up, introducing yourself (if necessary), and beginning your story with no one else present. Stage presence is how well you carry yourself and present yourself to your listeners. Many people get nervous speaking in front of groups. So take it slowly! Get to know the story so well that you're comfortable changing, deleting, or repeating sections based on reactions from the audience. Readiness means not only preparing your story, but being prepared to respond to the audience while you're telling the story.

• **Relax** right before beginning your story. Stop worrying about what people think! Your students want you to be comfortable, successful, and at ease speaking to them. They don't want you to be scared or embarrassed or afraid. So, face your audience, use good posture, and smile at them. If you're nervous, squeeze your thumb and forefinger together and then relax. Then take a few deep breaths to compose yourself. Remember; when you relax, the story spills out.

• **Remember** the advice of Paul in 2 Corinthians 10:5, "We take captive every thought to make it obedient to Christ." Now, what does that mean? "Taking every thought captive" means that we capture, or think purposely about every dream, memory, goal, and story in our mind in order to "make it obedient to Christ." How do we make our thoughts "obedient to Christ"? By making sure that our thoughts are pleasing to God and are useful to him. All that we see, read, imagine, recall, or learn, we give to him! God wants it all. So saturate your stories with his Spirit, and let God immerse and guide your thoughts. When you yield your thoughts to him, he does amazing things!

• **Remove** distractions. Do you have keys in your pockets? Get rid of them. Remove everything from your pockets except what you need to tell the story. Is something happening behind you that will be distracting? Move to another place in the room. Remove anything that might distract you or your listeners.

Myth Four: "But I don't know any stories!"

I'm always amazed when I meet people who tell me they don't know any stories. We're immersed in hundreds of stories every day. We hear news stories on the radio as we drive to work, we witness little tragedies and comedies throughout the day, we read about current events in the newspaper, we watch stories unfold on the evening news. And then we entertain ourselves by reading books, watching movies, and going to the theater! Our lives are rich in stories. We're like fish who don't notice the water—we're so immersed in the stories that swirl around us, that we don't even notice them! We already know enough stories to last a lifetime.

Perhaps what people mean to say isn't, "I don't know any stories," but, "I can't remember any stories right now," or "I don't know any stories well enough to tell them in front of others." Focus on what you do know, rather than on what you don't. In this book you'll learn natural ways to remember stories more clearly and accurately, and you'll discover the difference between conversation and presentation. For now, let's remember that we all know many stories that can help us in our teaching.

For example, you already know . . .

- Bible stories that you've heard, read, and retold;
- personal stories that show how God has worked in your life;
- fables, legends, myths, and folktales that can be used to illustrate biblical truths and concepts.

What's the secret to remembering the stories you've heard and already know? Like starting a fire, it only takes a spark.[1] Think of your fears and dreams, your triumphs and traumas, your struggles and discoveries. And share with your students how God has impacted and affected your life.

Myth Five: "No one will listen to the stories I tell!"

One thing is safe to say—children love stories. They'd rather you tell them a story than give them a lecture any day!

Storytelling is the natural way to teach. It immediately captures the attention of the students, it helps them remember the lesson, and it allows them the chance to more easily apply truth to their lives. Believe me, the more stories you tell, the more stories your students will want to hear!

A story doesn't just touch heads, it touches hearts. Through their emotional appeal, stories don't overwhelm us, they "underwhelm" us. They sneak past our natural defenses, slip into the important parts of our hearts, and impact us with the truth.

As you develop your storytelling skills, you'll be able to make your stories more suspenseful, interesting, or humorous. But for now remind yourself, "The audience is on my side. They're not out to get me, or laugh at me, or embarrass me. They want to hear a good story. They want to learn more about Jesus!"

Summary

You are already a storyteller. God doesn't need you to be a gifted speaker. You can stop being nervous because God is the one responsible for results; your only job is to be a faithful servant. You already know enough stories to last a lifetime. And, children *will* listen to your stories! They love them!

Whew! That's a lot to chew on!

As you get ready to embark on the journey of becoming a better storyteller, here are eight practical tips to help you gain confidence telling stories.

1. Connect with your listeners.

One of the greatest compliments I ever received in my storytelling career was when a 250-pound biker dressed in a leather jacket came up to me after I'd finished telling a story about two frogs.

"Hey, storyteller," he barked. "C'mere! I wanna tell you something!"

I gulped and looked up at his rugged face. "What's that?"

"You know when you were telling that story? Well, I felt like that big fat frog. You kinda remind me of the skinny frog. Maybe I could tell that story with you. You could be the skinny one and I'll be the big one!"

Whoa! That's not what I expected him to say! Anytime you can make a 250-pound man feel like an amphibian, you know you've connected with your audience!

Remember that when you tell a story, you're telling it to real people. Part of your job as a storyteller is to relate to and respond to your listeners. Enjoy interacting with them! Flirt with the audience! Have fun, smile, laugh, shout, joke, hug, wink, or do whatever will make you and your listeners both more comfortable.

---

[1]Appendix C contains more than 385 story starters to ignite ideas for stories you can tell from your life.

2. Connect with the story.

You need to be emotionally connected to your story if it's going to have an impact on the hearts and lives of the listeners. Maybe it's the mood of the story, or the message, or the images, or the humor, or the poetry of the language that draws you in. Maybe you don't even know what it is, but the story has grabbed you and won't let you go! That's a story you should tell! Your heart is in it! If you don't care about the story, no one else will. You need a genuine passion for the stories you tell.

Sometimes, a story seems to find you. It just resonates with who you are and fits the shape of your soul. That's natural! God created each of us with certain holes that will be filled by differently shaped stories. Tell the stories that matter to you—that scream and fight and need to be told. If you aren't telling a story from your heart, it won't reach the hearts of the listeners. Remember, a story told from the head reaches the head. A story told from the heart reaches the heart. A story told from a life reaches a life.

Tell stories you can't shake. If it's a story that doesn't linger in your mind or echo in your thoughts, don't tell it. Tell the stories that matter to you.

3. Believe the story.

No one ever challenged Jesus on the truth of his stories. No one ever said, "Oh yeah, was there *really* a farmer who sowed his seeds? Did that actually *happen?*" Even when the Pharisees plotted to arrest Jesus because of a story he told (Mark 12:12), it wasn't because they didn't believe the story, but because they *knew it was true about them!* When you tell made-up fables, parables, or folktales that teach important lessons, believe them! You don't necessarily need to believe that the story actually happened, just believe that it's worth telling and speaks a truth worth hearing.

4. Trust the story.

The natural curiosity of your students is one of your greatest assets as a teacher and a storyteller. Children want to know what will happen in a story, how the story will end, and what it has to do with them. So, as you teach and tell stories, avoid the temptation to explain everything. Instead, create an atmosphere in which curiosity is encouraged, wonder is facilitated, and meaning is discovered rather than explained.

For example, if you are telling "The Good Samaritan" don't say, "Today's story is about a man who helps someone he doesn't know." Instead, spark your listeners' curiosity by asking questions that relate to the meaning of the story. Ask, "What would you do if the kid you always pick on suddenly offered to help you with your homework?"

Always wait until the end of the lesson before telling people what the lesson was about. Jesus took the time to answer the questions his followers had, but he waited until they'd had a chance to think about the story first.

5. Picture the story.

If I asked you to tell me about a time when you were in an accident, or were hospitalized, or when you were scarred in some way, you would immediately be able to do so. You wouldn't have to practice the story, you could tell it to me naturally! You can naturally remember it because you experienced it and can vividly picture what happened. It's always easier to tell a story when you can picture it in your mind.

To apply this truth to your storytelling, don't try to *memorize* stories, just visualize them, experience them in your mind so that you can tell them in your own words in a way that feels natural. Practice the introduction to your story, the beginning, and the ending, so that you don't have to concentrate on the words as much as on seeing and telling the story. As you tell the story, don't just recite words, but try to really *see* the story. As you talk about what you are picturing in your mind, your listeners will picture it as well.

Four Keys to Opening Yourself Up to Storytelling

**Key One
Open Your
Heart**

Jesus said, *"For out of the overflow of the heart the mouth speaks"* (Matthew 12:34).

As we prepare to share stories with the children we teach, we need to remember that the first step is to open up our *hearts* to God. We have his promise that his Word will not return to him without being effective (Isaiah 55:10, 11). When you prayerfully prepare your lessons, you're not alone! You can rely on the person and power of the Holy Spirit to impact the lives of your listeners when you're faithful in telling the stories of God.

Care about the story you're learning. Find a personal connection to it. If you're not passionate about learning and telling the story, your lack of zeal will show through to the audience.

**Key Two
Open Your
Mind**

"After three days they found him in the temple courts, sitting among the teachers, listening to them and asking them questions" (Luke 2:46).

"Then he opened their minds so they could understand the Scriptures" (Luke 24:45).

Even as a boy, Jesus was serious about learning God's Word. He opened his *mind* to God. Later, when he became a teacher, he still used stories and questions to inspire reflection in his followers.

Opening your mind to God means being a serious student of his Word. It also means embracing and fostering imagination and taking your job of learning stories seriously. God wants to be the one fueling our passions and igniting our dreams. He wants us to let go of our safeguards, trust wholly in his promises, and open our minds to the truth of his Word!

**Key Three
Open Your
Eyes**

Solomon noticed things. He was an astute observer of life. His dad (King David) was one of the nation's foremost poets and musicians and, like his dad, Solomon was always on the lookout for truth and for parallels between everyday situations and spiritual lessons. He knew that spiritual truth may be found everywhere, if only we have the eyes to see it.

One day, as Solomon was looking out the window, he saw a married woman flirting with a man other than her husband. He used this illustration from everyday life to teach the importance of

6. Step into the story.

Great storytellers take your hand, disappear into the story, lead you through it, and then reappear at the end. When you're watching and listening to them, you feel transported into the story yourself! Try to become part of the stories you tell. See the story happen around you. Before you tell a story, try it out. Make sure that the way it's told fits you as a storyteller and fits your listeners as an audience. Some stories won't be a good fit. They may need to be modified so that they feel natural for you to tell and really connect with your audience. Then, as you tell the story, step into it and become part of it.

7. Strive for excellence, not perfection.

Too many people try to tell "the perfect story." I've told thousands of hours of stories and have yet to tell one perfectly. Be faithful. Be prepared. Do the best you can. But don't worry about getting the story "right." One of the wonderful things about storytelling is that everyone adds a part of himself to the story he tells. Let the story change itself to fit the audience and atmosphere of the storytelling event. And stop trying to do something only Jesus can do—tell a story perfectly!

fidelity and purity (Proverbs 7:6-27). Throughout Ecclesiastes, he lists other observations and the lessons he learned from them:

Ecclesiastes 3:9-12	Thoughts about work
Ecclesiastes 3:16-18	Thoughts about judgment
Ecclesiastes 4:1-4	Thoughts about oppression
Ecclesiastes 9:13-19	Thoughts about wisdom

One of the keys to wisdom is interpreting life and finding truth in the things you observe. In the following verses, note how Solomon observes something from everyday life, reflects on it, and then applies what he has seen:

"I went past the field of the sluggard, past the vineyard of the man who lacks judgment; thorns had come up everywhere, the ground was covered with weeds, and the stone wall was in ruins. I applied my heart to what I observed and learned a lesson from what I saw: A little sleep, a little slumber, a little folding of the hands to rest—and poverty will come on you like a bandit and scarcity like an armed man" (Proverbs 24:30-34).

Like Solomon, an effective Christian storyteller is always on the lookout for stories that reflect truth. Notice the pattern Solomon followed: First, he would carefully *observe* a situation. Then he would *reflect* on it and consider parallels to scriptural truth. Finally, he would *apply* the story or situation to life. Open your *eyes* to truth and to the stories around you.

**Key Four
Open Your
Ears**

Jesus said, *"He who has ears, let him hear"* (Matthew 13:9). An effective storyteller is observant, both toward the story he is telling, and toward his listeners. Even though it might sound strange, a storyteller listens to himself, his story, and his audience during the storytelling event. How does a storyteller listen to the audience? By observing the body language of the listeners, and then responding to how they respond to the story! So open your *ears*, listen, and respond.

8. Be yourself.

As you develop your own style of storytelling, seek to honor God by telling stories that make the most of the gifts he has given you. Rather than trying to be as funny as someone else, or use movement as well as another storyteller, or copy someone's style, seek ways of using your own strengths, talents, personality, interests, and skills to become a unique storyteller. Let the story flow out of who you are, rather than out of what you wish you were like.

Don't be ashamed of your gifts. God packaged them in you for a reason. Rather than imitating someone else, search for your own special style of storytelling. And don't try to impress anyone—people can see right through that! Develop a storytelling style that is comfortable and uniquely you. Then relax and have confidence that you're using your gifts to share God's message the way he intended!

Chapter 2

Preparing Your Listeners

How to Prepare Your Audience and Room

NATHAN WAS A wise storyteller. He confronted King David about his adultery with Bathsheba by telling him a story. And this subtle confrontation worked! The story impacted King David and led to his repentance (2 Samuel 12:13).

Nathan made no mistake in telling King David a story about a man who stole another man's lamb. Remember, young David had been a shepherd! David could identify with the characters in the story and because of that, the story was effective in reaching him. There is a vital relationship between a storyteller and his audience. An effective storyteller understands his audience, addresses their needs, and prepares his material with them in mind.

This relationship between the storyteller and the audience is one of the biggest differences between acting and storytelling. When an actor goes onstage, he pretends the audience isn't there. And the audience, in turn, pretends that the actor can't really see them. But when a storyteller steps onstage, he addresses the audience directly. And the audience expects the storyteller to look at them rather than pretend he can't see them.[1]

If you wrote a story, you'd experience it when you wrote it. Your readers would experience the story later, when they read it. Told stories, on the other hand, are experienced by teller and listener at the same time. Therefore, they experience the story in *community*. Storytelling, unlike reading, is a shared experience. Even so, when you tell a story, everyone in your audience hears the same words, but each sees a different set of images in his or her head. If you showed a video to your children, they would all see the same thing. But when you tell them a story, they all see something different!

Listeners are an integral part of the storytelling experience. They're not just observers, they're participants. And the way that the story is formed and told and communicated results from the relationship of the storyteller and the audience.

The goals of the storyteller and the expectations of the audience will affect the way a story is told. Jesus told different types of stories to different types of audiences for different purposes. In this chapter, we'll look at this relationship of storyteller to audience, and learn how to prepare a room for the storytelling event.

Understanding Your Audience

Think of how you talk to your friends—casually, informally, joking around. Now, think of how you speak to someone when you're interviewing for a job, or getting a formal reprimand.

---

[1]Storyteller Ed Stivender first explained this to me.

How do you talk when you're alone with your spouse or another member of your family? Each time is different! You naturally adapt the way you speak to the group you're speaking to!

Each storytelling event has its owns expectations—a Sunday school class, a church picnic, a campfire at summer camp, a Wednesday night outreach program, a closing program for VBS—each is a little different. Sometimes people expect to be entertained, other times they expect to be taught a lesson.

How can you tell what your class expects? One way is to get to know them. If you work with the same group of children each week, you'll soon learn their expectations about how long they think the story should be, what types of stories they like, how much fun they expect to have, and how much exaggeration is acceptable.

On the other hand, you may find yourself telling stories for a group of children you've never met! Perhaps, you're telling stories for your VBS program and there are many visiting children from the community. If so, look at them closely. Are they leaning forward with anticipation as you begin the story, or leaning back with their arms folded as if to say, "I'm too cool for this. I dare you to reach me." Clues from the setting, the children themselves, and the event at which you are telling stories will help. Check with your supervisor as well, to make sure you're meeting his or her expectations!

You can even help the audience clarify its own expectations. When I tell the "Parable of the Lost Sheep" (Luke 15:3-7), I use a wolf puppet who continually interrupts the story and mixes it up by saying things like, "And then the shepherd ate up his sheep," and I correct him, "No! He was a shepherd, he took care of his sheep!" and the wolf responds, "Gimme a fork—I'll take care of the sheep!" The audience quickly realizes that the wolf is mixing everything up and their expectations of the story shift from, "This is a Bible story told exactly as Jesus told it" to, "This is a creative retelling of the Bible story. It isn't word-for-word, but it has the same point as Jesus' story."

Preparing Your Audience

Do your best to keep everyone close together, instead of scattered all over the room, gym, or auditorium. If people are sitting on the fringes (something older children may try to do), audience participation may be hampered. Make sure structural barriers such as posts, pillars, basketball hoops, and bookshelves don't block the view of the children.

Help your listeners understand how you except them to respond to you and your story. Do you expect them to actively participate, or sit quietly and listen? Is the primary goal of this story to teach, or to entertain? The way you relate to them will communicate your expectations of how they should act during this storytelling event. Be aware that you, the teller, determine how much audience interaction will occur while you tell your story. When you begin speaking, the audience doesn't know how much interaction you expect. So, it's your job to clearly communicate how much you want the listeners to participate in your story. The younger the group, the more the children need to move around and become involved through the use of repetitious stories, stories with simple plots and simple resolutions, and plenty of songs, actions, and chants. (See "Teaching Children How to Participate" on page 40 and "Encouraging Participation" on page 45.)

Preparing the Space for the Storytelling Event

"That same day Jesus went out of the house and sat by the lake. Such large crowds gathered around him that he got into a boat and sat in it, while all the people stood on the shore. Then he told them many things in parables" (Matthew 13:1-3).

Imagine what it was like that day to stand on the shore and listen to Jesus tell stories. We don't know what the weather was like, but try to picture the blue sky high above and the wisps of clouds floating past. . . . Hear the waves lapping gently onshore and the birds calling overhead. . . . Feel the cool breeze coming in off the water. . . . Jesus used the natural amplification of the water to make sure he was heard and the outdoor environment to relate to his stories about seeds, weeds, yeast, birds, trees, rocks, and thorns!

The environment in which you tell stories affects how easily people can pay attention, how they feel about the story, and how well they can listen. Many educators overlook the importance of the classroom space, the seating arrangement, lighting, sound, and the mood of the room when they plan their lessons and tell their stories.

Let's look at few steps you can take to make sure your classroom environment is best suited for storytelling!

1. Find a neutral background.

Some classrooms have so many posters, bulletin boards, and colorful pictures on the walls that no matter where you look, your eyes are busy. While colorful walls can serve good educational purposes, they can also create distractions for children during story time. In a theatrical production, the background always serves to draw attention to the actors and the story, rather than divert attention from them. The same is true for a good storytelling background.

Look for a neutral background or a plain wall. You want to focus as little attention past yourself as possible. Typically, it's good to stand in a corner because the converging walls naturally serve as a way of focusing the audience's attention on the storyteller. You want the attention of the group focused on you. This might mean changing the layout of your stage area or classroom. Do it!

2. Stand in the light.

Before beginning to tell stories, look around and see if you can move into better light. Always face the brightest lights of the room. For example, if you have a window in your classroom, never stand in front of it while you tell stories because the light streaming into the room will be shining into the eyes of the students. As a result, they won't be able to see you clearly, and will look away from you to rest their eyes.

The most light should be on you, or in the space in which you'll be telling your stories. If there is light in the back of the room (behind the audience), it will disperse the attention of your listeners. Also, if you choose to use wigs or hats, be aware that they often cast shadows over your eyes and face, making it harder to see your facial expressions.

Even if you have spotlights available, you may not wish to use them. Most storytellers like to be able to see the faces of the people in the audience so they can naturally respond to the audience's reaction during their story.

> *When you tell a story, everyone in your audience hears the same words, but each sees a different set of images in his or her head. If you showed a video to your children, they would all see the same thing. But when you tell them a story, they all see something different!*

3. Remove distractions.

Movement is an attention magnet. You can be telling the most amazing, engaging, imaginative story ever, but if someone walks across the room behind you, every eye in the room will follow his movement! So, when you set up your space to tell stories, don't do it in front of a door that people might use, near a window that people might pass, or in a room where other activities are occurring. If there is a teacher behind you preparing crafts, pouring drinks, or even just looking at her watch, the children will be distracted from the story.

Before beginning your story, remove everything from your pockets (keys, coins, pencils) except what you need to tell the story.

4. Arrange the seating to your advantage.

Are the children seated in straight rows? Are they seated on the floor or on chairs? Are the chairs the right size for the students or are they adult-sized chairs? If people are uncomfortable or have difficulty seeing you they'll have a tough time paying attention to the story.

Different seating arrangements affect the mood and setting of the storytelling event differently. Slanted rows will create a less formal feel than straight lines. If the students are seated in a semi-circle, the children themselves will draw attention away from the storyteller because they are in each other's line of vision. This seating arrangement also creates a feeling of equality between the storyteller and the listeners, which you don't necessarily want.

When I tell stories to families, I prefer having children sit by their parents rather than inviting them up front. When you separate children like that, adults tend to *watch* the storytelling rather than participate in it as part of the audience. Keep the audience seated close together, and near you.

If you plan on inviting children to participate in your story, make sure there is room for them to move around comfortably and safely. Also, be aware of levels. If you're standing up while the children are seated on the floor, you'll look like a giant! Rather than making them comfortable with the story, you'll intimidate them! So, sit down or move further back away from them.

5. Make sure you can be heard.

In some larger classrooms or churches, you may be telling stories to dozens or even hundreds of children. If so, you'll need to use a microphone. Here are a few things to check before the children arrive:

- Are the batteries new and properly installed?
- Can I move freely through the room without the speakers squealing?
- Have I practiced moving through the story to make sure that I don't get tangled in the microphone cords?
- Will this microphone pick up all the sounds (both loud and soft) that I make during the story?
- Is the power switch turned to "on"? (Be aware that some microphones have two switches. Check them both.)
- Is the volume set to a comfortable level?
- Is someone positioned to adjust the volume level after I begin talking to make sure that everyone can easily hear the story?

Summary

Get to know your listeners, connect with them, and make sure you've prepared them for the storytelling time. Find a neutral background. Stand in the light. Remove distractions. Arrange the seating to your advantage and make sure you can be heard. Follow these steps and your students will be even more ready to hear the stories you tell!

Chapter 3

Understanding Your Story

The Seven Parts of a Story

BEFORE WE START looking at how to understand different types of Bible stories, let's try a little riddle. What well-known story contains . . .

Sea monsters, dragons, magicians, and spies!
Riddles and mystery! Intrigue and surprise!
Heroes and villains and giants and midgets,
Palaces, dungeons, and madmen and witches!

Kings, queens and emperors, wise men and fools;
Miracles, plagues, hidden treasure and jewels!
Angels and demons, rebellion and war,
Deception, disaster and mayhem and gore!
(Ew . . . yuck . . .)

Time travel! Romance! Adventure! Betrayal!
Freedom from slavery! Escaping from jail!
Soldiers and warriors and healers and saints,
And poems of thanksgiving, praise and complaints!

Partying prophets and killers who preach,
Fish who eat people! Donkeys that teach!
Shipwrecks and journeys and blessings to give!
And the world's greatest SUPERHERO ever to live!

If you said "God's story in the Bible!" you're right! The Bible is the most amazing book of all time! It's the greatest love story ever written and the most thrilling adventure story ever told. It has everything you could ever hope for in a story—from once upon a time in the garden, to happily ever after in the King's palace!

The Bible is the life-changing account of God's grace and forgiveness offered to a planet of rebellious people. It's the ultimate bedtime story for the human race. Yet, all too often in children's ministry, when it comes time for telling the Bible story, kids groan with boredom. We've somehow managed to drain the wonder out of the most wondrous story of all!

In this chapter, you'll learn how to look at Bible stories with new eyes to see what they're really about, to uncover the transformation in the lives of the characters, and to begin retelling them with energy, enthusiasm, and creativity.

What Is a Story?

Once, when I was leading a workshop on creative storytelling at a church in Ohio, I took some time to explain how understanding story structure can help teachers in their lesson preparation. After I was finished, a first-grade teacher asked me, "Why don't they put that information in the lesson? That seems like the most valuable thing you've said all day!"

That teacher was ready to take a deeper look at Bible stories, draw out their truths, and apply them in the lives of her listeners. I'll bet you're ready to do the same!

We can all tell that a book report, a shopping list, a table of contents, or a description of a lawnmower isn't a story. But why not? What makes a story, a story?

Every story is about transformation—either the transformation of an individual (in character-driven stories) or of a situation (in plot-driven stories). In a story, this transformation is unveiled. Usually, something goes wrong, a character has to face a conflict, and he or she is changed as a result. The main character is then different at the end of a story. He or she has changed as a result of facing the struggle or problem at the heart of the story.

For example, in the story of the creation of the world found in the first two chapters of Genesis, nothingness was transformed into a world, dust was transformed into human beings, and God's situation was different—he now had humans to love and to love him. In the next chapter when humans sin, they're transformed from sinless to sinful, from immortal to mortal, from life to death. In each case, the change occurs because of choices made by the characters in the story.

Let's look at this a little more in-depth. Here's the definition of "story" that my friend in Ohio found so helpful:

A story is the purposeful account of a vulnerable character who faces a struggle and makes a discovery that changes his life.[1]

"A story is a purposeful account..."

A story leads somewhere. Every event or image is included for a specific purpose. They build on each other to reach a climax of action or interest within the story. The scenes and events in a story are all connected to each other. One thing causes the next. The action isn't random, instead everything that happens in a story happens for a reason. A story has closure and all of its pieces fit together to form a completed picture. Even when Jesus' stories didn't have happy endings there was still unity and coherence.

It's important to realize that just listing one thing after another doesn't necessarily result in a story. The beginning of a story isn't just the first event in a list of events, but the originating event. The middle isn't just what comes next, but the muddle, or conflict, of the story. And the end isn't just the last event in a story, but the culminating event that leads to, or hints at, resolution. Events in a story are purposeful, causally related (rather than random), and create a unified whole. For a series of events to become a story, they need a reason for existing. They must point to something, unveil something, or reveal something new to the listener.

---

[1] Although based on many definitions of story, this definition focuses on the same four story elements Donald Davis describes in his article "Creating Family Stories" in *Storytelling Magazine,* September 1997, pp. 16-17. I'm indebted to Donald Davis for his insights into family stories, which helped shape and influence my understanding of story structure.

"...of a vulnerable character..."

At the heart of most stories is a character with a problem or an unfulfilled desire. At the beginning of the story that character lacks something. I call the character "vulnerable" because he or she needs to grow in some way, or needs to learn something. Please note that God isn't vulnerable in the same way we are, but he does have desires that are not always met. For example, God wants all people to love and obey him but he doesn't get what he wants.

Be aware that when you tell your story, your audience must care about the main character of the story; if they don't, they're not going to care about the outcome of the story! Story characters have a unique personality, specific traits, and consistent characteristics. As you tell a story, the actions and words of the characters reveal their personality.

"...who faces a struggle..."

The Bible contains genealogies, poems, letters, doctrinal teachings, and wise sayings. But in themselves, none of these things are stories. In a story, something must go wrong. If nothing goes wrong, you don't have a story. Stories don't just describe or explain, they reveal transformation. A story involves real choices, real struggles, and real discoveries.

Whenever you have a character with a struggle, you have emotion. This is one of the most important ingredients in the story. We, as listeners, are drawn into a story by identifying with the emotions of the characters. Whether it's fear or hope or sadness or joy, try to identify what emotions run through the story you're working on and then let yourself be touched by them as you tell the story.

The secret to discovering what Bible stories are really about is to ask, "what goes wrong?" rather than just asking, "what happens?"

"...and makes a discovery..."

Since stories are about transformations, they revolve around struggles and discoveries. There is a moment of discovery or revelation in stories when the main character realizes something he hadn't noticed, seen, or understood before. This results in a change that determines a new course for his life.

Sometimes, the resolution of the problem and the discovery made by the main character are only hinted at. Almost none of Jesus' stories ended with people living happily ever after. Most of his stories were rather shocking! But the listeners could discern the new direction the life of the main character would (or should) take.

Where struggle meets discovery, there is action! Action moves a story along and helps keep the attention of the audience. Often, the setting in which the story takes place is crucial for creating the struggle or showing the discovery. For example, in the story of Jesus and Peter walking on the water, the setting of the stormy sea is a powerful backdrop to what's going on in the hearts of the disciples.

"...that changes his life."

A character will always be either better off or worse off at the end of the story than he was at the beginning. For example, preceding the crucifixion, both Peter and Judas faced a struggle: what should I do about my loyalty to Jesus? Both made a choice: I will place my personal interests above my loyalty. Both made a discovery: I have wronged my innocent friend! And both were different from then on: Judas gave up on life and killed himself, while Peter repented and his relationship with Christ was restored and deepened. See how each of them was changed?

Where discovery meets the change, there is a choice. The character has struggled and glimpsed a new way of looking at things. Now, he or she must make a choice. The choice will set the course for the change in his life.

Be aware that many folktales (and parables) don't show us the inner change or growth of the character, but we can see how the circumstances changed so that the person's situation was different at the end of the story than it was at the beginning of the story. For example, in the story of "The Good Samaritan" we don't hear anything about the way the characters felt, just how they acted. When the man from Samaria approached the injured Jewish man, we don't know what the injured man was thinking—was he relieved to see potential help, or was he frightened because Jews and Samaritans didn't get along? All we are told is how the injured man's situation was changed when the Samaritan arrived.

Here is one way to look at the seven different parts of a story:

A story is the purposeful account of . . .

| a vulnerable character . . . | who faces a struggle . . . | and makes a discovery . . . | that changes his (or her) life. |

So What?

So, how can understanding the structure of stories help you become a better storyteller? Well, by looking for the character who struggles, you can identify who the story is really about. And, by finding what goes wrong, you can naturally remember the story more easily!

I was asked to write a version of the story of the first miraculous fish catch (recorded in Luke 5:1-11) for a preschool lesson to appear in a Christian publishing company's Bible curriculum. "We want the story to talk about how Jesus had power over the fish," my editor told me. So I looked at the story. In the story, Peter, James, and John have spent the entire night trying to catch fish, but have come up empty. In the morning, as they're wearily bringing in their nets, Jesus asks if he can stand on Peter's boat to preach to the growing crowds. Peter agrees and after the message is finished, Jesus asks Peter to go a little farther out and put the nets down on the other side of the boat.

If I'd been Peter, I'd have been thinking, "OK, Jesus, there aren't any fish on *this* side of the boat, they must all be over *there*. Right!" But Peter does as Jesus asked and the nets fill with fish. The disciples worship Jesus and, when they reach shore, they leave their nets, and follow Jesus.

Now, as I looked at the story, I asked, "Who is this story really about?" To find out who a story is really about, look for the person (or the group of people) who
- has a problem, struggle, desire, need, or question;
- learns a lesson or matures in some way during the story;
- changes his (or their) action or attitude by the end of the story.

Jesus doesn't have a problem (apart from needing a better place from which to preach), a struggle, or a question. He doesn't learn a lesson, mature, or grow as a result of the action of the story. And he doesn't change his action or attitude at the end of the story. So is this story about Jesus? Not primarily.

What about the disciples? Do they have a problem? You bet. Not only are they fish-less, they don't truly recognize Jesus' identity. Do they learn or mature in some way during the story? Yes! Peter recognizes his sinfulness and Jesus' holiness (Luke 5:8). And do they change? They make the biggest change of all! They leave their nets (bursting with freshly caught fish!) and follow Jesus (Luke 5:11). They leave everything they own and have lived for until then to become Jesus' followers!

Is this a story about how Jesus has power over fish? Not primarily. Instead, it's about the change that occurs in someone's life when he realizes the true identity of Jesus Christ! As you might have guessed, I didn't end up writing a lesson about how Jesus had power over fish!

Summary

Do you see now how understanding story structure will help you as you prepare your stories? You'll be able to identify who the story is really about and what the story really teaches. You'll also remember the story more easily because you won't worry about remembering the plot, but will naturally remember the struggles and the resulting discoveries of the characters!

Chapter 4

Studying Your Story

How to Understand, Interpret, and Apply Bible Stories

THIS CHAPTER provides you with an in-depth process for studying Bible stories. Please note that you won't need to study every story you tell in this much depth! The detailed questions and discussion points are there to provide you with guidance and direction as you seek to study, apply, and learn stories from Scripture.

Questions to Ask About Your Stories

What is this story really about?

First, find the main point. Ask, "What is God telling us in these verses? What lesson is being taught?" Strive for a clear understanding of the story rather than a neat little summary of the story.

Read the text and look at what's going on in the story. See what type of a story it is (history, autobiography, biography, or parable) and look at the context in which it was told.

For example, Luke 19:11 says, "He went on to tell them a parable, because he was near Jerusalem and the people thought that the kingdom of God was going to appear at once." This comment explains why Jesus decided to tell this specific story! It serves as a clue to help you interpret the story.

Look for key verses, summarizing thoughts, or conclusions. Very often you can find words such as "therefore" or "from then on" or "so." These words usually signal that the main point of the story is coming up. Also, if you can find a phrase or thought that's repeated throughout the story, it's a good clue that it might be what the story is really about.

Jesus often asked probing questions to guide his listeners to discover the point of his stories, rather than tell them specifically what he was talking about. Instead of answering all their questions, he led them to discover truth for themselves. Look for key questions to help you understand the meaning of the story, too.

Finally, some stories are complete in themselves, while other stories need context to make their point. Some *make* a point, others *are* the point. Ask yourself whether this story serves best standing on its own (as a way of revealing truth), or relying on the rest of your lesson (as a way of illustrating truth).

What is the context of this story?

Looking for context means looking at what precedes and what follows your story. Each little story is embedded in a bigger story that helps you understand what the littler story is about.

The key to understanding context is to discover who told the story, who listened to the story, and why it was told. To do this, you look at three things: the storyteller, the audience, and the context of the storytelling event.

In Luke 15, Jesus told three stories. By looking at verses 1 and 2, you can see who the storyteller is (Jesus), who the audience is (the Pharisees and teachers of the law), and what the context of the three stories is (the men were complaining that Jesus was associating with and eating with sinners).

In Matthew 13, Jesus told eight stories about the kingdom of Heaven. Four stories are told outside the house, to the crowd. The last four stories are told inside the house, to his disciples. After reading through the eight stories, can you discover the difference in perspective or meaning? Can you see why he chose to tell the different stories to the different audiences?

You can see that in each case, the audience was different and the stories were told for a different purpose.

When you study parables, ask yourself who the characters in the story refer to in real life. For example, when Jesus explained "The Parable of the Weeds" (found in Matthew 13:24-30), he showed his disciples how each character in the story referred to a person or group of people in real life. (For his explanation, see Matthew 13:36-43.)

Be careful to get the whole story. This may take some research! For example, if you're telling the story of Cain and Abel (Genesis 4), it would be easy to think that the difference between whether or not God was happy with their sacrifices was based on what they were offering to God. But Hebrews 11:4 explains that it was the condition of their hearts, not the type of sacrifice that made the difference! Cain's sacrifice was better because it was brought in faith. If you didn't take the time to look up the reference to this story in the book of Hebrews, you might miss the entire point.[1]

As you study your story, you may wish to consult a concordance or a Bible commentary for more information.

> **To figure out what a parable is about, ask yourself**
> - Who is the storyteller?
> - Who are the listeners?
> - What is the context of the storytelling event?

What is the structure of this story?

Next, look for patterns or repetition. You may discover a question repeated over and over ("Will you let God's people go?"), a person who appears again and again (like Peter), or a problem or cycle of events that repeats itself (Psalm 107 contains five stories of different types of people who all suffered hardship, cried out to God, and were rescued).

To whom does this story happen?

To tell where one story begins and another ends, look at the struggles, discoveries, and growth of the characters. Who struggles? Who discovers? Who changes? If you find this process of transformation in a character's life, you'll have found a complete story.

- Examples of struggles—mistakes, temptations, questions, regrets
- Examples of discoveries—decisions, lessons, choices, consequences

Often, a story isn't about whom or what it first appears to be about.

For example, the book of Ruth begins by introducing a woman named Naomi. When her

---

[1]For more information on how God reacts to sacrifices that aren't brought for the right motives, see Isaiah 1:10-13.

Story Patterns

Look for the following patterns in the stories you tell. They will help you understand as well as remember your stories.

- **Repetition**—Very often words, ideas, and images are repeated in a story or section of Scripture. Repetition is a way of emphasizing a point. For example, in Psalm 119 there are 177 references to God's Word. Guess what that chapter is all about! In addition, Jesus often introduced his stories by saying, "The kingdom of God is like . . ." Sometimes a problem, question, or series of events is repeated. In the book of Judges the cycle of sin, slavery, submission, and savior is repeated twelve times!
- **Refrains**—A series of words may be repeated throughout the story, making a natural refrain that will help in your retelling. For example, after each of the days of creation the Bible says, "And there was evening, and there was morning—the _____ day."
- **Reversals**—Often in Bible stories, the exact opposite of what you'd expect to occur, happens. In the story of "The Good Samaritan" (Luke 10:25-37), you'd think the priest or the Levite would help the man, but instead, his despised enemy helped him. When Zacchaeus went looking for Jesus, Jesus was the one who found Zacchaeus (Luke 19:1-10). In the story of "Lazarus and the Rich Man" (Luke 16:19-31), everything is turned upside down in the afterlife—the rich man becomes poor while the poor man becomes rich; the happy man suffers while the suffering man becomes happy—everything is reversed!
- **Ruin to redemption**—A common pattern for Bible stories is for characters to travel from being ruined because of their choices, to being redeemed because of God's grace. Peter is a good example of someone who went from ruin to redemption!
- **Rags to riches (or riches to rags)**—In the Old Testament, Joseph went from riches (in his father's house), to rags (as a slave), to riches (as the ruler of Potiphar's house), to rags (in prison), to riches (as a ruler in Egypt)!

sons die, she becomes angry and bitter, even changing her name to "Mara," which means "bitter."

Her daughter-in-law Ruth shows devotion and faithfulness not only to Naomi, but also to God. As a result of seeing Ruth's example of faith and devotion, Naomi gets over her bitterness and (through Ruth and her new husband Boaz's son) receives a new son to raise!

Who has the struggle? Naomi. Who discovers something as a result of the action of the story? Naomi. Whose life is different at the end of the story? Well . . . Ruth's life is different (she's married), but so is Naomi's (she has a son again)!

Surprise! A careful reading of the text reveals that the book of Ruth isn't about Ruth as much as it's about Naomi! Ruth is a static character who, while important to the story, doesn't mature, change, or grow. She is obedient and faithful at the beginning and at the end. Naomi's character is dynamic. The story begins and ends with her, she is the one who faces the greatest struggle, and the solution in the story comes to her. A story is nearly always about one central character, and in this story that character is Naomi.

Where does this story take place?

Changes in time and scenery mark important moments in a story. For example, in 1 Samuel 3, we read the story of when God first spoke to Samuel. The chapter begins by saying that "In those days the word of the Lord was rare; there were not many visions . . . Now Samuel did not yet know the Lord: The word of the Lord had not yet been revealed to him" (1 Samuel 3:1, 7). At the end of the story, the problems that introduced the chapter are resolved—1) God has a new spokesperson; 2) Samuel now knows the Lord; 3) God's Word has been revealed to him, and 4) Samuel is faithful in sharing God's Word with the people!

The first scene happens at night (v. 2), the second scene happens in the morning (v. 15), and the third scene summarizes Samuel's life from that day on (v. 19). Changes in time and place signal the changes of the scenes of this story!

Applying the Story

The four following questions don't deal as much with discerning the content of the biblical story, but rather with looking for ways to faithfully apply and tell the story to others.

1. How do I need to change this story?

Matthew, Mark, Luke, and John each told the story of Jesus' life. But they each told it differently. Why? Because they were four different storytellers writing for four different audiences with four different goals in mind!

Author	Audience	Purpose	Characteristics
Matthew	Jews	To show Jews that Jesus is truly the promised Messiah.	Matthew includes lots of references to the Old Testament and emphasizes how Jesus fulfilled ancient prophecies concerning the coming Messiah.
Mark	Romans	To show Romans that Jesus is truly the Son of God.	Mark shows Jesus as a man of action, power, mystery, and authority.
Luke	Theophilus, a Greek man	To prove that Jesus really was whom Theophilus had heard him to be (Luke 1:4).	Luke pays careful attention to historical detail and chronological order.
John	Spiritual seekers	"That you may believe that Jesus is the Christ, the Son of God, and that by believing you may have life in his name" (John 20:31).	John includes many teachings of Jesus not recorded anywhere else.

Each author told the same story (the story of Jesus' life) from his own perspective. God inspired and guided them, but they weren't robots. He created them with individual gifts and talents and then relied on them to be faithful as his Spirit guided them in telling his story in their own way. You are another one of God's storytellers telling his story to yet another audience! You, too, will tell God's story in a unique way. Don't be afraid of telling God's story in a way that your audience can understand and relate to. Ask yourself, "What changes (in wording, content, or order) could I make to this story (without changing the meaning of the story), to make it easier to tell to this audience?"

See the workshop notes on this chapter, and the other chapters of this book to address these last three questions in greater depth.

Hints and Tips on Changing Stories

God's Word is God's Word. We don't want to change the meaning of it, but there may be times when you'll need to change certain aspects of stories when you tell them.

- **Condense time.** Skip over long periods of time or long genealogies. In the book of Acts, Paul told the story of his conversion several different times. Each time it was a little different. He left some things out, he rearranged the order of events, and he condensed or expanded the story for his different audiences. This shows us that stories may contain changes in order of sequence of events (flashing forward or backward) and changes in duration of time (expanding or contracting the time an event could take).
- **Limit the number of characters.** As you craft your story for telling, remember that you may need to limit the number of characters you include in the story. Usually, stories told orally have fewer characters than written stories. We just can't keep as many characters "onstage" in our minds.
- **Leave out objectionable content.** Some material isn't appropriate for young children. Leave out references to sexuality and violence, and other adult themes.
- **Explain difficult or foreign ideas and concepts.** Some terms, traditions, and cultural conditions are hard for children of today to understand. Don't assume too much. Explaining that Jews were forbidden to take care of pigs will help children understand how desperate the prodigal son was to get a job!

2. How can I best tell this story?

Consider your own gifts and storytelling abilities, your audience, and the creative storytelling techniques you wish to use.

3. How shall I introduce and wrap up this story?

Think about how this story fits in with the rest of your lesson, and your educational goals.

4. How shall I apply this story?

Consider how this Scripture passage applies to life today and brainstorm activities that you can include in your lesson to apply this story to life.

Summary

As you study your story, consider the message, context, structure, characters and scenes of the story. Think about changes you might need to make to the story, what techniques you'll use to tell the story, and how it applies to life today.

Chapter 5

Growing Your Own Tale

Hints on Rehearsing and Learning Your Stories

"HE [JESUS] ALSO SAID, 'This is what the kingdom of God is like. A man scatters seed on the ground. Night and day, whether he sleeps or gets up, the seed sprouts and grows, though he does not know how. All by itself the soil produces grain—first the stalk, then the head, then the full kernel in the head. As soon as the grain is ripe, he puts the sickle to it, because the harvest has come'" (Mark 4:26-29).

Jesus explained that the kingdom of God is like a growing seed—the process is mysterious and much of it happens beyond the control of the farmer! Taking a story into your heart and letting it grow into one that you tell is a similar process. It's not step-by-step and mechanical. It's more like a growth process that happens in overlapping phases. It's a little unpredictable and hard to control! Rather than a checklist of things that you can do to assure that your story is properly prepared, you sort of mix everything together to create the right kind of environment for story growth.

During the process of learning and rehearsing your story, you must prepare yourself (chapter one), consider your audience (chapters two, nine, and ten), and understand the story (chapters three and four). As you practice, you'll naturally think about ways you might include audience participation (chapters six, seven, and eight) and ways you might improve your delivery (chapters eleven and twelve). Finally, as you practice and learn your stories, you'll strive for excellence (chapter fourteen) and consider how this story fits in with the rest of your lesson (chapters thirteen and fifteen).

Because of all these factors, *this* chapter might seem like a mini-summary of this entire book! You'll find concepts introduced in this chapter that are expanded and developed in-depth elsewhere in the book. So, use this chapter to get acquainted with the ideas and to prepare the garden of your imagination for the rest of the book!

If you're ready, let's get started!

Phase One—Getting to Know the Story

Before beginning to tell your story, you need to get acquainted with it. You need to get to know your story. Notice, I didn't say you need to know your story, I said you need to get to know your story. What's the difference?

The process of getting to know someone takes time. You can meet someone in a moment and say that you know him, but really getting to know him takes longer. Only through the process of becoming better acquainted is a deep relationship built. The better you know someone, the easier it is for you to introduce that person to others. Only then are you really familiar with the characteristics that make that person unique! So it is with your story. The more familiar you are with the story, the easier it will be to tell it to someone else. The deeper the relationship you have with your story, the deeper you can plant it in the hearts of your listeners. So, read it aloud several times. Ask yourself, "What would I be experiencing if I were in this story? What would I see? What's the main point? What's this story really about?"

Look at what's happening in the story by 1) identifying the main character, 2) noticing what he or she struggles with, and 3) seeing how he or she grows or changes as a result of facing that struggle. Then tell yourself about the story. Explain it in your own words. Walk through it. Watch the story happen. Don't worry about performing it. Just imagine it happening around you. Before introducing others to your story, take the time to get acquainted!

Getting to Know Your Story

- Think about the story.
- Talk about the story.
- Tell people about the story.
- Tell the story to yourself.

Phase Two—Test-Driving Your Story

If you were shopping for a new car, you'd probably test-drive it before handing over your money. You'd want to know how it feels, if it's the right color and size for you and your family. You'd want to consider whether the options are right for you. You'd evaluate the whole package to see if it really fits your needs and lifestyle.

You need to test-drive stories, too. After you've become acquainted with your story, hop into it and start the engine. Tell the story to yourself. Test how fast it should go, how smooth it feels, how it handles curves and the traffic of real life. Ask yourself, "Where does this story really take off? Where is it too slow? Where does it meander too much? Is it even the right story for me to tell?"

If you're working on a Bible story, read it aloud to yourself, and then put the Bible down and tell the story to yourself. As you do, look for surprises in the story. Try to notice something new in the story every time you tell it.

Try it on for size. How does it fit? How does it feel? Don't try to polish or perform your story. Don't worry about that! Just talk through the story and try to notice what's going on within it.

Stories grow as you tell them. So, get to know your story inside and out. But don't try to learn it word-for-word. Instead, explore the story as you practice it. As you develop the story, add details and descriptions where appropriate or necessary.

Always take your story for a test-drive by yourself before you invite any listeners to ride along with you!

Phase Three—Paying Attention to Your Story

Your attention is like a river wandering through the countryside. There may be many dry creek beds in which it can flow, but the more divided it gets, the less force the river has until finally it slows to a trickle or dries out completely. Don't let too many distractions drain the impact and presence of your story.

Even when you're rehearsing, it's easy to get distracted by things that have nothing to do with your story—how cold the room is, how you forgot to eat lunch, or how your ankle hurts from twisting it last night. You may even be worried about how well your listeners will like your story, or how well they'll like you!

All these factors (and many others) vie for your attention. And as they do, they distract you from the task at hand—connecting with your story and your listeners. So, as you work on developing your story, focus on being present in the moment. Take the time to iron out difficult sections, develop your ideas, rehearse intricate phrases, and practice moving from your introduction into your story. But when you're actually telling the story, don't let those preparation details distract you! As strange as it may seem, your goal when practicing a story is to learn to *forget!* Forget your practice time. Forget the script. Forget everything that might divide or distract your attention.

I find that the stronger the images I have of the story, the less likely I am to get distracted. The more I can step into a story and imagine it happening, the more my audience will be able to imagine it as well.

Several factors contribute to how well I'm able to imagine the story:
• my familiarity with this story;
• my confidence level in telling this story;
• my level of comfort with this particular audience;
• my ability to clearly see and experience the details in this story.

As you become more familiar with the story and practice telling it a few times, try to observe what's happening in your story and tell it as you see it—don't try to just remember the words you used the last time you told it.

Phase Four—Navigating Through Your Story

Imagine that you're driving home when you come to a "Road Closed" sign. If you're familiar with the streets of your town, you could drive an alternate route and still make it home. But if this route is the only route you know, you'd be stuck!

Memorizing the words of a story puts you in the same position! What would happen if you forgot the next word? The road ahead would be closed off! You'd be stuck! It's happened to me and to most people who have memorized a story—we've lost our way and never made it home. But, if you know the story so well that you know alternate routes through the story, you can maneuver through forgetting a word or two and still make it safely home to the end of the story!

So, as you begin to learn your stories for telling, don't think of it as a process of memorizing and reciting the right *words,* but of remembering and then telling the right *story.* Storytellers are concerned with helping their listeners picture the story in their minds. Because of that, images are more central to storytelling than printed letters and words. Storytellers typically don't memorize their stories because
• memorizing doesn't allow you to change the story for different audiences;
• memorizing makes you focus on remembering words rather than on picturing images.

So, practice the story, not the words. This is where I think some Bible curricula publishers miss the point. They write out precisely what to say and encourage teachers to read the story or lesson as printed. But who is to say that their route through the story is the best one for you and your students? As you develop skills, you'll find that you can steer many different ways through a story and still be effective.

Rather than learning the words that make up a story, I encourage you to learn the *terrain* of a story.[1] Know the story so well that you can take alternate routes through it, if another route seems like the best way to tell that story that day.

---

[1] Storyteller Jim May calls this "learning the whole landscape" of the story. See *The Storyteller's Guide,* written and edited by Bill Mooney and David Holt (Little Rock, AR: August Publishing House, 1996), p. 54.

Phase Five—Growing Your Story

As you read through the Bible story you're preparing to tell, think about the feel of the story and try to reflect that feel in the way you tell the story. For example, when Jesus told the story of the lost sheep (see Luke 15:3ff), he began by asking a series of hypothetical questions: "Suppose one of you has a hundred sheep." As you tell this story to children, you can keep the same feel in your telling of the story by saying, "Kids, pretend you have five pet kittens. If one got lost, you'd look for it, wouldn't you?" See how the question mirrors the text?

Let the story grow from the text. If a story has lots of emotion, or music, or action, weave that into the way you tell that story.

The story of Shadrach, Meshach and Abednego being thrown in the fiery furnace (Daniel 3) is a bold story of courage, power and faith under fire (literally)! This is not a wimpy little story! The courage and faith of those three young men reshaped the way an entire empire worshiped! When you tell this story, look for ways to reflect the same power and energy in your telling.

Also, make the story personal. Find a way to connect with the characters of the story on a personal level. For example, if you were telling "The Four Soils" (Matthew 13:3-9) you might think of a time when you sowed the Word. Or when the Word didn't take root. Or when you saw weeds choking the spiritual life out of someone. Or when you saw someone produce fruit. How did you feel? What did you learn? How did you change? Find a way to identify with the characters and emotions of the story.

Even if you're telling a Bible story that you've never heard before, find a way to connect with it. Let it become a story that matters to you, not just a lesson you're trying to get through!

Phase Six—Developing Your Story

Practice your story with your audience in mind. Think about what you want the listeners to do, feel, believe, think, or learn by the end of your story. This is the destination your story is attempting to reach. If you can't explain it in specific words, don't get frustrated. Can you feel it? Can you imagine what emotion you want the listeners to experience? That's good enough. Go from there. Always aim for the heart, not just the head.

Consider how you might include the students by letting them act out part of the story, create sound effects that set the mood for the story, and even repeat key phrases of the story. As you develop ideas on how you plan to deliver your story, ask yourself how you could include

- music, sound effects, or singing;
- movement, gestures, or actions;
- refrains, rhythms or rhymes;
- participation, role-playing or humor.

Let your understanding of your students help shape the way you prepare your story. Think about what techniques will best communicate this story and reach them. Avoid techniques that might distract your listeners or make them uncomfortable. You can derail children from listening to your story by choosing material that isn't age-appropriate, that contains adult themes, or that uses words they don't know. You can ask too many questions, bore them with long descriptions, or choose audience participation techniques they think are stupid.

By the way, don't tell a story that's so close to your heart that you lose control of your emotions. Storytelling may be therapeutic, but not on your listeners' time. Tell stories *for* them, not *to* them. Of course, some stories may shake people up, or be confrontational. But let people be offended by the message of the gospel, not the manner in which you share it. Stay in control of your emotions; it'll help your listeners feel comfortable.

Be Willing to Make Mistakes

Anytime you try something for the first time, you risk failing. When you're telling a story, don't think of making a mistake as failing, but as learning and contributing to your growth as a storyteller!

If you forget something in the middle of the story, don't correct yourself. You might cover by saying, "Something I didn't mention earlier is that Samson was the world's strongest man!" And then just go on with your story. Most kids in the class won't even notice the mistake!

Don't let your listeners think you're nervous, or that you messed up, even if you did! You might even laugh at your mistake, but don't nervously or awkwardly try to cover it up.

If you can't remember what comes next, you may wish to repeat the last line or description and see if it sparks your memory. If not, and you're completely stuck, smile and say, "I have no idea what comes next. Let's take a break from this story!"

Once, when I was telling a rhyming story in front of about eight hundred children, I forgot the next line! I tried to remember it, but I was totally clueless. I tried making up my own line, but it didn't even rhyme! Finally, I just skipped to the last two lines of the poem, finished it and moved on. And guess what? I survived!

Listeners will feel uneasy if they think you forgot your line or your place in the story. So if you get lost or confused, plug on confidently, don't get all upset and flustered.

If you make a mistake that seems to add to the story—keep it! Don't apologize for it. It's just a discovery about what works in this story!

Summary

Get to know your story—really get acquainted with it. Test-drive your story to make sure it's the right one for you to tell. Focus your attention on the story as you practice it and as you tell it. Become familiar with the terrain of the story rather than memorizing one version of the story. When working on telling a Bible story, let the way you tell it grow from the way it's told in Scripture. And finally, practice your story with the audience in mind.

Now, I should mention that even if you follow these suggestions, there's no guarantee that your story will be a success. Even in Jesus' story the farmer had to trust the process! But these procedures will nurture the right environment for your story to grow and mature.

And, God willing, it *will* produce fruit!

Flight Instructions: Cruising Up to Altitude!

Now that you've prepared yourself through prayer and Bible study, now that you've studied your story, taken steps to understand your audience, and prepared the storytelling space, you're ready to really take off!

In this section, you'll learn how to
- incorporate music, chants, and refrains in the stories you tell;
- encourage children to creatively participate as you tell stories;
- include dozens of creative dramatics activities in your storytelling;
- use costumes and creative props to add flavor to your storytelling;
- tell stories that relate well to young children;
- connect with preteens through humor, audience involvement, and creative storytelling techniques.

It's time to let the brains of your students *fly*. So, let's soar!

Chapter 6

Sing It Out!

How to Tell Stories with Music, Chants, Rhymes, and Refrains

When Using Audience Participation

- Read the audience—to see if they're ready and willing to participate.
- Respect the audience—by asking them to join in only as much as they're comfortable.
- Respond to the audience—by changing what you've asked them to do if it's too difficult (or boring); or, by adding more participation if they're really enjoying it!

AFTER CROSSING the Red Sea, Moses and the Israelites sang to the Lord, and then Miriam led all the Israelite women (up to 600,000 of them!) in a praise dance! When Mary (the mother of Jesus) met Elizabeth, she burst into song. David sang and danced before the Lord. Jesus sang hymns on the night he was betrayed. And of course the book of Psalms has 150 songs that range from praise to despair!

Truly, music and the spoken word are rooted deeply in Scripture. The Bible is alive with all the sounds, rhythms, and music of language and life!

In this chapter, you'll discover ways to incorporate music, chants, rhymes and refrains in the stories you tell.

Developing Chants and Refrains

Repetition occurs naturally in many types of stories. For example, think of the stories of "The Three Bears," "The Three Little Pigs," and "The Three Billy Goats Gruff." See how the number three occurs in each of them? Now, think of Scripture. How many times did Peter deny Jesus? Three. How many times did Jesus ask Peter if he loved him? Three. How many people came up to the Good Samaritan as he lay in the ditch? Three. How many times did Jesus return to the sleeping disciples in the Garden of Gethsemane? Three! See all that repetition? God knows we remember things best when they're repeated. That's how we're wired to remember them! So he imbedded repetition into his story!

Many Bible stories already contain refrains or repetition. In the creation account, we hear the refrain, "And God looked at what he'd made, and it was good." In the story of the Exodus, we see Moses repeatedly saying, "Let my people go," and Pharaoh repeatedly saying, "No!"

Every time you find repetition, you can invite the audience to say or act out a refrain with you! For example, you might say, "And God looked at what he'd made . . ." and the students could respond, "And it was good!" It can be that simple!

When telling about the Exodus, half the group could shake their fingers and say, "Mister King! Mister King! Let us go out!" and the other half could respond, "Not by the hair on my chin or my snout!" OK, maybe not "snout," but you get the idea!

Be sure to explain when you want the children to join you and when you wish for them to stop. As each section of participation ends, make sure they're quiet and ready to listen to the next part of the story.

Let's look at two creative techniques for using repetition to your advantage in telling stories!

Teaching Children How to Participate

1. Say the words to the refrain once without the audience joining in.

2. Repeat the first line or phrase and have the audience repeat it after you're done. Mouth the words, or say/sing them softly as you listen to the audience repeat the line. Continue with the remaining lines, teaching each line separately.

3. Put it together. Go through the entire section slowly and mouth the words so that each audience member can understand and remember his or her part. Don't expect them all to join you the first time, and don't expect those who do join you to say or do their part flawlessly the first time through. Be patient—a few more times through and they'll have it!

4. Be aware that, in some repetitious or cumulative stories, the audience will naturally begin to anticipate what's about to occur. In those cases, you won't need to teach them what to say or do, they'll see it coming and join in naturally!

Technique One—Call and Response Storytelling

With this style of storytelling, whenever you come to a certain phrase in the story, the audience joins in with you. You can have the entire audience respond to what you say, or you can have a section, or small group respond.

Let's look at an example based on the story of "The Good Samaritan." In chapters four and five of this book we learned that when studying a story, we follow the process of

1. finding the main point;
2. looking for patterns that will help us remember and retell the story;
3. letting the way the story is told in Scripture help shape the way we retell it today.

The main point of the good Samaritan story is that we need to love others with actions, not just words, by reaching out to anyone in need. There is an easy-to-remember pattern in the story—1) a man is hurt, 2) the first guy to walk by doesn't help, 3) the second guy doesn't help, 4) the third guy (who is the man's enemy!) does help and the hurting man gets better.

Finally, even though we don't know what the injured man said as he cried out for help, we can guess and create a refrain that he might have used. Page 41 contains an example of using the "Call and Response" technique in retelling the story "The Good Samaritan."

Technique Two—Group Refrain Storytelling

This technique is similar to "Call and Response Storytelling." The biggest difference between the techniques is the number of groups and parts. Since there are more groups involved in "Group Refrain Storytelling," this creative storytelling technique works best with larger audiences.

1. Identify three or four characters that appear in each scene of the story. If a character appears only once in the story, don't assign that character a part.

2. Write refrains or create actions that are fun to say or do. Each refrain/action should reveal something significant about that character and add depth and clarity to the story. Give it a little thought. Put some time into coming up with something fun, meaningful, and memorable. Your students will appreciate your effort!

• The Good Samaritan •

(based on Luke 10:25-37)

Notes for the storyteller: Before beginning to tell this story, divide the audience into two groups. Call the first group "The Injured Man Group." Call the second group "The Unhelpful Holy People Group." Explain each group's part and teach them the words to their refrain. If you have a small class, just teach them all to say the hurting man's part.

Don't worry about memorizing the storyteller's parts, just use your own words to narrate the action of the story. You may, however, wish to memorize the short rhyme at the end of the story. Also, consider adding gestures that the groups can do as they say their lines!

Storyteller: Once, a man was walking from Jerusalem to Jericho when he was attacked, beaten up, and robbed! The thieves took his money. They took his coat. They even took his pants . . . and his underwear! Yikes! He lay in a ditch by the side of the road and he called and he called and he called for help . . .

Injured group: Anybody, anybody please help me!
I was beaten and robbed and I have an owie!

Storyteller: Soon, a priest came by. Of course the man expected the priest to help him. But do you know what happened instead?

Unhelpful group: The priest walked by with his nose held high,
Pretending that he didn't hear the hurting man cry.

Storyteller: The man lay there getting weaker and weaker. He couldn't even crawl out of the ditch! So he did the only thing he could do, he called and he called and he called for help . . .

Injured group: Anybody, anybody please help me!
I was beaten and robbed and I have an owie!

Storyteller: Soon, a Levite came by. A Levite was someone who helped make sure everything was prepared for the worship services. Kinda like a janitor. The injured man was sure the Levite would help him. But you know what happened instead . . .

Unhelpful group: The Levite walked by with his nose held high,
Pretending that he didn't hear the hurting man cry.

Storyteller: By now, the man was getting desperate! He was too weak to yell anymore. All he could do was whisper and whisper and whisper for help . . .

Injured group: (whispering) Anybody, anybody please help me!
I was beaten and robbed and I have an owie!

Storyteller: Well, who should come along that same road but a Samaritan—a man this guy didn't like. He didn't like anyone from Samaria! He made fun of the people who lived there! He expected the Samaritan to walk on by, or maybe even hurt him worse! BUT . . .

The Samaritan stopped. He offered his hand.
He bandaged his wounds, and he helped the man.
He put him on a donkey, he took him to an inn,
And he paid the innkeeper to take care of him!

Here's the moral of the story, if you don't yet know it:
"Don't just say you love your neighbor, find a way to show it!"

See how the repetition of the story lends itself to using refrains? Also, notice that I included a moral for the story. You may choose to leave it out, but I like how it summarizes the story!

How to Create Refrains

Sometimes, the story itself will include a refrain that you can use. More often, you may need to make up your own refrain based on what's going on in the story. There are four ways to develop refrains:

Refrains can **echo the meaning of the text.** They can reflect what a character in the story might have said, thought, or done.

In the story of "Balaam and the Donkey" (Numbers 22-24), King Balak hires a sorcerer named Balaam to curse the Israelites. But rather than cursing them, he keeps blessing them instead! Here are possible refrains you could use. (By the way, see how Balaam's refrain applies to us today as well?)

(Group #1) Balak:
Quiet! Don't bless them! Don't say something good!
I told you to curse them and curse them you should!

(Group #2) Balaam:
But when God wants to bless, then I have to confess:
I must do what he wants—nothing more. Nothing less.

Refrains can **summarize what's going on in the story.** They can be used to describe a character or event every time it appears in the story.

In the story of "The Four Soils" (Matthew 13:3-9), Jesus shares how a farmer tried to plant his seeds, but only a small number of seeds survived. You could use the following refrain to summarize the big question of the story:
Seeds, seeds, which ones will grow?
With roots spreading out in the soil below . . .
With rocks and thorns and a hungry crow—
Seeds, seeds, which ones will grow?

Refrains can **reflect the change in direction** of the story,

In the story of "The Rich Man and Lazarus" (Luke 16:19-31), Jesus paints a vivid picture of the contrast between a rich unbeliever and a poor believer named Lazarus. In this life, Lazarus has nothing but hardship. As you tell the story, the rich man can say:

3. Remember that you want each group's part to be about the same length. Also, count up how many times each group does its part. Add or delete sections so that each group has about the same number of speaking parts. For fun, find a section of the story where one group has to do their part several times in a row!

4. As you write your version of the story, try to place cue words in places where it's natural to pause as you speak, such as at the end of sentences. The ending can either point to the application of the story, or include a transition into the application of the story.

5. Assign one part to each section of the audience. Choose groups by where they are seated or by who they are. For example, "All the adults will be Noah, all the boys will be animals, and all girls will be raindrops!"

6. Teach the groups their parts and the cue words on which they'll each say or do their part.

7. As you read or tell the story, be sure to pause after each cue word. Nod to each group to signal to them when they're to say their part.

"The Tale of the Evil Farmers" on page 44 is an example of a "Group Refrain" story.

I am rich, and you are poor.
I am healthy, you are sore.
I have good things, you have bad.
I am happy, you are sad.

But then, after they die, the tables have been turned. There is a great reversal and the rich man says:
You are rich, and I am poor.
You are healthy, I am sore.
You have good things, I have bad.
You are happy, I am sad.

In retelling the story of Christ's resurrection, you want the excitement of the news to spread into the hearts of your listeners. One way to do that is to tell the story with this refrain (pat your legs to create a rhythm and build enthusiasm each time you say it):
Have you heard? Have you heard?
Have you heard the news about Jesus?
Have you heard? Have you heard?
Have you heard the news about Jesus!

Here are good times in the story to use the refrain:
- When the women find the stone has been moved.
- When the angels tell the women that Jesus is alive.
- When the women tell the disciples what has happened.
- When Jesus reveals himself to Mary Magdalene.
- At the end of the story say, "Today, our job is the same as the woman who shared the good news. We can ask everyone we meet, "Have you heard. . . .""

Adding Music to the Stories You Tell

Scripture tells us to sing and make music to the Lord (Ephesians 5:19). A great way to do this is by adding music and singing to the stories you tell!

Make music with instruments. Use simple instruments such as kazoos, bells, xylophones, rain sticks, wood blocks, drums, maracas, or tambourines to allow children to make music during some (or all) of the story. You can use an instrument yourself, have a small group of children accompany you, or you can give instruments to the whole class.

You may wish to create your own simple rhythm instruments with beans, sticks, cardboard tubes, sand, or shells. Pour beans or sand into a container, seal the opening, and you've got a shaker! You can also use instruments to create background sounds or music for your story.

Some churches have hand bells available for their children's ministry. Find out if your church does and think of ways to include them in your story time, too!

Make music with your body. Children can join you by clapping their hands, tapping their feet, snapping their fingers, slapping their knees, or rubbing their hands together!

Make music by singing. Songs often appear in Bible stories. Many times when David

• The Tale of the Evil Farmers •

(based on Mark 12:1-9)

Notes for the storyteller: Divide the audience into four groups and assign each a part. If desired, have them stand up to say their part. As you teach each part, say it as silly or as exaggerated as possible. Add actions if you desire. Explain the cue words for each group. By the way, to build a lesson around this story, look up Isaiah 5:1-7.

Orchard Owner: *(in a funny vampire-like Transylvania accent)* We'll grow some green grapes!

Servants: *(sounding really stupid)* Duh, would you like some water?

Farmers: *(with a crazy, evil laugh)* We'll have the vineyard to ourselves! Ha, ha, ha, ha!

Vineyard: *(in an itty, bitty grape voice)* Oh, no! Don't step on me! Ahh! *(Squish!)*

Once upon a time, there was an *orchard owner* who planted a *vineyard.* He put up a wall, dug a pit for the winepress, and built a watchtower.

Then he went away on a journey and rented it to some *farmers.*

At harvest time, the *orchard owner* sent a *servant* back to the *farmers* to collect some of the fruit of the *vineyard.*

But they took him and beat him! And threw him out of the *vineyard.*

So, he sent another *servant.* And another *servant.* And still another *servant!* Some were beaten, others were killed by those wicked *farmers.*

Finally, the *orchard owner* said, "I'll send my son. Surely those wicked *farmers* won't hurt him!"

But, when the son arrived, they said, "If we kill him, we will forever own the *vineyard!*" So they took him, and killed him, and threw him out of the *vineyard.*

And then Jesus told the church leaders, "Therefore I tell you that the kingdom of God will be taken from you and given to a people who will produce its fruit" (Matthew 21:43). Jesus wants all of us to share the fruit and invite others into his kingdom! Let's all do the grape's part one more time together! *Vineyard!*

was going through a tough time, he wrote a song about it! As you tell those stories, sing the psalms he wrote.

Make up simple melodies for the refrains of your stories, sing worship songs, or listen to songs that summarize Bible stories. You may wish to sing a popular song or hymn and then tell the story about the person who wrote it, or when and why it was written.

Make music with a cheer, chant, or rap. Make up a song that retells a Bible story, or put a Bible verse to music. Think of a cheer, chant, or rap that you can use as a refrain for the story. Create a way of telling the whole story, or part of the story, in rhyme!

You may wish to divide the audience into sections or groups and assign each a different part or refrain to say or sing. For example, page 45 contains a copy of a rap I made up for a creative retelling of the Pentecost story for preteens. I taught three groups of students the first line of each stanza, and they repeated that line while I rapped the rest of that verse. We practiced until we could do it as a round!

Make music by adding a choral response. When using "Choral Response" you may read or say a section of the story and the audience will respond, or you can divide the group in half and teach each group a response. For example, if you were retelling the story of when David was anointed king of Israel (1 Samuel 16:1-13), you could have half of the class say, *"I'm not too big or brave or tall or strong or cute or smart!"*

And the other side could respond, *"But God sees what you're like inside, God looks at the heart!"*

Some psalms are set up this way. See Psalm 136 for an example of a simple story-song that includes a refrain your children could say or sing!

• The Pentecost Rap •

Each of them was speaking in a language not his own. (Group one repeats this line.)
Saying things that sounded very foreign and unknown,
(Sounding like your teenage sister on the telephone!)
Each of them was speaking in a language not his own.

Each of them had little flaming fires on his head. (Group two repeats this line.)
Filled up with the Spirit and not wine like people said.
No lighters, just ignited by the Holy Ghost instead!
Each of them had little flaming fires on his head.

Each of them was saying things he could not understand. (Group three repeats this line.)
But God was using all their words to spread throughout the land,
The message of his Son and what he'd done—he rose again!
Each of them was saying things he could not understand.

Encouraging Participation

Listed below are several introductions you can use to encourage the audience to become involved:

- "Now, in this story I'm going to ask you to help me with certain parts. Don't worry! I'll tell you what to do when it's time for you to do it! Okay? Here we go!"
- "This story is for kids of all ages. That means there may be times in this story when I'll ask you to act like a kid! Do you think you can do that? Good!"
- "Kids, I want you to help me make sure that the grownups are paying attention. When we get to _____ in this story, look around and make sure they're doing the actions, too!"

Don't force people to participate. Instead, encourage them to become involved. Sometimes in the middle of a story you may need to remind them to get involved. Try saying:

- "Here's where you come in."
- "This is your part."
- "I'll need your help with this section of the story!"
- "Wait, we have to try that again, I didn't see the girls dancing!"
- "Okay, now this time let's all try it!"
- "Everybody!"
- "Help me out!"
- "One more time!"
- "I can't hear you!"

Add mood music. Find instrumental music that reflects the mood of the story. For example, play light, airy instrumental music when telling about creation. Use somber or scary music when telling the story of David and Goliath. Use fast-paced, hip music when telling about one of Paul's missionary journeys. Or, look for CDs with sound effects that a helper can cue during the telling of the story. You may even have a talented instrumentalist at your church who can improvise music on a keyboard or guitar as you tell the story!

Add sound effects. A story rich in sounds is the story of Noah's Ark (Genesis 6-9). You could reenact the sounds of the building process (cutting wood, stacking, painting), the sounds of the animals (roaring, chirping, howling), the sounds of evil people (grunting, screaming, cackling) and the sounds of the storm (raining, blowing, thundering).

Sound effects are easy to add whenever there are animals, specific environments in your stories (such as jungles, night scenes, or crowded markets), or weather-related scenes (such as storms, wind, or thunder). Cue the audience when to participate, when to get louder, and when to be as soft as possible. You can also invite the audience to join you by humming or whistling during different sections of a story!

• Noah, Won't Ya Build Me an Ark •

(based on Genesis 6-9)

Here is an example of a story-song about Noah's Ark. Create your own tune for it, or just chant and rap it. Consider teaching the students actions to do during the refrain.

Chorus:
Noah! Go-n build me an ark,
Noah! Go-n build me an ark!
Uh-huh!
Noah! Go-n build me an ark,
Noah! Go-n build me an ark!

Well, God looked down, one sunny summer day,
He saw Noah sitting there on a pile of hay,
He said, "I'm not happy with the people of today,
I'm gonna send a big flood, gonna wash 'em all away." Saying . . .

Chorus

"It's gotta be a waterproof floatin' boat,
To hold bumblebees and frogs that croak,
It's gotta hold alligators, hold dinosaurs,
Gotta hold reptiles and a whole lot more!" Saying . . .

Chorus

"It's gotta hold lions, bears and tigers, too.
It's gotta be a great big floatin' zoo.
It's gotta hold giraffes with their stretchy necks,
And don't forget about Tyrannosaurus Rex!"
Saying . . .

Chorus

"I wanna save you, save your family, too.
But you gotta get aboard when the animals do,
I'll send 'em in coming at you two-by-two.
Line 'em up. Count 'em out. Fill the floatin' zoo!"
Saying . . .

Chorus

So Noah built, and he waited, and the animals came,
Two of each one, yeah, two of the same.
Then the rain came rainin' down on the land,
The ark started floatin' up from the sand . . .
And they floated and they floated all over the sea
While the whole wide world was as wet as can be.
And all the time Noah was a-feedin' that bunch,
Not a single dragonfly ever missed his lunch!
Saying . . .

Chorus

Then the rain stopped raining and the ark stopped flat—
Sitting on top of Mount Ararat.
And the sun dried the water as the cow chewed his cud,
And everyone stepped out, sloshing in the mud . . .
Saying . . .

Chorus

And that's about that, they started all anew,
Noah and his family and the animals, too;
And even today when you see a rainbow—
You can think back to what happened long ago,
When Noah went and built him an ark
Noah went and built him an ark.
Uh-huh!
Noah went and built him an ark.
Noah went and built him an ark!
Yeah, boyz!

Summary

You can create your own refrains to involve the audience. You can also add music to your storytelling by playing or handing out instruments, by using your body, singing, cheering, chanting, rapping, or responding. You can even add mood music or sound effects to the story!

Have fun making music to the Lord!

Chapter 7

Act It Out!

How to Tell Stories with Movement and Creative Dramatics

ONE OF THE BEST ways to help students remember stories is by getting them actively involved in the storytelling process. You can do this by adding creative dramatics and movement to the stories you tell.

You can use creative dramatics to set the stage before the story begins, to actively involve your listeners while you tell the story, or as a way of review after the story is completed. In this chapter, you'll learn ten creative storytelling techniques that actively involve your audience. The first activity is for use *before* your story.

1. Imaginary Journey

A great way to prepare children for the story you're about to tell is through an activity I like to call "Imaginary Journey."

Here is an example of how an Imaginary Journey could be used to prepare your listeners for a lesson on the Sermon on the Mount (found in Matthew 5-7).

> OK, kids let's all stand up! I want you to imagine that we're no longer here in this classroom, but that we're walking along a path that leads up the side of a mountain. Walk with me, everyone! Whew! It's hard work! It sure is steep! What's the weather like? Hot! OK, pretend you're really hot and tired. . . .
>
> What kinds of animals might we see? Oh, no, not a bear! Run! . . . Climb! . . . Run! . . . Climb! . . . Pretend to run along this dirt road! But it's been rainy and you don't have any shoes on . . . feel the squishy mud ooze between your toes? Doesn't that feel nice? . . . OK, the bear is gone. Whew!
>
> Now, let's climb up the side of this mountain for story time today! . . . Climb over the boulder. . . . Now be careful as you cross this little mountain stream. . . . Tiptoe. Tiptoe. Tiptoe. Good. . . . Wait a minute! Look at all these people! . . . There must be thousands of them! I wonder if someone important is coming? Maybe the president? Nope. Someone even more important. Look! . . . It's Jesus! Wow! He's gonna talk! Let's all sit down and be quiet so we can hear what he has to say.

As you can see, this type of activity effectively prepares children to listen to your story. They're actively involved, their imaginations are ignited, they can picture what's happening in the story, and they're curious to see what will happen next.

Here are some steps to help you create your own Imaginary Journeys:

• Look for stories with specific environments—jungles, forests, beaches, mountains, or nighttime scenes. As you read through the story, try to notice sights, sounds, and smells. Why types of things might you see if you were on your way to this story? What sounds would you hear?

- Let the children suggest things that you might see or dramatically act out on your journey. What would you be thinking about? Where are you going?
- End your "Imaginary Journey" by directing the children to quietly sit down and prepare to listen to the rest of the story.

The next seven ideas are ways to weave creative dramatics *into* the stories you tell.

2. Organic Storytelling

Closely related to an "Imaginary Journey" is "Organic Storytelling." With this technique, you begin with the story outline, or framework, and then with the help of the audience, you add details to the story.

For example, when Jesus told the story of "The Lost Coin" he said, "Or suppose a woman has ten silver coins and loses one. Does she not light a lamp, sweep the house and search carefully until she finds it? And when she finds it, she calls her friends and neighbors together and says, 'Rejoice with me; I have found my lost coin.' In the same way, I tell you, there is rejoicing in the presence of the angels of God over one sinner who repents" (Luke 15:8-10).

This is a very short story. To retell it to children you could use "Organic Storytelling" to fill in details to the story. Have the children pat their legs to keep a rhythm and then have them repeat after you,

Once there was a lady who lost her coin and she didn't know where to look. . . . (Repeat.) Now, kids, where would you look for something important that you might have lost? (Allow them the chance to respond.) OK, under the couch. Let's try that! Once there was a lady who lost her coin and she didn't know where to look . . . so she leaned on over and looked under the couch, and she poked her finger and said, "Ouch!" but she didn't find her coin, no she didn't find her coin. Once there was a lady who lost her coin and she didn't know where to look. . . . Where else might she look for her coin?

After a few times through, let the woman find her coin and then finish the story. By using this technique, you encourage children to use their imaginations, participate in the storytelling event, and cooperatively come up with a unique way of retelling the story.

Here are some steps to help you create your own "Organic Stories":
- Look for stories with simple plots and lots of possible variations. For example, getting on Noah's Ark (have the audience give you ideas for the different animals), or looking for the lost sheep (have the children suggest places to look, such as behind a rock, in a cave, on the mountain, etc.).
- Allow the audience to provide suggestions and then use them without embarrassing the child, even if his or her suggestion seems a little silly.
- Stay within the framework of the story, but use your imagination to explore possibilities.
- Limit the responses and your reaction to them. One way to do this is by attempting to make your suggestions rhyme. It sounds hard, but for a lot of people it's easier than it sounds!

3. Masks

Use masks to portray characters or emotions related to the story. Masks can be real or imaginary. To put on an imaginary mask, cover your face with your hands, then pull your hands away to reveal a different emotion! Have the children practice putting on the same masks that you put on.

You may wish to make real masks by cutting out eye holes from a paper plate and gluing a craft stick on the bottom of the plate as a handle. Then draw faces and expressions on the plate. Make one mask for each of the characters in the story, or for each of the different emotions expressed in the story.

- **Partner Masks**—Tell the story with a partner. Every time you switch to a new character or emotion, your partner puts on the mask for that character or emotion.
- **Group Masks**—Invite three children to the front of the room. Assign each child a different imaginary mask (for example, happy, sad, and surprised). Then divide the audience into three groups and, whenever you point to their leader, the audience members put on the imaginary mask of the child leading their group! Before class, go through your story and identify when the characters felt these three different emotions. Then when you tell the story, remember to pause long enough for the groups to put on and take off their masks.

4. Pantomime

Pantomime, or "mime," is typically thought of as "silent acting." However, world-famous mime, Tony Montanaro, defines mime as "physical eloquence." In other words, mime is the art of using your body well to communicate. Using mime doesn't mean you can't talk, or that you have to wear white makeup, or that you pretend that you're inside an invisible box! It simply means you're communicating effectively by the way you move your body through space.

Mime can be used in many ways to creatively retell Bible stories:

- **Human Video**—Choreograph the movement of children to correspond to a favorite song or instrumental piece. As the music plays, the children act out ways of visually representing a story that relates to the song. They don't necessarily act out every word of the song, but show instead how the song moves them and makes them feel. You can use either instrumental music or music with words.
- **Human Sculpture**—As you read the story, one student moves a partner in ways to reflect what is happening in the story. This can be a very funny activity to do with older students!
- **Human Clay**—As you tell the story, have the children pretend to be the different characters or animals in the story. Encourage the children to become different story characters by reshaping their bodies. For example, say, "Let's all act like the lions in Daniel's den. Great! Now let's pretend we're Daniel praying to God. Good! Now turn yourselves into the angel that shut the mouths of the lions!" This technique works well when you have different animals or distinctively different people in a story.
- **Silent Story**—Children simply act out a Bible story with no musical accompaniment or narration.
- **Narrative Pantomime**—While one person reads or tells a story, a small group of children act out the story. This can be done improvisationally (where children make up their movements on the spot) or it can be rehearsed and then reenacted for another group of people.

Let's look a little more in-depth at using narrative pantomime. There are a few simple techniques you can follow to make it an even more successful activity.

First, look for stories with lots of action and not much talking. The more action, the better! If there's a lot of dialogue, descriptions, flashbacks, or too many characters, you'll need to rewrite that section of the story or leave it out. You want the characters to say as few words as possible.

Next, go through the story and choose how many characters you need. Obviously, you'll need actors to play all the people in the story. But don't limit yourself to that! You can have people play animals (such as snakes, fish, or donkeys) and inanimate objects (such as boats, rocks, wind, or doors)! It can be fun to use people in unexpected ways—such as having a boy play a girl's part or vice versa. Make a list of how many characters (both boys and girls) you'll need.

Practice reading the story aloud and see where you might want to pause. This isn't tough, just remember to pause after every action verb! In other words, you want to pause long enough to give the actors time to act out what you just read. As you read through the story, think about how you may need to coach the actors or encourage them as they do the different actions.

Finally, as you invite volunteers up front, define the role each student will play. For example, if I invite Tammy up front, I might shake her hand, whisper to her what character she will be playing, tell her where she should stand to start, and explain when she will come onstage. I may also reassure her that she doesn't need to say anything (if that's the case). Let's see how this all works together!

Jesus' parable of "The Terrible Tenants" found in Mark 12:1-9 is an example of a story that works well for narrative pantomime. He starts his story by saying, "A man planted a vineyard. He put a wall around it, dug a pit for the winepress and built a watchtower. Then he rented the vineyard to some farmers and went away on a journey" (Mark 12:1). Notice all the verbs Jesus used? "Planted, put, dug, built, rented, went." Because this section is packed with action and little dialogue, it's easy for folks to act out as you read aloud. Before beginning, call up ten or twelve volunteers and assign them their parts.

- Owner (one person)
- Tenants (two or three people)
- First servant (one person)
- Second servant (one person)
- Third servant (one person)
- Many other servants (two or three people)
- Owner's son (one person)
- Wall (one or two people)

Here is how it might sound with pauses and prompts for the actors:

> "A man planted a vineyard. . . . GO AHEAD AND PLANT SOME SEEDS . . . LOTS OF SEEDS . . . MORE SEEDS! MORE! . . . GOOD. . . . He put a wall around it . . . dug a pit for the winepress . . . DON'T FALL INTO THE PIT! . . . I THINK IT WAS A LITTLE DEEPER . . . and built a watchtower. Then he rented the vineyard to some farmers. . . . FARMERS! WHERE ARE YOU? . . . WAIT, DON'T WALK THROUGH THE WALL! USE THE GATE! . . . and went away on a journey . . . BYE-BYE!" (Mark 12:1).

As you can see, the comments inserted into the text are responses to what might be happening onstage. You may wish to plan some humorous comments beforehand, but you'll need to watch what's actually happening and be prepared to respond to it. Also, you need to watch your actors so you can give them verbal cues about when to come onstage, exit the stage, etc.

OK, let's move through the story. I've inserted ellipses (. . .) in the places you may wish to pause.

> "At harvest time he sent a servant to the tenants to collect from them some of the fruit of the vineyard. . . . But they seized him . . . beat him up . . . REMEMBER, WE ARE ONLY ACTING! NO REAL BEATINGS PLEASE! . . . and sent him away empty-handed. . . . Then he sent another servant to them . . . they struck this man on the head . . . OUCH! THAT'S GOTTA HURT! . . . and treated him shamefully. . . . He

sent still another . . . and that one they killed. . . . He sent many others; some of them they beat, others they killed. . . . BY THE END THERE WERE BODIES EVERY-WHERE . . . IT LOOKED LIKE THE SET OF A KUNG FU MOVIE . . ." (Mark 12:2-6).

Wow. Still no dialogue. See all the verbs? Notice the action? This is the ideal type of story for a "Narrative Pantomime!"

By the way, as you probably noticed, this story includes lots of violence. Obviously, you don't want the students to really beat each other up! Although I wouldn't use this story with younger children, I would use this story with preteens. They'll probably think it's cool! Be careful to make sure the story isn't too scary for your students.

Some dialogue appears in the next section, but to make it easier to act out, I've edited it to make it shorter. Here is how the story might finish . . .

"He had one left to send, a son, whom he loved. He sent him last of all, thinking they would respect him . . . But they grabbed him . . . and killed him . . . and threw him out of the vineyard . . . because they wanted it all for themselves. So what did the owner do? He went and got rid of those tenants . . . so that the fruit could be shared with everyone . . . The end" (based on Mark 12:7-9).

5. Gestures and Finger Plays

Whenever you invite the audience to join you in movement or creative dramatics, be sure to create an atmosphere in which participation is safe, encouraged, and fun. Invite people to participate, but don't force them to. Clearly explain when you want them to join you, what you want them to do, and when they should stop. You might say, "When I point to your group you'll start making the sound of the lions in the lion den, but when I pull my hand back and stop pointing, you'll stop. Let's practice." Cue the audience on when to do their part by gesturing to them, saying a word or phrase, or by the tone of voice you use as you tell the story.

You can invite the audience to do gestures with their hands, arms, or feet whenever you come to the refrain in a story. Consider using sign language, bouncing in place, pretending to walk, waving arms, tapping feet, or using other simple movements. (Be aware that younger children may have a tough time clapping and singing at the same time.) Exaggerated actions are funniest, so let loose and have fun!

You may wish to have a group of students join you, or you might want everyone to participate. You can have the audience do the actions with you, right after you're done, or you can start a movement on one side of the room and pass it along like "the wave" that spectators do in baseball stadiums!

6. Audience Echo-Mime

For this technique, as you tell the story, you do (or a storytelling partner does) actions that correspond to what is happening in the story. The audience then does the same action, as if they were echoing or mirroring what's happening. You can use this technique for sections of a story, or for an entire story.

Explain that every time you do (or your partner does) an action, the audience is going to repeat it. Before class, read the entire skit at least once to become familiar with the story. I'd suggest selecting a volunteer to lead the pantomime actions. Give him or her a copy of the script. Have your helper read and practice her part before performing it with you.

During the lesson, invite students to join in by acting out parts of the story. Tell students to act out what you say by imitating the actions of your partner. Then begin reading the skit.

• Big Bad Naaman's Big Bad Bath •

(based on 2 Kings 5)

What to Say	What to Do
Naaman was an army commander for Aram.	Salute.
He was used by God to lead his army to victory!	Put one arm up in victory and stand tall.
He was very strong ...	Flex your muscles.
and very brave ...	Make fists and place them on your hips confidently.
and feared no man!	Shake head back and forth.
But, he had leprosy, a dreaded and deadly skin disease for which there was no cure.	Bite nails on both hands.
Naaman thought he was a goner.	Make a throat-slitting gesture.
He was hopeless.	Two thumbs down.
But wait!	Hold one finger in the air.
A slave girl from Israel had an idea!	Tap your head with your finger.
She'd heard of Elisha, one of God's prophets in Samaria.	Point off into the distance.
And she said, "He'll cure you of leprosy!"	Two thumbs up.
So Naaman asked his boss for sick leave.	Kneel and pretend to plead.
The king told him, "Yes! Hurry and get cured!	Point off into the distance.
Here, take this note and give it to Israel's king."	Pretend to hand the note to someone.
So Naaman packed a lot of money and nice things in his suitcases ...	Rub fingers together like you're holding money.
and took many camels ...	Make two humps with your hands.
and servants ...	Bow down with your hands stretched out.
and his king's note.	Make a box with your fingers.
When he arrived in Israel he gave the note to Israel's king.	Pretend to hand the note to someone.
The note said, "This is my brave soldier Naaman,	Make fists and place them on your hips confidently.
please cure him of his leprosy."	Two thumbs down.
But the king was angry and frightened by the note so he ripped his clothes.	Pretend to rip your shirt.
He said, "No one can cure this guy! He's a goner!	Make a throat-slitting gesture.
I think Naaman's king is trying to start a war with me!"	Shake one finger up and down, scolding style.
Then Elisha the prophet heard that the king had torn his clothes.	Cup a hand behind your ear.
So, he sent a message that he would cure Naaman ...	Two thumbs up.
And fix the king's problem ...	Put one fist on top of the other.
(but not the king's clothes.)	Hold shirt and look at "ripped" spot.
So Naaman took his riches ...	Rub fingers together like you're holding money.
his camels ...	Make two humps with your hands.

his servants . . .	Bow down with your hands stretched out.
and his note . . .	Make a box with your fingers.
and rode to Elisha's house.	Pretend to ride a horse.
But Elisha stayed inside when Naaman knocked on his door.	Pretend to knock at a door.
He sent his own note to Naaman.	Make a box with your fingers.
"Go wash yourself seven times in the Jordan River . . .	Pretend to wash armpits.
Your skin will get better . . .	Look over your whole body and smile.
and you will be healed."	Applaud!
But the note only made Naaman angry!	Look angry and clench fists.
Naaman said, "I thought the prophet would come out and call on God's name . . .	Lift up your hands in praise to God.
wave his hand over me . . .	Wave one hand over the other.
and cure me of leprosy!	Two thumbs up.
Why should I wash in the Jordan river?	Hold hands up, palms out, in a questioning manner.
Our rivers are better than any flowing in Israel!	Make ocean waves with hands.
Who needs this guy or his river!"	Wave hand away and look disgusted.
And Naaman went off in a rage.	Punch one fist into the other.
But Naaman's servants said to him, "Wait, Naaman!	Put one hand up like a stop sign.
Think about this for a minute!	Tap head with one finger.
If the prophet had told you to do something great,	Hold both hands up in victory.
wouldn't you have done it?	Hold both hands palm up and look curious.
Why not do this simple thing—wash and be healed!"	Pretend to wash armpits.
So Naaman walked down to the river,	Walk in place.
And washed himself seven times.	Wash armpits.
And his leprosy was gone!	Look over entire body, then put two thumbs up.
And Naaman was very happy!	Huge smiles.
Naaman quickly returned to Elisha.	Run in place.
And praised God for what he'd done.	Put hands up in praise position.
Naaman thanked Elisha	Shake someone's hand vigorously.
and promised to worship the One True God from then on.	Hold both hands up in praise position.
The End.	Bow, and have a seat.

7. Devotion in Motion (Creative Movement and Dance)

When Jesus told the story of "The Prodigal Son," he mentioned that the people celebrating the return of the younger son were dancing (Luke 15:25). David danced before the Lord and encouraged others to do so as well. Scripture even encourages worshipers to "praise his name with dancing" (Psalm 149:3)! Dance and creative movement are important expressions of celebration and worship!

Strobe lights or black lights with white clothing can create very interesting visual effects for stories. I once saw a group of children wearing black clothes (with white skeleton bones

The Language of Movement

We can express lots of emotions through the language of movement. As you craft your story, look for ways to include creative movement into the telling!

Types of movement	bend, crawl, float, gallop, grow, hop, jump, leap, march, roll, run, shake, shrink, skip, slide, slink, slither, soar, spin, stalk, stomp, stretch, sway, swing, tiptoe, trip, twist, walk
Directions of movement	up or down, in or out, over or under, frontward or backward, together or apart, curving or straight, sideways or diagonally
Qualities of movement	sustained or percussive, staccato or flowing, vibratory or suspended, swinging or straight, smooth or choppy, fast or slow, strong or weak, hard or soft, heavy or light, moving or still
Levels of movement	high, middle, low
Sizes of movement	small or big

painted on them) present a very cool, black light choreographed movement presentation of "The Valley of the Dry Bones" (see Ezekiel 37)!

8. Add-On Storytelling

Sometimes you'll be teaching or telling a story that your students have heard before. A great way to keep their attention is through "Add-On Storytelling." With this technique, each student adds one line to the story, and the goal is to tell the complete story by having everyone in the class contribute! So, you'd begin by saying the first line of a story. The next person would continue from where you left off, and so on.

It can be hilarious to see how different this story ends up being from the one recorded in the Bible! After everyone has had a turn, look up the Bible story and identify the differences and similarities between the two stories.

You can also do this as a review activity after you've finished telling the story!

Use these last two creative dramatics activities *after* your story.

9. Improvisation

When you've finished telling a story, you can use role-playing to extend the learning and to apply the lessons of the Bible story. When improvising, children create their own dialogue, action, or characters based on situations or scenes related to the Bible story.

To create your own improvisational situations based on a Bible story, first identify what the main point of the story is. For example, "The Good Samaritan" (found in Luke 10:25-37) is about treating people of a different race, gender, political, or religious background with respect and compassion. To translate that into language kids can understand, you might say,

- Don't pick on people who are different than you.
- Don't look down on others.
- Be nice to everyone, not just the people who are nice to you.
- Be kind to the kids no one else likes.
- Help people who are hurt, even if they're not your friends.

The Good SamarSKITan

Use the following improvisational drama activities to bring up issues related to the story of "The Good Samaritan." Discuss the improvisations before the close of class.

1. You and your friends are playing basketball when a new kid you don't know shows up. He looks a little weird. Act out what happens when he tries to join your game. (Three or four people.)

2. Two kids are going to the park. Act out a scene of what happens when one kid's younger brother tries to tag along. Neither of the older two want him to come! (Three people.)

3. Your mom was driving you to school when the car stalled by the side of the highway. After three hours, someone finally stops. Act out your conversation. (Two or three people.)

4. Two people walk by a beggar. A father tries to explain to his child why he didn't give the man any money. The boy doesn't understand. (Three people.)

5. A couple of bullies have beaten you up and stolen your bike. Someone you always pick on and make fun of is coming your way—you don't know if she wants to help you or hurt you. Act out what happens. (Two people.)

6. For the first time ever you're chosen captain of a team! You get to pick teams! You want to pick one of your friends, but you notice a kid who always gets chosen last. You wonder if you should choose him. Your friends will probably laugh at you if you do. Act out what happens. (Two or three people.)

7. Johnny always plays by himself on the playground. One day, you invite him to play kickball with you and your friends because you want to be nice. He swears at you and gets angry. Act out what happens next. (Two or three people.)

8. You see your Sunday school teacher walk right by this one kid who is sitting in the corner, crying. You wonder if she saw him or ignored him. You decide to talk with her. Act out the conversation. (Two people.)

9. Your mom has asked you to do the dishes tonight, even though it's your brother's night to help. Your brother claims he's sick. Act out what happens. (Two or three people.)

10. Susie always pretends she's hurt or sick so she can spend time with the teacher. One day, when she's crying, you and your friends laugh at her. She runs to the teacher. How do you feel? What do you do? (Two to four people.)

Then create situations that portray these principles. See the box above for examples.

Improvisation can also be used in the middle of a story. Have a group of students improvise how they think the story might end, and then go back and read or tell the rest of the story to see how close they were!

10. Guessing Games

Guessing games work great as a way to review stories at the end of a unit or a series of stories. Here are four creative guessing games to use when reviewing stories.

Frozen Poses—Create frozen statues of Bible characters, scenes or objects; then have others guess who you're supposed to be portraying. You can have the students freeze their faces in a moment of emotion from the story, or freeze their bodies in a moment of action from the story.

If you choose, have the statues come to life for five seconds before letting the other children guess who they're supposed to be. You might wish to have the actors act out the jobs or activities of the different characters.

Another variation is to have one person onstage be the statue, and have a partner shape his or her body into the frozen pose of a story character. Then have the audience guess who the shaper was trying to portray!

A variation of this activity is to mime objects that appeared in the stories and then guess what they are.

Scripture Snapshots—Create frozen scenes from pivotal parts of Bible stories with small groups of students. Practice the poses and then present the snapshots as part of a special program. Here is a list of some scenes I've used for a Good Friday service:

Snapshot 1—Jesus Reveals the Betrayer (Mark 14:17-21)

Snapshot 2—Jesus Institutes the Lord's Supper (Mark 14:22-25)

Snapshot 3—Disciples Sleep While Jesus Prays (Mark 14:32-34, 40; Luke 22:45a)

Snapshot 4—Judas Betrays Jesus (Mark 14:43-45)

Snapshot 5—Guards Beat Jesus (Mark 15:16-20)

Snapshot 6—Peter Denies Jesus (Matthew 26:73, 74; Luke 22:56-58; John 18:25-27)

Snapshot 7—Guards Crucify Jesus (Mark 15:24, 25)

Begin with a blackout. As the reader begins speaking, slowly bring up the lights so that as he finishes each reading, the light allows the audience to see the "Scripture Snapshot." Go to blackout again as the actors quickly and quietly move to create the next "Scripture Snapshot." Slowly raise the lights as the reader begins the next scene. Allow only three or four seconds of darkness between each scene.

Backward Stories—Read a story backward and have the students guess which story it is!

Acting Up or Acting Out?

How do you control your students when you start doing all these active stories? The first key is to make it clear when the children are to participate and when they're to be silent. Be sure they understand clearly what to do, when to do it, and when to stop. If things get out of control, it may mean you didn't clearly communicate how much participation was appropriate.

Have a control device. Perhaps turning off the lights, raising your hand, pulling out a favorite puppet, putting on a special hat, or a saying a word such as "Freeze!" I made a small musical chime that grabs attention and helps calm the children. Take fishing line and tie it around a stick or small board. Hang keys at various lengths so that when they dangle against each other, they sound like chimes. (You can usually get leftover keys free from hardware stores.) Whatever the device, use it to get their attention and make sure they know when to be quiet and listen to the story.

Respond to distractions. For example, if a bell or cell phone rings in the middle of the story, pause until the noise is done, then mime picking up a telephone and say, "Hello. Mom? Why are you calling me in the middle of my story? I have a whole classroom full of kids here waiting to see if Daniel makes it out of the pit and you're just calling to say 'Hi'? Goodbye, Mom!"

Keep calm and remain in control. Change the pace of the story or redirect the listeners back to the story. You might say, "Hey, kids! You sure do know how to act like great snakes! Let's all slither back to our seats so we can listen to the rest of the story and find out what happens to Adam and Eve."

You don't want to play the role of disciplinarian. Instead, put a finger to your lips say, "Shhh," then quickly continue the story. If a child is continually disruptive, you may need to ask another leader to escort him or her to a seat in the back of the room.

If the audience stops paying attention, it does you no good to continue telling your story. You may need to shorten your story, switch to another story, or switch to a different activity: "We'll get back to Balaam and his donkey in a few minutes. Let's take a little break and make our craft project."

End your program with a clear application, a cool-down activity, and remember, kill it while it's still kicking! Don't wait until the story or the activity is getting tedious and boring, instead end it while the kids are still interested and excited!

Chapter 8

Costumes and Props

How to Use Stuff to Tell Stories

GOD HAS ALWAYS used the unusual, the weird, the shocking, and the surprising to get people's attention. In fact, once God
- told Jeremiah to wear a yoke;
- used a ghostly hand to write an ominous message on a wall;
- spoke to Moses through a burning bush that wasn't consumed;
- told Isaiah to preach naked for three years;
- had Ezekiel eat a scroll, lay on his side for 390 days, use excrement for fuel, and shave his head;
- turned water into wine, withered a fig tree, and fed thousands with a little boy's meal!

We can use the unusual, the weird, and the shocking to grab people's attention and make the message more memorable, just like God did!

Some stories naturally lend themselves to the use of props. You can tell stories with paper, clay, hats, costumes, etc., but remember that the props are there to serve the story, not the other way around. Don't get so gimmicky that people remember the object, but forget the story!

Using Costumes

One time when I was telling stories at a church in Tennessee, I met a seminary professor of Old Testament theology. He explained that before the stories of the Old Testament were written down, they were retold and passed on orally. One example he noted was the story of Joseph. Whenever there is a change of scenery, there is a change of clothes! Joseph starts with normal clothes, then he gets a fancy coat, then slave's clothes, then manager's clothes, then prisoner's clothes, then rich ruler's clothes! This professor suggested that these costume changes were probably used by ancient storytellers to help them (and their audiences) remember the story! Cool, huh?

Simple costumes can add lots of fun and flavor to the stories you tell. Consider these possibilities:
- **Hats**—wear a different hat for each character, or wear one hat different ways to represent the different characters in the story.
- **Canes**—use a cane as a shepherd's staff, a club, a sword, or another prop.
- **Wigs**—create funny characters with wigs. If you invite volunteers up and have them wear wigs, the kids will love it!

- **Glasses**—wear oversized glasses or sunglasses to create unique characters.
- **Blankets**—turn a blanket into a cape, a robe, a snake, a child, or a hat depending on how you manipulate it.

When I tell the story of "The Three Billy Goats Gruff," I use a baseball cap as my only costume piece. I turn it three different ways on my head to represent each of the three billy goats, and I take it off when I become the troll. In this way, a simple costume piece can be used quickly and easily to portray four different characters in the same story. You could do the same when portraying the characters in a Bible story.

Whatever you wear is your costume! Think of the messages you give just by the way you dress. Be aware that your choice of clothes affects the storytelling event.

Using Objects and Props

The only limit to the props you use is your imagination! I've seen people use magic tricks, balloon twisting, string, paper, food, and numerous other props when telling stories. Be aware, however, that the more elaborate the props, the easier it is for the audience to become distracted from the story.

Here are some problems I've seen with props:
- **Too small**—The audience needs to be able to see your objects! I once saw a lady use a test tube to tell a story to more than one thousand people. No one beyond the first few rows could see what she was doing. It was embarrassing to watch.
- **Too distracting**—The props become the focus of attention rather than the story. This is a problem I've seen with felt boards.
- **Too complicated**—Keep your props simple. If your props are too complicated, you'll spend too much time and energy concentrating on using them correctly, and your story will suffer. This happened to me one time when I was trying to do an illusion that related to my story. It backfired completely! The more intricate a prop, the more likely it is you'll drop it, break it, or mishandle it.
- **Too unique**—Avoid using objects that are so interesting or unique that they draw attention away from the story. This may happen if you have an elaborate coat, cane, hat, or costume piece. You don't want the audience thinking about how clever or interesting the prop is, you want them paying attention to the story.

Anything that can easily be manipulated or shaped can be used to tell a story. Here is a partial list of objects to consider using as you tell your stories:

1. Story sack—Use a small pouch to hold objects related to the story. Kids will wonder what you're going to pull out next!

2. Overhead projector—Use objects, action figures, and cutouts to tell a story on an overhead projector. Add a glass pan with real water for storm or sailing stories. Add food coloring, antacid tablets, etc. to the water for special effects!

3. Toys—Use stuffed animals, toys, dolls, army men, and action figures as props.

4. Dowel rods—Manipulate a dowel rod to represent different objects or images from the story. Also consider using chopsticks, branches, or sticks.

5. Food—Eat foods that are referred to in the story, eaten in the story, or that are related to the story. Create your own edible object lessons using pretzels, gum drops, marshmallows, raisins, crackers, cheese, apple slices, or peanut butter. (Warning: some children are seriously allergic to peanuts!)

6. Felt board—Use felt figures and a colorful background to tell the story. There are many fine felt boards and figures commercially available.

7. Magnet board—Glue magnets on the backs of small cutouts and place them on a metal board, similar to a felt board.

• Reunited! •

(a stick gospel presentation)

Notes for the storyteller: I've used this presentation with thousands of children around the country. Once, at a large church in Akron, a lady told me, "I've been in children's ministry for twenty years and that's the best and clearest gospel presentation I've ever seen." Here it is.

Invite two volunteers to come up front. Have each of them hold onto the ends of a stick that's about three feet long. Then explain that one of them will represent Eve, the first lady ever. And the other child will represent God. I usually say something like this,

"OK, Susan, we're going to pretend that you're a human being. Do you think you can do that? Good. And John, we're going to pretend that you're not a human being, but that you're really God. OK? Now, we know you're not God. Not really! But for this story, that's the part you'll be playing. *(Have the kids stand on either side of you, each holding one end of the stick.)*

Now, long ago God created a huge and beautiful world. And he put two people in a place called the Garden of Eden. Their names were Adam and Eve. *(Turn to Susan.)* Your husband's name was Adam. *(Suggestively)* Wooooo!

Every evening Adam and Eve would go walking with God in the garden. They were so close to God that nothing separated them. This stick shows how close and connected they were to God.

But then, Adam and Eve disobeyed God and their closeness with him was broken. *(Take the stick and break it over your knee. Then hand one of the sticks to each child.)*

The people could no longer enjoy being close to God because they'd done what he told them not to do. Now they were separated from him. Go ahead and back up, Eve . . . farther! Farther! . . . God didn't go anywhere. He just waited.

And all throughout history, people tried to get close to God by being good. *(Turn to Eve.)* You were good!

Come a little closer to God . . . but then you were bad—back up! Then you were good. You were really good! Come closer . . . but then you were bad! So bad! Really bad! Back up . . . then you were good. . . . *(Go on and have fun with this part, but be sure that the students understand that no matter how good people were, they weren't good enough to be close to God again.)*

In fact, the Bible says all people have sinned and fall short of God's perfect standard of holiness (Romans 3:23; 5:12). And so, since people could not be good enough to bridge the gap from earth to Heaven, *(invite Susan closer)* God built a bridge from Heaven to earth *(take the stick from John)*. Jesus was born fully God *(hold up the stick representing God)* and fully man *(hold up the other stick; then bring them together)* together in one person.

And Jesus lived a perfect life. *(Invite John and Susan to each hold one end of a short stick again, you keep the other stick.)* Then he died in our place so that we could experience true closeness with God once again. And he provided the way for us to be close to God again . . . *(hold your stick up against the one the children are holding to form the shape of a cross)* at the cross.

Let's thank John and Susan for helping me tell that story! *(Lead the audience in applause for the two volunteers.)*

8. **Books**—Show children books or pictures. Remember, when you're reading a picture book to children, show them the pictures after reading each page. Hold the book up so that it's easy for all the children to see, and, remember that the smaller the pictures, the closer the children need to be to see them. The younger the children, the fewer lines you'll be able to read per page and still keep their attention.

9. **Drawings**—Draw shapes, figures, or pictures that reveal the action or transformation in the story.

10. **Dual props**—Consider holding up two different objects and waving or wiggling them to represent the different characters in a story. For example, when Jesus and the devil were talking the desert, you could hold up a crown for Jesus (He is our King!), and a rubber snake for the devil!

11. **Musical instruments**—See chapter six.

12. **Attention-getters**—Use unusual items, illusions, or science experiments (object talks)

Signal Cards

When telling the story of Samson and Delilah, have three signal cards:

- Hold up the "Ohh!" card whenever the Philistines appear.
- Hold up the "Ah!" card whenever Samson is on the scene.
- Hold up the "Ooh, la-la!" card when Delilah appears.

Here are some more ideas for phrases to use on signal cards:

Whoa!	Curses, foiled again!	Duh, OK!
My hero!	Radical, dude!	(Gasp!)
I'll save you!	Bummer, man!	(Cheer!)
Boo!	Wipeout!	(Sigh)
Hooray!	Whoa, baby!	(Look surprised!)
Eek!	Look out below!	(Evil laughter!)
Oh, no!	Yikes!	(Wild applause!)
Cool!	That last step's a doozy!	(Hiss!)

---

to grab and keep the attention of the children. Any story with a transformation will work well for an illusion.

13. Scarves—Use crepe paper, ribbons, streamers, banners, or scarves to represent fire, wind or water. Have children wave them at appropriate times in the story.

14. Tangram—Arrange tangram shapes into images that correspond to images from the story. Choose a story with specific objects, transformations, or distinctly different characters. (The pattern for this Chinese shape can be found in most dictionaries or online. Pre-cut pieces can also be purchased at school supply or craft stores.)

15. Bubbles—Blow bubbles whenever God or an angel speaks in a story.

16. Crafts—Use carefully planned craft projects to reinforce the lesson.

17. Signal cards—Use cue cards throughout the story to signal when and how the audience should participate. Include either words for the audience to say, or actions for them to do at specific points in the story. You'll want to choose simple words or short phrases. With younger children, use pictures rather than words.

18. Manipulatives—Use anything that can be changed into another shape or form.
- Paper can be cut, crinkled, or folded.
- Aluminum foil can be squeezed, flattened, or molded.
- Pipe cleaners can be bent, twisted, or curled.
- String can be cut, tied, or designed.

19. Sensory Props—Use props that specifically appeal to various senses to facilitate learning and to help the students remember the story.
- **Sight**—Turn off the lights, flicker them, or use filters to create different-colored lighting.
- **Touch**—Use squirt guns when telling stories of storms, rain, or floods. Use finger-paints with younger children. Use a fan to create wind, or a hairdryer to create a desert wind!
- **Hearing**—Add music, sound effects, or funny noises to the story.
- **Taste**—Eat food that relates to the story. Something sweet (like honey) can represent manna or God's Word!
- **Smell**—Place candy or fruit in a bag to create a sweet smell. Use stinky garbage to represent sin!

20. Puppets—Consider using finger puppets, hand puppets, or arm puppets. Anything that opens (like pliers or a folding chair) can be manipulated like a puppet! The type of puppetry you use will be based on your skill, the age and interest level of your audience, and the types of puppets you have available.

• That Was Good! That Was Bad! •

(a signal card story)

Notes for the storyteller: Create two signal cards, one that reads, "That was good!" and the other, "That was bad!" You could also have students give a thumbs up or a thumbs down. Invite two volunteers to the front and give them each a signal card. Explain that as you tell the story, they'll hold up the card whenever you point to them. Half of the audience will say, "That was good!" and half will say, "That was bad!" Practice. Then tell the story!

Once long ago, God created a beautiful world.	*That was good!*
But Adam and Eve disobeyed God and had to leave his special garden.	*That was bad!*
But God gave them a promise of someone to come—a Savior, to bring them hope!	*That was good!*
But all throughout history a lot of people did not believe God's promises.	*That was bad!*
Then one day a little baby was born who came to make all of God's promises come true.	*That was good!*
Mean people tried to kill him.	*That was bad!*
But he escaped to Egypt.	*That was good!*
But when he came home and grew up, the religious leaders didn't like what he had to say about God.	*That was bad!*
But he went right ahead, teaching people about God, healing them, and forgiving their sins.	*That was good!*
But the leaders were so mad that they had him arrested, tortured and killed!	*That was bad!*
But three days later he came back from the dead!	*That was good!*
And he told his friends he was going home to Heaven.	*That was good!*
And he said that he would come back again one day to take all of his followers to be with God.	*That was good!*
And the promise is still true today—for all who believe,	*and that is GREAT!*
Let's thank these two people for coming up here!	

21. Going Skit-So!—Give students a variety of odd props and clothes and assign them a Bible story to retell or act out.
- Give each team of four to six students a bag full of bizarre props to use in their skit.
- Each group has twelve minutes to prepare the skit and then three minutes to perform it.
- Each student must participate in some way in the skit.
- When choosing Bible stories, stick to the more familiar ones.
- Have the students choose who will tell the story and who will act it out. Have them practice at least once. Remind them they will only have three minutes to perform.
- Take turns watching each group perform its story!

22. Claymation Celebration—Mold clay into different shapes to represent what's happening in the story. See the example on page 62.

• The Creation of the World •

(based on Genesis 1)

Notes for the storyteller: This story will work best with a small group. The children will stay focused because they'll be curious what the next shape is going to be! Practice creating the shapes in the story before attempting to actually tell the story.

Make sure you can create the suggested shapes and that you feel comfortable with the timing and pauses of the story. In this story, hold up the clay whenever a word is boldfaced.

Long ago, the world was **shapeless** . . . like a big glob of clay.	*Hold up the blob. Begin forming the clay into a ball.*
But then God spoke, and he shaped our world and made it just the right **size**.	*Hold up the ball.*
Then he said, "Let there be light" and there was!	
On the second day, he separated the waters from the **sky**.	*Pull the clay apart . . . and begin forming mountains.*
On the third day, God made the plants and the **mountains**, the oceans and the land.	*Hold up the mountains . . . begin forming a crescent moon.*
On the fourth day, God made the sun and the stars, and . . . the **moon**.	*Hold up the moon . . . begin forming a simple fish shape.*
On the fifth day, God made the birds in the sky and the **fish** in the waters.	*Hold up the fish . . . begin forming a human face (or body).*
On the sixth day, God made the land animals, and . . . from the clay of the earth, he formed a man. He named him **Adam**. He was handsome!	*Hold up the face (or body).*
God breathed on Adam and created life in his soul.	*Hold up the human and breath on it. Then if you wish to be a little silly, wiggle it around and say something like, "Wow! It's good to be alive!" Begin forming a pillow.*
God also made a wife for Adam. Her name was Eve. And then, on the seventh day, God rested from all the creating he'd been doing. God taught his people to **rest** on the seventh day as well. The end.	*Hold the pillow up to your head and pretend to go to sleep.*

Variations

1. Add other props to tell a more elaborate story. For example, you could shine a flashlight on the clay and turn it on and off to represent the passing of each day. (Or have an assistant turn the room lights on each time you say, "On the ____ day.")

2. Give clay to the children and allow them to join you as you create the various shapes.

Summary

There's no limit to the number of ways you can use stuff to tell stories. Keep your objects and costumes simple and relevant to the story. Be creative and explore the unusual—just like God did!

Have fun!

Chapter 9

Wiggles and Giggles

How to Creatively Tell Stories to Young Children

YOUNG CHILDREN present special challenges for the biblical storyteller. Their little bodies aren't made for sitting still! They wiggle and squirm and run around and look at birds flying past the window and play with their shoelaces and just want to have fun! In this chapter, you'll learn five characteristics of young minds and then discover four storytelling techniques that work great with preschool and kindergarten-aged children.

Abstract vs. Concrete

Young children don't think in abstract terms. They don't understand the hidden meanings, metaphors, and symbolism in stories. Usually, the power of parables comes from weaving a spiritual truth into a story that's essentially about something else. The more abstract the parallels, the less young children will understand them.

For example, when Jesus told a story about a lost sheep, he was using a story about an event from his culture to show the similarities of how we wander from God spiritually, and how God takes the initiative to look for us and rescue us—and then celebrates when we're found! But for young children, it's a story about a lost sheep. Period. They won't understand the spiritual parallels!

This doesn't mean you should never tell parables to young children, just be aware that you may need to explain the symbolism in as concrete a way as you can. For example, "That shepherd cared for his sheep enough to go and find it and bring it home. God loves us just like that. He loves you and wants to bring you home to Heaven." As you craft stories for young children, look for simple, clear, easy-to-understand stories that are concrete rather than abstract.

Sitting Still vs. Paying Attention

One day I dropped my four-year-old daughter off at a church's day care program. When I picked her up a few hours later and asked her if she had fun, she shook her head no.

"Why not?" I asked.

"I had to sit still," she told me. She explained that the teacher had told them that if they moved or talked while they watched a movie, they wouldn't get a snack.

"What was the movie about?" I asked.

"I don't know," my daughter replied. She'd been concentrating so hard on not moving, that she couldn't pay attention to the movie!

Don't mistake sitting still for paying attention. Listening is not the same thing as sitting still! For many young children, sitting motionless is much more work than paying attention.

Listening, really listening, is tiring. It's not the same as watching TV since listening to a story requires the listener to create all of the images in his or her head. Be aware that listening to a story is usually something that a child will consider fun, but sitting still while someone tells a story is something difficult and not very enjoyable. Focus more time and energy on grabbing and keeping the attention of the children than on trying to get them to sit still.

The key to keeping children interested is realizing that they're more easily distracted and more easily bored than adults. So, the challenge is to tell stories in a way that they can understand and relate to, that engages their imaginations, and that actively involves their bodies.

How do you do this? By choosing appropriate material, taking the time to prepare and shape it so that it relates to your students, and then telling your stories with energy, imagination, enthusiasm, and participation.

During lulls between stories, chant a Bible verse with the children, do an object lesson, have a short contest, or introduce a skit. Give them a mental break! Then move into the next story.

> *If kids aren't having fun, they probably aren't learning. And if kids are interested and engaged in the lesson, they probably aren't misbehaving.*

Reading vs. Telling

One night, I finished reading a bedtime story to my oldest daughter (who was two years old at the time) and closed the book.

She snuggled close to me and said, "Daddy, can you tell me a story with your mouth?"

"What do you mean, honey?" I said, "I just read you a story!"

And then it hit me! She wanted me to tell the story from my mouth, not from the book!

"Do you want me to tell you a story without the book?"

Her eyes lit up. "Uh, huh!"

I learned an important lesson that day. I realized that she didn't want a story from the pages of a book, but from the pages of my heart. She wanted me to tell it with my mouth!

Many educators simply read each lesson or story from their curriculum. While there is nothing wrong with studying the ideas found in your curriculum, be aware that the way the story is written is not necessarily the right way for you to tell it. You're a different storyteller than the author, and your class is unique! It's much more important for you to connect the story to the lives of your students than get through the material in your lesson. Your job isn't to get through the material, but to get through to your students.

Look for ways to learn and tell the story yourself (from your mouth!) rather than just reading it from your teacher's guide.

Explaining Stories vs. Telling Stories

For the most part, children (and adults) will pay attention only as long as they're curious about what's happening. In other words, if you're telling a story and the children know how it will end, they begin to lose interest. Children will start thinking about snack time, crafts, or playing on the playground!

Use your children's natural curiosity to your advantage. Don't tell them what the story will be about. Instead say, *"Raise your hand if you've ever ridden on a donkey! Wow! Raise your hand if you've ever eaten a donkey! Yuck! This story isn't about eating donkeys, but it is about a man who rode a donkey. I wonder who he was and where he was going? Let's all be quiet and listen to the story to find out!"*

I've found that the more time I spend preparing my lessons, the less time I end up lecturing, yet, the more the children end up learning! But the less time I spend preparing my lessons, the more I lecture and the less they learn!

If kids aren't having fun, they probably aren't learning. And if kids are interested and engaged in the lesson, they probably aren't misbehaving. So spend more time preparing your lessons and thinking through transitions from one activity to another. Look for ways to include more learning activities, attention-getting object lessons, and application games in your teaching time.

If things get boring, direct the attention of the students to another activity. Remove distractions and keep the children focused. Be prepared. And remember, your lesson begins when the first student arrives!

Asking Questions vs. Telling Stories

Have you ever heard (or said!) something like this?

"OK, boys and girls, today we're going to learn about Noah and the ark! Noah took lots of animals on the ark. What were some of the animals? That's right, he took horses. Horses live on farms. Has anyone ever been to a farm? What did you see? Were there cows there? Cows give us milk to drink in our cereal. What's your favorite type of cereal?"

I can just picture what happens when the parents pick up their children, "So, Joey, what did you learn at Sunday school today?"

"I don't know . . . something about how Noah fed Fruit Loops to the horses on the ark!"

Asking children questions while you tell a story can bewilder children, distract them, and lead you into tangents. So, ask fewer questions and don't be afraid to just tell the story.

Sometimes teachers ask all these questions hoping to get their students to pay better attention. But a poorly directed question will distract more than focus children!

Many educators, when telling the story of "Jonah and the Big Fish" say things like, "Boys and girls, today's story is about a great big fish. Ooh! Who likes to go fishing? Wow!"

Now, the problem with this approach is that, without realizing it, you've just changed the subject! Instead of thinking about Jonah, the children are thinking about a fishing adventure they've been on! And then when the children want to talk about their fishing trip, the teacher feels like they aren't paying attention to the story. In truth, they were paying attention, but got sidetracked by the teacher's questions. And besides, Jonah has nothing to do with a fishing trip! No one goes fishing in the story!

Whenever you ask questions, make sure they're not open-ended questions that will get the children thinking about something other than the story you're telling.

If you ask any questions, let them direct attention to the main point of the story. For example, *"Kids, how many of you have ever been afraid of getting in trouble? (As you ask this, raise your own hand so they know to answer with their hands, not their mouths.) How many of you have ever said 'No!' when your mommy or daddy asked you to do something? Me, too! Today's story is about a man who lived long ago who said 'No!' to God."*

Remember, every question you ask must move the story forward, not cause your children to become distracted from the story.

Four Storytelling Techniques

Let's look at four key stories from the life of Jesus and explore four storytelling techniques that work well with young children. In each example, you'll see how the content and message of the story help to shape the way it is told!

• **The Birth of Jesus** •
(based on Luke 2:1-20)

Notes for the storyteller: This story naturally has lots of sounds in it. After all, Jesus was born in a barn! This opens up the opportunity for you to include sound effects and audience participation in your story. As you tell the story and include sound effects, encourage the children to join you! The ideas given below are meant to spark your imagination. Insert your own sound effects wherever you think it's appropriate!

Mary and Joseph came into the town. They were looking for a place to stay. But no one had room! The streets were full of people! Pretend that *you're* getting smushed by all kinds of people ... good acting! So Mary and Joseph went into a nearby barn to sleep.

They heard the sounds of sheep ... Baa! Baa! ... And cows ... Moo! Moo! ... And horses ... Neigh! Neigh! ... And crickets ... Chirp! Chirp! ... And maybe even roosters ... Cock-a-doodle-doo! Cock-a-doodle-doo!

Soon, the time came for baby Jesus to be born. And when he was born, he started to do what all babies do ... he cried! Pretend to cry like a little baby ... Waaaa! ... Waaaa! ... Good!

Now, outside of town, there were some men on the hills. They were making sure no one hurt their sheep. Some sheep were probably sleeping ... Zzzzz ... Zzzzz ... But some were probably awake! ... Baa! Baa! ... Baa! Baa! ...

Suddenly, an angel came! The shepherds were scared! Show me how they might have looked! ... Good! ... But the angel said, "Don't be scared, your Savior is born!"

Then more angels came! They all praised God! Let's lift our hands up like we're praising God ... Good!

After the angels went back to Heaven, the shepherds went to the barn and found the sheep ... Baa! Baa! ... And cows ... Moo! Moo! ... And horses ... Neigh! Neigh! ... And crickets ... Chirp! Chirp! ... And roosters ... Cock-a-doodle-doo! Cock-a-doodle-doo!

And best of all, they saw the baby Jesus for themselves.

Maybe he was crying ... Waaaa! ... Waaaa! ... Maybe he was sleeping ... Zzzzz ... Zzzzz ... But whatever he was doing, they knew right away he really was their Savior!

And from then on, they told everyone they met, "Jesus, the Savior has been born!" Let's say that together, "Jesus the Savior has been born!" Hurray!

• **Jesus in the Temple** •
(based on Luke 2:41-52)

Notes for the storyteller: This story has a sense of mounting danger and mystery in it—where is Jesus? There is also action—Jesus' mother and father look frantically for him! As you tell the story, build in this sense of mystery and action.

You may wish to create simple gestures for the children to do during the refrain.

When Jesus was a boy, his parents took him to the worship place for a special time of praying and singing. But now that they were going home, they couldn't find Jesus anywhere!

Where is Jesus?
Where is Jesus?
Where could he be? *(Repeat and invite the children to join you.)*

They realized Jesus was missing! So what do you think they did? Right! They looked for him! They looked high! (Look up.) They looked low! (Look down.) They looked this way (Look left). They looked that way. (Look right.) They looked all around! (Stand up, turn in a circle looking.) But they couldn't find Jesus anywhere!

Where is Jesus?
Where is Jesus?
Where could he be?

Boys and girls, they were getting scared that something bad might have happened to Jesus! They went to their friends and looked even faster! (Encourage the children to join you. This time do the actions faster than before.) They looked high! They looked low! They looked this way. They looked that way. They looked all around! But they couldn't find Jesus anywhere!

Where is Jesus?
Where is Jesus?
Where could he be?

By now, they really were scared! They went back to town and looked fastest of all! (Do the actions even faster!) They looked high! They looked low! They looked this way! They looked that way! They looked all around! But they couldn't find Jesus anywhere!

Where is Jesus?
Where is Jesus?
Where could he be?

Finally, after *three days,* Mary and Joseph found Jesus sitting in the worship place! He was talking to the teachers and leaders about God! His parents didn't know what to think! But Jesus told them, "You should have known I'd be here because God is my Father! And this is his house!"

So they went home, and Jesus obeyed his parents. He grew bigger and stronger and smarter, and even closer to God than ever before.

The end.

Sample Story Three—Adding Refrains and Rhymes to a Story

• Jesus Tells a Story About Loving Others •
(based on Luke 10:25-37)

Notes for the storyteller: Repetition occurs naturally in "The Good Samaritan." There is also lots of action! Whenever a story has repetition, it allows you to include the audience. Invite the children to join you on the refrain.

Once a man was talking to Jesus and he asked, "Who are the people I should love?" So Jesus told him a story.

A Jewish man was walking
Along a desert road.
When robbers came and hurt him!
They even took his clothes!

The man was hurt! And he was sad.
He felt lonely. He felt bad.

A pastor who was walking,
Came down the road that day.
He saw the man, but didn't help!
He just went on his way!

The man was hurt! And he was sad.
He felt lonely. He felt bad.

A worker from the temple
Walked right up to the man.
But did he help? No, he did not!
He left him in the sand!

The man was hurt! And he was sad.
He felt lonely. He felt bad.

Soon, a stranger came, and saw the man was hurt.
But he didn't leave him all alone, lying in the dirt.
He put him on his donkey. Gave him a place to stay.
Paid for food and medicine, and helped him on his way!

The man was happy! He wasn't sad!
He felt thankful! He felt glad!

"Which man showed the most love?" asked Jesus.
"The stranger who helped him," answered the man Jesus was talking to.
"That's right," said Jesus, "Now, go and show that same kind of love to other people."

Sample Story Four—Adding Movement and Imagination to a Story

• Jesus Is Alive! •
(based on Mark 16:1-8)

Notes for the storyteller: Young children love playing pretend! As you look at Bible stories, think of ways you can help them picture what's happening by pretending to be present in the story. Some ideas are included to get you started.

Before asking young children to act out a story, tell it to them first. That way they'll be familiar with the story when they act it out!

On the Sunday morning after Jesus had been put in the grave, his friends went to put spices on his body. It was so early in the morning that the sun was just coming up. The friends were talking about their problem. Jesus was in a cave. And the rock in front of the cave was too big to move! So, they were trying to think of a way to move it.

But when they got to the cave, they saw the rock had been moved already! Even though it was a very big rock, it was rolled out of the way!

Then they saw an angel! The angel told them that Jesus was alive again! No one had to move the stone because the angel already had!

God wanted everyone to know that Jesus was alive!

Kids, let's pretend we're trying to move that big rock! OK? Everyone stand up and let's try to lift a giant imaginary rock. Put your hands out and feel the rock. Feel how high it is . . . feel how smooth or rough it is. Now, it's gonna be too big to lift, but let's try anyway! Ready? Get your hands under the edges . . . one, two, three—lift! . . . Ugh! The rock is just too BIG!

OK, let's try to push the rock out of the way! Maybe that'll help! Ready? Put your hands on the imaginary rock. OK. Here we go . . . one, two, three—push! . . . Ugh! The rock is just too BIG!

OK, let's try one more thing. Let's try to karate chop the rock and see what happens. Ready? Get your karate chopping hands up and . . . one, two, three—chop! . . . Ouch! The rock is too HARD and it's just too BIG!

Now pretend you're that angel, moving the rock out of the way for God! Get a little tiny finger ready . . . OK, push it out of the way! Ping!

Wow! That was easy!

Now pretend you're that big strong angel and let's all say together, "Jesus is alive!" Let's say it loud because it's good news we want everyone to hear. Ready? "JESUS IS ALIVE!"

Chapter 10

"Been There, Done That!"

How to Connect with Older Elementary Students

YOU STEP TO the front of your sixth grade class. And there they sit—twenty-five preteens—staring at you lazily from around the room. "OK, boys and girls," you say, "today's Bible story is called 'Jonah and the Big Fish.'"

And then it happens. The sighs start coming. The heads start shaking. The mouths start yawning. One student looks at his watch. Another student passes a note to her friend. One kid in the back of the room (the one who likes making noises with his armpits) rolls his eyes and says, "Oh great. This one again!"

You take a deep breath and continue, "So, as I was saying, once upon a time, there was a man named Jonah. . . ." But inside, you wonder if maybe next quarter you oughtta volunteer as a janitor instead of as a Sunday school teacher.

Does this scenario sound even remotely familiar? If so, this chapter is for you!

As children mature and grow through elementary school, they change. But not just physically! Rather than just wanting to have fun when they come to class, they also want to be cool. And to a lot of kids, part of being cool means looking uninterested in anything the teacher has to say!

In addition, because of the similarity between so many Bible curricula, children tend to hear the same Bible stories year after year as they get older. This makes your job even more difficult! In this chapter, you'll learn how to tell stories in creative ways that reach preteens. You'll discover how to involve the students, use humor, and tell stories in fresh and relevant ways that your students will relate to and enjoy.

What Preteens Are Like

- They're becoming more concerned about what other kids think of them.
- They're more savvy and can sense a lecture coming a mile away.
- They're beginning to think abstractly and can more easily understand longer, more complex stories and the symbolism found in many parables.
- They enjoy comedy, suspense, action, and mystery.
- They don't want to act like, or be treated like, babies.
- They don't want to be embarrassed (especially in front of the opposite sex)!
- They're very concerned about things being fair.
- BUT, they still want to have fun!

Technique One: Tandem Storytelling

Tandem storytelling simply means that two people tell the story together. They may either tell the story directly to the audience, or interact with each other. Here is a humorous, tandem version of the story of Jesus' birth. "Teller 1" plays the straight person, and "Teller 2" keeps getting everything mixed up. The script could be memorized, read in front of the group, or rehearsed and remembered without being performed word-for-word. You could also perform this script as a puppet play!

• No Iguanas Allowed! •
(based on Luke 2:1-20)

Teller 1: Long ago—

Teller 2: When a guy named Caesar Augustus was ruling the land,

Together: There was a census.

Teller 1: Which means that everyone had to be counted—

Teller 2: One, two, three, four—

Teller 1: To see if there were fewer people, or many more!

Teller 2: Hey, that rhymes! *(getting into it)* five, six, seven, eight, who do we appreciate?

Teller 1: Eh, hem. So they headed to their home-towns—

Teller 2: *(clicking heels together)* There's no place like home! There's no place like home!

Teller 1: Oh, brother! *Anyway*, a man named Joseph

Teller 2: who was living in Nazareth—

Teller 1: went to the town of Bethlehem, the place where King David was from—

Teller 2: because King David had been his great, great, great, great, great—

Teller 1: Alright, that's enough!

Teller 2: Great, great, great, great—

Teller 1: OK, I think they get the picture . . .

Teller 2: Great, great, great—

Teller 1: Alright, already!

Teller 2: Grandpa.

Teller 1: Thank you.

Teller 2: You're welcome . . . *(clicking heels together)* There's no place like home! There's no place like home!

Teller 1: He went with Mary, his girlfriend.

Teller 2: Wooooo!

Teller 1: The lady he was planning to marry.

Teller 2: He was gonna marry Mary! They were gonna have a merry Christmas!

Teller 1: She was expecting a baby who'd been specially sent by God.

Teller 2: So, while they were there in Bethlehem—

Teller 1: the time came for her to have her baby.

Teller 2: So she went to the hospital.

Teller 1: They didn't have hospitals.

Teller 2: Oh. Then where did she go?

Teller 1: The barn.

Teller 2: The barn? I'm sure glad we have hospitals today!

Teller 1: Because there was no room for them at the—

Teller 2: Motel 6 *(or the name of another local hotel)*.

Teller 1: Inn! At the inn! There was no room for them at the inn!

Teller 2: Or at the hospital.

Teller 1: *(getting exasperated and shaking his head)* So, she wrapped him in swaddling clothes

Teller 2: That means itty bitty blankets.

Teller 1: And placed him—

Teller 2: *(singing loudly)* Away in a manger, no crib for a bed. The little Lord Jesus lay down his sweet head; The stars in the sky looked down were he lay, The little Lord Jesus asleep on the hay *(smiles and bows to the audience)*.

Teller 1: That's right. Nearby, in the barn, there were—

Teller 2: Cows! Moo! Moo!

Teller 1: Uh, huh, and—

Teller 2: Sheep! Baa! Baa!

Teller 1: Right, and—

Teller 2: Alligators! Chomp! Chomp!

Teller 1: No! There were no alligators in the barn! Just sheep and cows and goats and things like that!

Teller 2: Oh. Were there mice?

Teller 1: Probably.

Teller 2: What about camels? Were there any camels?

Teller 1: There might have been some camels, yes.

Teller 2: And iguanas?

Teller 1: There were no iguanas!

Teller 2: Too bad. I like iguanas. And alligators. But I especially like iguanas—

Teller 1: Could we get back to the story, please?

Teller 2: Sure.

Teller 1: Good. Nearby, in the fields, were shepherds keeping watch over their flock by night. They were carefully watching their—

Teller 2: Iguanas.

Teller 1: Sheep! When all of a sudden—

Teller 2: *(loudly)* Poof!

Teller 1: *(startled)* Ah!

Teller 2: *(making a halo over his head)* There was an angel!

Teller 1: And God's holy light shone on them. And they were so scared—

Teller 2: —they almost wet their togas.

Teller 1: What did you say?

Teller 2: Never mind.

Teller 1: But the angel said—

Teller 2: Nice iguanas!

Teller 1: There were no iguanas! The angel said to them, "Don't be afraid!"

Teller 2: The iguanas won't bite.

Teller 1: Would you forget about the iguanas! The angel said, "Don't be afraid! I've got good news! It's good news for everyone! Tonight in Bethlehem, a baby has been born. And he is the Savior and the Lord! You'll find him lying—"

Teller 2: *(singing)* Away in a manger, no crib for a bed. The little Lord Jesus lay down his sweet head; The stars in the sky looked down were he lay, The little Lord Jesus

asleep on the hay *(smiles and bows to the audience).*

Teller 1: And all of a sudden, the sky was full of angels all shouting praises to God!

Together: Glory to God on high!

Teller 2: And peace on the earth below!

Teller 1: Then the angels were gone.

Teller 2: Poof!

Teller 1: And the shepherds all said to one another,

Teller 2: "Forget these sheep, let's get some iguanas!"

Teller 1: No! They said, "Let's all go to Bethlehem and see this child for ourselves!"

Teller 2: So they ran!

Teller 1: And found Mary

Teller 2: And Joseph

Teller 1: And the baby.

Teller 2: And the iguanas.

Teller 1: NO IGUANAS! Just the baby lying—

Teller 2: *(singing)* Away in a manger, no crib for a bed. *(To audience):* Everyone! The little Lord Jesus lay down his sweet head; The stars in the sky looked down were he lay, The little Lord Jesus asleep on the hay *(smiles and bows to the audience).*

Teller 1: And after they'd seen him with their own eyes, they couldn't keep the news to themselves but told everyone they met about the child. And everyone who heard it was impressed—

Teller 2: and amazed!

Teller 1: And Mary thought about it all and stored the memories of that night in a special place in her heart. And the shepherds returned to their sheep and praised God that everything the angels had told them was true.

Teller 2: A Savior had been born!

Teller 1: He is Christ the King.

Together: The end.

Technique Two: Fill-in Storytelling

When telling a fill-in story, write out the story before class, leaving out important words. When class begins, ask the students for words to fill in the blanks of the story without telling them what the story is about. Write their suggestions in the blanks and then read the story aloud to the students.

After reading the story, say, "Now, who can tell me something that appeared in our version that doesn't appear in the Bible's version? *(Allow them to respond.)* Right! Let's take a closer look at the Bible's version of this story."

For example, if you are telling the story of Jonah, you might use the following story format:

• The One That Didn't Get Away •
(based on Jonah 1–3)

Once there was a guy named _____ *(a boy's name from your class, it will be repeated throughout the story)*. He was one of God's chosen men and served God as a _____ *(name of a job you wouldn't want)*. One day, God told him "I want you to go to _____ *(name of a town nearby)* and tell them all about me!" But _____ *(the same boy's name)* got up and headed in the opposite direction. He went to the beach and bought a ticket for_____ *(name of a far away town)*. Then he hopped on a _____ *(a means of transportation)* and took off.

Well, as the _____ *(another means of transportation)* was _____ *(a verb ending in "ing")* along, suddenly a _____ *(a type of weather phenomena)* blew in! Everyone aboard was totally _____ *(an emotion)*!

But_____ *(the same boy's name)* knew what had happened. He told them, "Just _____ *(verb, present tense)* me overboard! This whole thing is my fault!"

So, the men took him and *(use same verb)* him into the _____ *(an object)*! It was really _____ *(adjective)* and _____ *(adjective)* in there!

Suddenly, a gigantic _____ *(animal)* swallowed him up! He slide down into its stomach where it smelled just like _____ *(something gross)*.

While he was there, he realized he'd done the opposite of what God wanted. He finally changed his mind and prayed. After _____ *(number between one and one million)* days, the beast spit him out onto the shore, right where God had wanted him to go in the first place! And _____ *(the same boy's name)* learned it's always best to do things God's way—rather than our own way—the first time!

The end.

Technique Three: Contemporary Retelling

With this technique, retell the Bible story in your own words and look for ways to connect it to the lives of your listeners. Try to find parallels in the Bible story to the world of your students today. Set the story in a contemporary setting and rewrite it with the names, places and terms popular with your students. Paraphrase it in your own words.

This technique can really bring the message home and help your students understand the application and relevance of the gospel to their lives.

• The Party •

(based on Luke 15:11-31)

Once there was a father with two sons. One day, the younger son went up to his dad and said, "Listen old man. I'm sick and tired of hanging around here waiting for you to keel over from a heart attack, or whatever. Gimme my inheritance now, while I'm still young enough to enjoy it."

So, his father handed the young man his money and the son set off on a long trip to The Big City (probably Las Vegas or something). When he got there, he was a party animal—staying up late, throwing his money around, and purposely doing all the stuff his dad had warned him never to do. Yeah, you know what I'm talking about. . . .

Finally, the money was gone and the boy had nowhere to go. So he got the only job he could—working at a homeless shelter cleaning up the bathrooms where the homeless people threw up and passed out on the floor.

He was really hungry, not even making enough money to buy food. *Even these homeless bums have more to eat than I do,* he thought. *You know what I oughtta do? I oughtta go back home. Every year my dad hires migrant workers to work in the fields. I'll bet if I told him I was sorry, he'd hire me and at least then I'd have something to eat!*

So, he got up and headed home. All along the way he rehearsed what he was gonna say to his dad. But when he got close to home, his dad was watching out the window for him. And he ran out to greet the boy without even changing out of his pajamas! And he just stood there in the middle of the road, hugging his son.

"Dad, I'm sorry I messed up—" the son began. But he couldn't even get out his apology for all the hugging his dad was giving to him.

"Welcome home, Son!"

"But, Dad—"

"Welcome home!"

His dad turned to a friend and said, "Order an extra large pizza with lots of pepperoni. Break out the nachos and root beer. Tonight, we celebrate!"

Pretty soon, the boy's older brother got home from work. He smelled the pizza, he heard the music, he saw people playing Twister on the back porch and he knew what has going on. They were having a party!

He refused to go in. Finally, his dad came out to invite him in, but he said, "What's the deal? I work for you twenty-four/seven and I can't even invite a few friends over to play video games! And then this son of yours goes and wastes all his money and you throw him a big homecoming party!"

And his dad said, "You live with me all the time and you can have anything you ask for. But your brother was lost and hopeless, but now he's home. He was as good as dead, but now he's got a second chance at life. Don't you get it? I had to throw a party! I had to! Come on in—the pizza is hot and the root beer is cold and the party is just getting started!"

Jesus ended the story there. We never find out if the older brother joined the party or not. The last we hear about him, he's standing there outside with his arms folded, staring at the open door.

Technique Four: Reader's Theater

In reader's theater, a small group of students is invited forward to dramatically read a story. Each student is given a script from which to read. The advantages to this type of creative dramatics activity are that no one has to memorize anything, it's relatively easy for you as a teacher to include in your lesson, and the students really enjoy it.

Here are the five steps to using reader's theater:

1. Choose your story and decide how many readers you'll need.

2. Rewrite the story (if necessary) and photocopy the story so that you have enough copies of the script for each reader. Decide if you want to use any costumes or props.

3. Highlight each reader's part. If necessary, cross off words like "he said" and "she said."

4. Choose several students to dramatically read the parts. Hand each of them a script.

5. Allow them a moment or two to familiarize themselves with the script. Then begin!

A sample reader's theater script

• The Bravest Beauty Queen •

(based on the book of Esther)

Notes for the leader: You will need five readers for this story, preferably two female (Narrator and Esther) and three male (Haman, Mordecai, and King Xerxes).

Narrator: One day, long ago there was a king named King Xerxes.

King Xerxes: Gesundheit.

Narrator: I wasn't sneezing, I was telling them your name.

King Xerxes: Oh, right.

Narrator: Well, one day, he kicked his wife out of the palace because she wouldn't do what he asked her to do.

King Xerxes: Serves her right. That'll teach her a lesson!

Narrator: But then, he got really lonely.

King Xerxes: That'll teach me a lesson. What am I gonna do? I know! I'll search for a beautiful new queen. Why should I be lonely? After all, I am King Xerxes!

Narrator: Gesundheit.

King Xerxes: Thank you.

Narrator: So, he decided to throw the first beauty pageant ever. His advisors searched throughout the land until they came to a place where there lived a Jewish man named Mordecai

Mordecai: That's me!

Narrator: And his beautiful young cousin, Esther.

Esther: That's me.

Mordecai: Esther, you know that since your parents died I've raised you as my own daughter and I've always done what's best for you.

Esther: Yes, Mordecai. Why are you saying this? What's wrong?

Mordecai: These men are searching for a new queen for King Xerxes.

King Xerxes: Gesundheit.

Mordecai: Who said that?

King Xerxes: Never mind.

Mordecai: Anyway, they may try to take you away. If they do, don't tell anyone you're a Jewish girl.

Esther: But why not, Mordecai?

Mordecai: Trust me, Esther. There are people out there who don't like Jews.

Esther: OK, I promise. I'll do as you say.

Narrator: The advisors DID notice Esther and they DID take her back to the king. And when he saw her, his heart began to flutter.

King Xerxes: Esther wins the contest! She shall be my new queen!

Narrator: He placed a crown on Esther's head and threw a big party to celebrate. Now, one of the highest officials in the government, a man named Haman, was there.

Haman: So—the king has a new queen. I'm just glad she's not a Jew. I hate those Jews. I especially hate that guy Mordecai!

Mordecai: I don't care what you say about me, Haman. I'm not going to bow down and honor you.

Haman: You will, too! Or else you'll be sorry!

Mordecai: I never worship people, Haman. I'll never worship you.

Narrator: Then one day Haman had an idea.

Haman: I know what I'll do. I'll tell the king that all Jews are bad and should be killed! Then I can get rid of Mordecai, and all of his people at the same time!

Narrator: Well, Haman tricked the king into making a law that all the Jews should be killed. And when Mordecai found out, he was *very* troubled and sad.

Mordecai: What will we do? Unless something happens, we'll all be goners! I know, I'll send a note to Queen Esther and ask her for help.

Esther: *(pretending to read a letter)* Dear Esther, we're all in danger. Perhaps you've been placed in the palace at this time to help us. Will you ask the king to save us? Love, Mordecai.

Narrator: Now, you remember how the King reacted to queens who didn't please him—

Esther: What shall I do?

Narrator: And besides, talking to the king without being invited was dangerous—if the king didn't want to talk to you, he would have you killed! Esther didn't know what to do.

Esther: If the king isn't pleased with me, he'll have me killed! But if I don't say something, my family will die. Oh, what shall I do?

Narrator: Finally, Esther agreed to help her people. She went into the throne room and bowed low to the ground. She knew she might not walk out of there alive.

Esther: O king, have mercy on me.

King Xerxes: Arise, my queen! What do you want? Don't be afraid. I won't hurt you!

Esther: Please come to a special banquet. I'll ask you a favor then.

King Xerxes: Yes! Splendid! I'll see you there my dear!

Esther: And Haman is invited, too.

Haman: Oh, goody, goody. A party!

Narrator: Meanwhile, Haman was preparing to have Mordecai hanged. He had a long rope brought in, and ordered his helpers to build a place to hang Mordecai.

Haman: *(evil laughter)* He'll never bother me again!

Narrator: The first party went well and then, a few days later, Esther invited the king and Haman to a second banquet. It was finally time to ask for the king's help.

Haman: Oh, goody, goody! Another party! And by the end of the day Mordecai will be hanged. This is gonna be a day to remember!

King Xerxes: Esther, thank you for this party. Now, I think you mentioned that there was something important you wanted to ask me. What is it?

Esther: Save me, O King! Save me and my peo-ple from the man who wants to destroy us all!

King Xerxes: But who? Who would dare to harm my queen? Who would do such a thing?

Esther: *(point to Haman)* He would!

King Xerxes: What?

Haman: Uh-oh.

Esther: Our enemy is Haman!

Haman: This might not be good.

Narrator: About then, one of the guards mentioned that the place to hang Mordecai was ready.

King Xerxes: What? But Mordecai is a hero! He stopped an assassination attempt against me! You would kill my queen and the man who saved me?

Haman: Uh-oh. This is not going according to plan.

King Xerxes: Guards! Take him away! You know what to do with him!

Haman: Um . . . help?

Narrator: That day, Haman was hanged and the king did what he could to protect the Jews from those who wanted to harm them.

King Xerxes: Mordecai!

Mordecai: Yes, your majesty?

King Xerxes: Tell your people to protect themselves. I don't want any Jews harmed!

Mordecai: Yes, sir!

King Xerxes: And it seems that with Haman's departure we have a job opening. Would you be interested in being my chief advisor?

Mordecai: I would be honored, your majesty!

Esther: Oh, thank you, King Xerxes! You've saved my people.

King Xerxes: No, Esther. *You* have saved your people.

Narrator: And ever since that day, Jews around the world have celebrated parties of their own in honor of Esther and the time she helped rescue them from Haman's evil plan by talking to King Gesundheit—

King Xerxes: Xerxes!

Narrator: Oh, yeah.

All: The end.

Technique Five: "What If? Storytelling"

As you read the Bible story, ask yourself how the story might have ended if things hadn't happened as they really did. For example, ask what would have happened if the disciples had kept sleeping in the garden . . . if Jonah hadn't repented in the fish's stomach . . . if Lazarus had refused to come out of the grave when Jesus called him. . . .

This technique works especially well with popular or familiar stories. Have fun with this, but be sure to discuss it when you're done. Compare the differences between the "What If?" story and the real story recorded in Scripture.

• Edgar's Decision •
(based on Acts 3:1-11)

Many beggars sat along the road that led to the temple because every day, faithful Jews came to offer their prayers and sacrifices. Many of them carried extra money to buy doves and animals for their offerings. So, if you were poor or homeless, there was no better place to beg for money.

One sunny day just before the afternoon prayers were to begin, Peter and John went up to the temple to pray. Edgar, a man who'd been crippled since the day he was born, sat by the temple gate, his favorite spot to ask for handouts. Seeing Peter and John approaching the gate called Beautiful, he hung his head low and started his most successful begging routine, "Hey, you guys, do you have any spare change? I'm ashamed to ask it of you, but I'm crippled and can't work. I need to eat. Do you have a spare coin for a man who's down on his luck?"

Peter and John stopped. They looked at each other and then stared at the man. Peter said, "Look here! If you want us to help you, at least look us in the eye!"

Edgar smiled to himself before he looked up. *I'll bet these guys are loaded with dough,* he thought. *They'd have just walked on by and ignored me if they weren't gonna give me something.* Then Edgar looked up pitifully and held out his hand.

But instead of handing him money, Peter said, "I don't have any silver or gold or even spare change. But, what I do have I'll give you. In the name of Jesus Christ of Nazareth, stand up and walk!"

"What?" asked an astonished Edgar.

Peter repeated himself, "Stand up and walk."

Edgar looked from Peter to John, "Is this guy serious?"

John smiled, "Sure he is. Jesus is the guy who was killed and God brought back to life. There's unlimited power in his name. We're offering you a free gift, better than gold or silver."

Edgar stared up at Peter and John, looking from one to the other. "You guys are nuts," he said finally. "You're crazy! Do you really expect me to believe something like that?" He'd heard about kooks like this. His mother had warned him.

"I'm serious, stand up and walk," Peter said, reaching out his hand.

"I'm crippled! I can't walk! Now, get outta here before people see me talking to you. It'll ruin my business for the day."

Peter and John looked at each other. Finally, they shrugged their shoulders and continued walking toward the temple. They'd only taken a few steps and were about to enter the gate when they heard another man call. He was being carried toward the gate on a mat. Peter and John smiled and walked over to him.

Don't bother, Dave, they don't have any cash, thought Edgar, as he glanced at the man who was being lowered on the mat. Then, turning back to the crowds bustling toward the temple, Edgar called, "Hey, you! You there! Got any spare change for a man who is down on his luck?"

Application: God offers us gifts worth far more than gold or silver; life-changing gifts that bring us healing, hope, life, and peace. But we must believe in him to receive the blessings he has promised. Will you be more like Edgar who scoffed at the offer, or more like Dave who accepted? (Find out what happened to "Dave" in Acts 3!)

Technique Six: Monologues

Telling a story from the point of view of one of the characters within the story is called a "monologue." You can tell the story from the point of view of a person, an object, or an animal. Sometimes, the character really does appear in the story (as in a monologue from Peter about the day he walked on the water with Jesus); at other times the emotions and actions of a character may be inferred from the events of the story.

To use monologues

1. Look for an object, animal, or person in the story you're teaching or telling.

2. Consider what unique perspective this character can give to the story.

3. Reflect on a connection with the audience. In other words, try to see if what the character learns in the story could apply directly to your students.

4. Brainstorm ideas. Try to see the story and progression of events through the character's eyes.

5. If you've substantially changed the story or added lots of events that aren't supported by the biblical account, be sure that you point this out to your students. Say for example, "We don't know how the innkeeper responded to Christ's birth in his stable, but his story may have gone something like this . . ." (see the monologue "Those Rags" on the next page). You may wish to discuss how much, or how little, of his story is found in the Bible.

Here are some ideas to get you started.

Tell a story from another person's point of view:
- **Boaz** reflects on what it was like to see Naomi return to town and then to meet her young, honorable (and adorable!) daughter-in-law.
- **Esther** records in her diary what went through her mind the night before she went to talk to King Xerxes.
- **Onesimus** tells the story of how he stole money from his owner, met up with Paul, was converted, and then returned to face his old master.
- **Simon of Cyrene,** the man who carried Jesus' cross, tells how that day affected his life.
- **The Samaritan** explains what he was thinking when he decided to help the hurting man.

Tell a story from an object's point of view:
- The **star** tells what it was like to be chosen to point the way to Jesus.
- The **manger** tells how it felt to be the first place the Savior ever slept.
- The **whip** that Jesus used to drive out the moneychangers talks about the righteous anger of God.
- The **tree** that is cut down to form the cross tells what it felt like to be used for such a horrible purpose.
- The **rock** that covered the tomb tells his version of what happened on Sunday morning when Christ arose.

Tell a story from an animal's point of view:
- A **scorpion** retells the story of the Exodus: "I was just sitting there minding my own business when all of a sudden . . ."
- The **donkey** remembers talking to Balaam: "I still recall the day I spoke my first words. It was rather odd, considering I'm a donkey. Let me tell you about it . . ."
- A **lion** tells the story of when Daniel came to visit: "Boy was I hungry! I hadn't eaten anything in three days when they threw my supper down. He looked rather delicious, but before I could dig in . . ."
- The **fish** who swallowed Jonah remembers the story: "Talk about indigestion! You wouldn't believe the story if I told you!"

- A **scapegoat** tells what it was like to be sent out of the village: "They put their hands on me to signify all their sins going on my head. It was frightening! And then they sent me away. And all I could think was, *Why me? Why are they sending me away? What's the point of it all?*
- The **snake** who bit the apostle Paul tells what happened: "I couldn't believe it! The guy just shook me off his hand as if nothing had happened! Right into the fire! Ouch! I figured the venom would start working any minute, but—nothing!"

• Those Rags •

(a rhyming Christmas monologue)

I was half asleep when I heard the knock on the wooden frame of the door.
It was late in the night, I angrily rose. I was tired. I cussed and I swore.
I went downstairs and I walked outside. Found a man and a lady there.
In tattered clothes, worn and alone,
They shivered in the cold night air.

"Have you lodging for two?" the man spoke first. "It's urgent; a child's on the way!"
I glanced at the woman, but then he said, "I'm sorry we've no money to pay."
I felt sorry for them, but my inn was full and I couldn't take them in for free,
"There's room next door," I said to him.
"We've tried them," said he to me.

I thought for a moment, I saw his wife flinch; the child was soon to arrive.
"There's room in the stables," I said to the man. "At least your kid will survive."
We helped her back, sat her down, and I offered to help if I could.
"We'll need some blankets and clothes," said the man. "Can you find some?"
I promised I would.

I ran back to the inn in search of some clothes and I happened to wake up a guest.
"A woman outside is now giving birth," I said as he rose and got dressed.
We gathered some blankets and ran back outside where we heard the cry of a child.
The young wife took him and wrapped him up snug.
She held him. And hugged him. And smiled.

The three of them stayed in our home for a while and a loving friendship began.
They claimed that their babe was a gift from above—Son of God and also of Man.
I didn't believe he was really God's Son, but the shepherds and wise men arrived.
They'd heard of his birth from angels above,
And seen it proclaimed in the skies.

They worshiped and praised him. They bowed to the babe. They claimed that he'd free us all!
I doubted at first, but then I believed in the child from my manger stall.
He came in the darkness to bring us the light. A child. A boy. A son.
And I still have those rags that he wore on that night
When his work on this earth was begun.

Using Humor with Preteens

1. Impersonations—Preteens will laugh at silly impersonations of cartoon characters, actors, TV personalities, or sports heroes as long as they can identify who is being impersonated. Be careful not to make fun of the people you are impersonating!

2. Feigned stupidity—Kids will usually laugh if you act like you don't know something you should know, or mix something up that should be obvious, or pretend to forget a common name or place in the middle of the story.

3. You'll never guess!—In a story with repetition, you may come to a part where you quip, "You'll never guess what happened next! I mean you'll *never* guess in a million years what comes next—" They will, of course, guess correctly. Then you get to act surprised. "That's right! How on earth did you know that? Are you like a genius or something?" Have fun with this, but don't overdo it.

4. Exaggeration—Truth exaggerated or taken to an extreme can be very funny. One way to do this is to point out something that the Bible teaches that the students may never have noticed. For example, many preteens think gross things are cool, so when you tell the story of David and Goliath, you could mention that when David sliced off Goliath's head, blood went spurting all over.

5. Bizarre props—Use bizarre props to tell the story. Draw a story with whipped cream or spray paint. Use life-sized manikins, giant blow-up dolls, or cardboard sports hero cutouts!

6. Surprise!—The unexpected is funny. Tell the students something one way for a few times in the story and then change it. For example, you might point out several times in a story that Jesus was from Bethlehem. Then say, "By the way do you know where Jesus came from?" And they'll say, "Bethlehem!" Then shake your head and respond, "No. His momma!" Let them think that they know the answer and then surprise them!

7. Involvement—It's usually funny to bring volunteers onstage, give them goofy costumes and have them act something out. When bringing preteens onstage, give them a specific job and keep them involved. Allow them the chance to creatively express themselves and to enjoy the role. Don't let them stand up for too long with nothing to do.

8. Non-story material—Consider using jokes, silly words, tongue twisters, riddles, conundrums, rhymes, proverbs, puns, jingles, commercial themes, or ballads either as part of your story or between the stories you tell.

Technique Seven: Spontaneous Melodrama

This is similar to "Narrative Pantomime" (see chapter seven). The difference is that spontaneous melodramas tend to include more characters, be more silly and surprising, and involve more physical comedy. This technique works best with a large group where there is an audience to watch the show!

• The Adventures of Sam •

(based on Judges 14–16)

Notes for the storyteller: Invite seven volunteers forward. If desired, give them props. At least give a wig to Samson! As you tell (or read), the story, be sure to pause long enough for the actors to do their actions. This story would also work great using teen volunteers as your actors!

You'll need

Samson (a big guy)	Bad guys (four or five people)
Delilah (a girl)	Lion (a small guy or a girl)
Crowd (audience)	

Once upon a time, there was a guy named Sam. He would walk around saying things like, "I am Sam." "Sam I am." "Do you like green eggs and lamb?" Sam had the longest hair you've ever seen on a man, and he was *really* strong. He spent all of his time lifting weights . . . jogging in place . . . jumping rope . . . and doing pushups. . . . Sometimes he would do poses in front of the mirror to look at his rippling muscles. . . .

But Sam's great strength didn't come from his workouts. Nope, it was really his long hair that God's Spirit used to give him his great strength. When Sam was working out or posing people would walk by and say, "My, what big muscles you have!" . . .

And Sam would say, "All the better to beat up bad guys, my dear!" . . .

And the people would say, "My, what long hair you have!" . . .

And Sam would reply, "All the better to—hmm—that part is a secret!" . . .

Sam *was* strong—and brave. One day, he heard a roar from the side of the road . . . it was a lion! The lion ran toward him roaring loudly . . . even louder . . . even louder! Until it almost lost its voice. . . . Then Sam grabbed the lion . . . picked it up . . . and put it over his shoulder . . . then the other shoulder . . . spun around three times . . . and dropped it (gently!) on the ground . . . Then with his bare hands, he ripped the lion in half. . . . Yuck! Then he dragged the lion's body into the woods. . . .

Whenever the bad guys would come on the scene, Sam would do karate moves on them. . . . Once, acting like Jackie Chan, he took out one thousand men with the jawbone of a donkey! . . . When people saw Sam coming, they would bite their fingers . . . shake at their knees . . . and run away!

He ruled the land not five years, not ten, not fifteen, but twenty years!

Then he met this cute girl named Delilah. She walked up to him and said, "Hi, Sammy baby!" . . .

And Sam put his hand over his heart and said, "Hubba! Hubba!" . . .

When the bad guys found out that Sam had a girl-friend, they huddled up . . . to make up a plan. Finally, they said, "Break!" . . . and ran over to Delilah.

Using sign language, they asked her to find out why Sam was so strong. . . . She shook her head no. . . . They tried again, with even bigger gestures. . . . Again, she shook her head no.

Then they offered her lots of money. . . . Her eyes got really big. . . . She stuck out her tongue, panted like a dog . . . nodded . . . and then said, "I'll do it! I'll do it!" . . .

They left her alone with Sam. She walked over to him . . . pointed to his muscles . . . and asked him the secret of his strength. But he wouldn't tell her.

So she pouted . . . and begged . . . and pleaded . . . until finally, he pointed to his head and said, "There! There! My strength is in my hair!" . . . He liked the way it sounded so much, he said it again, "There! There! My strength is in my hair!" . . . He said it one more time, this time acting like a cheerleader as he said it. . . .

So that night, when he fell asleep . . . she invited in the bad guys. . . . They grabbed him and shaved his head *(by ripping off his wig)* which left him very weak. . . . Then they handed the money over to Delilah. . . . There was lots of money . . . more money . . . all kinds of money!

As she counted out her money she turned and said, "Bye, Sammy baby." . . .

And Sam, very sadly said, "Hubba, hubba" . . . as the bad guys led him away. . . .

Yes, Sam died as a prisoner, but before he died, he humbled himself and prayed. So I guess you could say that, at least in his heart, the story had a happy ending, after all.

The end.

Aerobatics: Reaching New Heights

Let's look at how to navigate to new heights of excellence in storytelling. This section is especially for experienced educators and storytellers who are looking for new ways of developing their craft. In this section you'll find dozens of practical ideas on how to
- develop vital storytelling skills such as voice, gesture, posture, and movement;
- tell stories that taste good to your listeners and will keep them coming back for more;
- orchestrate all the elements of storytelling into a whole that is greater than the sum of its parts;
- discover secrets to effective storytelling;
- tell stories with more impact;
- weave stories together into an integrated presentation;
- find stories from literature, imagination, folklore, and your own personal experience that you can use in your lessons;
- make stories stick by adding creative follow-up activities.

Maneuver to new heights by learning and applying the principles found in this section!

Chapter 11

Seconds, Anyone?

How to Cook Up a Tasty Delivery

WHEN I LEAD storytelling classes for children, I ask them, "If I were going to bake a cake, what are some of the things I'd mix together? What ingredients would I use?" The children yell, "Flour! Sugar! Chocolate! Cake mix! Spoons! Ovens!" They're full of ideas!

Then I ask, "Now, if I'm going to tell a story, what are some of the ingredients I need to tell my story?"

"Your voice! Funny faces! Hats and costumes! Words!"

Finally, I ask them, "When I bake a cake, what's the most important goal—to use lots of ingredients, or to make it taste good?"

"Make it taste good!"

They already know that the point of baking a cake isn't to use a lot of ingredients or be able to recite interesting facts about the ingredients—the whole point is to mix everything together so that the cake tastes good! Each ingredient serves to complement the others and the cake tastes better than any single ingredient would taste.

The same is true with telling a story. When you finish telling your story, you don't want people to walk away thinking, "My! What fine use of gestures and body language!" or, "Oh, what elegant pauses that storyteller used! Masterful! To die for!" Instead you want the story to taste so good that the listeners don't even notice the storytelling ingredients you mixed together. All you want them to notice is the story itself! They may even beg you for seconds! When your audience clamors, "Tell us another one! Tell us another one!" then you've cooked up a successful story!

In this chapter, you'll learn how to choose the right ingredients, stir them together, bake them into your story, and then serve the story to your audience!

Choosing Your Ingredients

Most storytelling books spend lots of time explaining voice, posture, gestures, dialect, and so on, but forget to emphasize the importance of making the story taste good. Because of this tendency, it's easy to lose sight of the whole point of storytelling and work instead on developing each specific skill. That's like a cook who goes to the kitchen and studies the history of each ingredient, practices pouring and measuring, memorizes the cookbook, and sets the table, but never actually cooks anything! It's much more important for a storyteller to tell a story well than worry about his or her proficiency at each specific storytelling skill. There *is* a time to develop your storytelling skills—as long as you remember to focus first on telling your story well!

So, let's identify the ingredients that a storyteller uses and take some time developing those skills. But remember; the goal isn't to use as many skills as possible, but to mix them together—naturally and organically—so that the end result tastes good. Remember the cake? The more you cook, the better your instincts will be so that you can start improvising on the recipes—and improving on them! Once you're thoroughly familiar with the ingredients of storytelling and how they interact together, you can begin mixing them together in new ways and start creating fascinating dishes on your own.

What are the ingredients you'll be using? Here is a list of eight important ingredients you'll use when serving up a tasty story.

Ingredient One: Voice

The most basic ingredient of all is your voice. While it's certainly possible to tell a story well without using your voice (mimes, dancers, and sign language experts do it all the time), most of us rely primarily on our voice to tell our stories.

You can use your voice to reveal different characters, develop sound effects, express emotions, and create suspense. Your voice becomes an artist's brush with which you paint word pictures on the minds of your listeners.

Care for your voice.

It's wise to take care of your voice. Many actors and singers spend long hours training their voices to be resilient and strong and to sound clear and pleasant rather than strained and weak. There are lots of books containing breathing exercises for the serious voice student, but let's be realistic—if you're telling stories once or twice a week you probably don't have time to train your voice like a professional singer!

Still, there are a few simple things you can do to care for your voice:
- Before telling your story, take the time to warm up your voice by singing a little, exploring different levels of pitch and volume, and trying out some of the different voices you'll be using when you tell your stories. Different voices add flavor and fun to a story.
- Relax your jaw muscles and loosen your neck, throat, and shoulder muscles before speaking. Tension in the throat, neck, and jaw causes vocal strain. Yawning is a great way to relax your throat muscles!
- In rehearsal, feel free to experiment with different types of sound effects or voices for your stories. But use only those that are comfortable for you. Don't strain your voice.
- Avoid yelling, screaming, shouting, or other activities that can damage your voice. Speaking in cold, wet weather can also cause you to lose your voice.
- Drink lots of water before and during your speaking engagements (rather than tea and coffee which actually constrict the muscles in your throat).
- If you find that you frequently strain or lose your voice, talk to a voice coach or singing instructor for more activities and guidelines on caring for your voice.

Make sure you are heard.

Speak loudly enough to be heard and, if you have more than fifty people in your group, consider using a microphone to amplify your voice. Many people shy away from microphones. But it's your responsibility to be heard! So, if there is a large group, one of the best ways to take care of your voice, and be easily heard by the audience, is to use a microphone.

Once I was speaking at a Christian camp of about 250 elementary students. The young lady who was leading songs before I went onstage told me, "I hate using a microphone. I'll be able to make the kids hear me." I encouraged her to reconsider, but she wasn't about to change her mind.

By the third day she'd lost her voice and someone else was leading the songs.

Use a microphone and take care of your voice.

Be careful to speak clearly so people can understand the words you use. Many of us have certain words that we mumble, especially at the end of sentences. Try to identify these words and then practice saying them more clearly.

One more thing: speak in a natural tone. Some people start talking with a preachy, scolding tone as soon as they step in front of a group. Other people talk with an annoying, condescending tone. Avoid both extremes and talk in a natural, pleasant speaking voice.

Ingredient Two: Face

Your face is a magnificent storytelling tool. With your face you can show nearly every emotion imaginable: from joy to sadness, from anger to peace, from fear to surprise, and from confusion to delight. Your face is an endless canvas that can reflect the emotions of your heart.

Try this at home. Turn away from a mirror and try to make a face that clearly expresses one of the emotions or attitudes listed below. Then turn and look at the mirror to see if you're accurately portraying it. You may be surprised to discover that some of the emotions you think you're clearly expressing actually look like something else!

afraid	determined	hateful	nagging	shocked
amazed	disappointed	hesitant	nervous	shy
angry	disgusted	hopeful	pleading	sick
bewildered	ditsy	infatuated	pouting	silly
bossy	enthusiastic	innocent	powerful	sorrow
concerned	furious	joyful	regretful	stressed
confident	grumpy	lonely	relieved	surprised
content	guilty	mean	romantic	thankful
depressed	happy	mischievous	sarcastic	tired

When you tell your stories, don't try to do too much with your face. You can overdo it. Just use this exercise to expand and refine the facial expressions you have in your repertoire so that you can naturally start using them in your storytelling. To communicate clearly, it's important to express the same emotions with your face that you feel in your heart.

Ingredient Three: Eyes

Most people have heard that public speakers should have good eye contact with the audience. But what does that mean, exactly? Does good eye contact mean looking at everyone in the audience? Or staring over their heads, as some people suggest?

Eye contact is the process of looking into another person's eyes. The use of eye contact by storytellers is one of the key elements that differentiates storytelling from drama.

To understand eye contact, you need to first understand a little bit about the way we tell stories. When you tell a story, you sometimes take on the role of the narrator and explain what's happening in the story. For example, if you were telling Jesus' story of "The Prodigal Son" (see Luke 15:11-32) you might begin, "Once upon a time, there were two brothers and the younger asked his dad for his inheritance." That's **narration**.

At other times, however, you might step into the role of one or more of the characters and talk as if you actually were that character: "Dad, give me my inheritance! I don't want to wait around here until you're dead before I get it!" "OK, son. I'll give it to you. Wait here while I go get your share." That's **dialogue**.

See the difference between narration and dialogue? When the storyteller is narrating, he's addressing the audience. When he's engaged in dialogue, he's actually talking to the other characters in the story.

The secret to good eye contact is for a storyteller to always look at whomever he or she is speaking to. When you're narrating, look at the audience. But when you're engaged in dialogue, look at the other characters in the story!

"Wait a minute!" I can hear you say. "The other characters aren't really there!"

That's right. They're imaginary, but they're still present in the story. So, you'd look, let's say, to your left to address the father, and then back over your right shoulder to talk to the son. You don't look at the audience; both you and the audience direct your attention to the place onstage where the other character would be standing if he were there.

Practice having a conversation like this with yourself. Pretend that you're having a dialogue with your friend or spouse about where to go for dinner. Go ahead, give it a shot!

By the way, when you look at the audience, avoid staring at any individual for too long. If you stare at someone for more than a moment or two, he'll begin to feel uncomfortable, and the attention of the audience will shift from you to him! If you find someone who is really enjoying your story, glance back at that person often for encouragement!

To summarize, good eye contact is natural, genuine, and directed at whomever the storyteller is addressing: either the audience or the other characters in the story.

Ingredient Four: Posture

Believe it or not, you communicate just by the way you stand and hold your body. If your shoulders are slouched too far forward, people will think you're sad, depressed, or shy. If you hold your shoulders too far back, people may think you're overly confident, proud, or even stuck-up. If you stand straight and tall with your shoulders comfortable and natural, people will think that you're confident and at ease with them.

To become more aware of how posture communicates, do some people-watching on a busy street, at an airport, or in the lobby of your church! Watch how different people carry themselves and see what impression they give you. Be aware of how stiffly or loosely they stand, how straight or crookedly they walk, and if they lean forward or backward when they stop. Notice how they hold their weight and balance their head, back, arms and legs.

How can posture affect your story? Well, how do you think Goliath would have stood? What about David? Or shy Saul who was hiding behind the luggage when the people were about to crown him king? What about Peter? Judas? Jesus? See? You can already imagine the way these people would stand because you know personality characteristics or traits they had—Goliath is huge and menacing, David is bold and confident, Saul is tall and shy, Peter is brash and impulsive, Judas is sly and deceptive, and Jesus is self-assured and compassionate. As you tell your stories, let your posture naturally reveal personality traits of the characters you're portraying in your stories.

Finally, be aware of your own posture as you stand in front of your audience. If you sit when you tell your stories, notice the difference between leaning back in a rocking chair, leaning forward on a musician's stool, kneeling on the carpet, or sitting cross-legged. Each communicates a different level of formality with your listeners.

Practice standing or sitting with your shoulders in a calm, neutral position. It will help you stand comfortably and confidently as you tell your stories.

Ingredient Five: Movement

There's more to a story than meets the ear—a story is also told for the eye! In a story, actions speak louder than words! Just to see how movement can portray different characters, take a moment and walk around the room pretending to be Samson, the muscle-bound hero from the Old Testament. Now, change to Delilah, the alluring temptress who led to his downfall. Then shift to being the sly Philistine who lurked in his room. Go ahead, try it!

Quite a difference, huh? Notice how each character leads with a different part of his or her body and moves differently.

The way you move your body communicates many things. Some storytellers are comfortable jumping around, skillfully changing their bodies into the shape of all sorts of different characters. They practically dance their way through the story! Other people are more at ease sitting in a rocking chair elegantly weaving their tale simply by using well-chosen words—without any movement at all. Do what's most comfortable for you.

The amount of body movement you include in your story will depend on

- Audience—how many people are in attendance (typically, the more people, the more movement).
- Proximity—how far you are from your audience, (typically, the more distance, the more movement).
- Story content—how much movement naturally occurs in the story.
- Your personality—how comfortable you are using body movement to tell your stories.

Movement and gestures must rise from your own comfort level rather than what you think you're supposed to look like or what your curriculum suggests that you do. Experiment with different ways of moving to find the balance that works best for you.

Ingredient Six: Gestures

Closely related to the way you stand or move your body are gestures—the way you move your arms and hands. Most people naturally gesture as they speak. Some people are so used to talking with their hands that they even do it while they're speaking on the phone!

Gestures should be consistent and committed. Don't hesitate. Don't do them half-heartedly. They must be done like the rest of the story, with confidence, sincerity, appropriateness, and authenticity. If you think you look stupid, you probably do! If you don't notice how you look because all you see is the story, you're right on track!

If you're going to use movement when you tell a story, use movement when you practice the story. That way, the movement and gestures grow naturally out of the story and aren't awkwardly grafted in at the end. Don't try to act out each word, rather look for a way to naturally embody the story as you tell it.

Gestures can be used for characterization, to show what's happening in the story, or even to misdirect the audience. Typically, gestures are most effective when they're done from the elbow or shoulder, rather than the wrist.

As you experiment with telling your story, explore how you could communicate the ideas in your story just by the way you stand, move, and gesture. If you're careful to observe and respond to the movements, you'll discover new and interesting ways to use your body to tell your story.

Try practicing the story

- with huge gestures, as if you're speaking to 25,000 people in a stadium;
- with tiny, finger-sized gestures, as if you're stuck in a broom closet;
- without any words, just move and mime your way through the story;
- without any gestures, just words;
- while sitting down;
- while standing up;
- with different props or costumes.

I call this, "brainstorming with your body." Don't try to rehearse one version of the story to get it right; instead, pay attention to the differences that naturally occur with each different way of retelling the story. Then keep the ones you like!

The secret to finding the right gesture is believing the story. You'll respond believably and naturally to what's happening in the story when you can vividly imagine it and experience the story.

Sometimes people practice a specific gesture so much that when they tell the story, the gesture looks rehearsed rather than natural. Avoid that! Gestures must flow naturally from the story rather than distract from it. It's much more important for them to be natural than "right." The secret to having believable gestures is to let them grow from the story as you tell it. Gestures, while polished, should never look rehearsed.

Ingredient Seven: Imagination

If voice is the way a storyteller relates to the audience, imagination is the way a storyteller relates to the story. Don't confuse imagination with make-believe. Imagination is not believing in something that is not true, it is the ability to picture something that is beyond our natural experience. Imagination lies at the heart of a faith that hopes for what it cannot see, a religion in which a lamb tramples a snake and immortal God dies as mortal man. Without imagination how can we *know* a love *that surpasses knowledge* (Ephesians 3:19)? Or *fix our eyes* on what is *unseen* (2 Corinthians 4:18)? Or be *certain* of what we *do not see* (Hebrew 11:1)? Without imagination, how can we accept a faith in which death is the beginning of life, weakness is the key to strength, and foolishness is the pathway to wisdom?

God wants us to love him with wonder, creativity, *and* imagination.

Go ahead; imagine something extraordinary. God calls us to imagine the impossible, and then promises to go beyond that in his good gifts to us. He is able to do *"immeasurably more than all we ask or imagine"* (Ephesians 3:20). Did you catch that? I can imagine a lot! But he can do immeasurably more!

Don't let yourself be like the Pharisees. They weren't willing to use their imaginations; they weren't willing to believe. They wanted everything spelled out. Sure, they knew the laws, they could quote them word for word, but they never understood that faith is more than knowing the right things.

Never be ashamed to nurture your imagination. Tell stories that inspire hope and ignite the imagination. Just like Jesus did.

Ingredient Eight: The Secret Ingredient!

The secret ingredient is yourself. Add yourself to the story. Tell it your way, with the gifts and personality God gave you. Don't be ashamed of who God designed you to be! Begin with prayer, rely on God, and then serve up the story with a good dose of yourself mixed in. If you do that, your presentation is gonna taste great to your listeners!

Summary

Watch any great storyteller and you may find something that he or she does "wrong." But often, despite not following the rules, the story works. Why? Because those tellers know that the tools of the storyteller are there to serve the story, not the other way around!

A well-told story is more than a sum of its parts. Just like a good cake is more than a bunch of flour, eggs, and milk, a good story is more than a well-trained voice, natural gestures, good timing, and eye contact. While all of these are important, how good the cake tastes—how well the story communicates with the audience—is even more important!

Chapter 12

Five Storytelling Secrets

Foolproof Ways to Improve Your Delivery

WHEN I WAS in middle school I entered the Conservation and Environmental Awareness Speaking Contest for Jefferson County, Wisconsin on a quest to win the whopping ten dollar first prize. For dozens of hours I labored over my three-minute masterpiece, carefully perfecting every gesture, pause, and facial contortion in front of our bathroom mirror. And it worked, too. Sort of. I placed in the top ten each of the three years I entered (even on the year it snowed and only one other contestant showed up). My monologue about the importance of soil conservation told from a worm's point of view left the judges in stunned silence. And my storytelling career was up and running.

Or, at least, squirming. I think I might even have won that ten dollar prize if the judges could have watched me rehearse—I was brilliant. Unfortunately, they couldn't come over, and at the time I didn't know these five secrets to practicing and telling stories.

Secret One: Recite Less, Respond More

My high school basketball coach had a saying, "Practice doesn't make perfect, it makes permanent. Perfect practice makes perfect." The same is true for storytelling. Practicing stories is important, no doubt about that. But practicing a story doesn't necessarily improve the way you'll tell it. It may improve how well you remember that story. It'll probably impress upon your mind and body one way of moving or acting or speaking. But if you practice your story over and over the same way in front of a mirror, you'll learn to tell it that way. Every time. Forever.

Practice doesn't make perfect, it makes permanent. So use practice time to develop proficiency at storytelling *skills*. Tell the story in a variety of settings to a variety of audiences in a variety of ways. Become so familiar with the story that when it's time, you'll be able to tell the most natural, appropriate, genuine version of your story to *your* students on *that* day. You'll know the *story*, not *one version* of it.

To shape stories, successful storytellers respond to the ongoing feedback of the listeners. They tell a story differently in front of a bathroom mirror than in front of a live audience. If a storyteller practices in front of a mirror, it shouldn't be to perfect the story, but to see what the listeners see during the story.

The delivery of your story is based on three main factors: the story, the storyteller, and the listeners. As with any message that needs to be communicated, each factor affects the communication process: **story** (content, truth and emotion) + **storyteller** (goals, attitude, personality, style) + **listeners** (response, expectations, mood) = **delivery.**

Think about the content of the story, the readiness of your listeners, and your own knowledge and communication skills. As a storyteller, you're responding not only to the listeners, but also to the story itself as it's told.

If you polish a knife too long, you'll only make it more brittle. It's the same with storytelling. Practice until the story is sharp, then stop. Don't over polish your stories or they'll lose their edge. The best stories are always polished, yet contain an air of spontaneity. Storytelling combines both preparation and alertness.

A technically perfect story may fall flat. Why? Because audiences would rather hear a storyteller who connects with them, who touches them with the story, who communicates with them, than watch someone go through the actions of telling a story that they don't feel a part of.

Don't make the mistake of trying to memorize your story. Do spend time learning and practicing your story! Take the time to really learn it. Yes, you need to be prepared. Yes, learn the story and practice your refrains or gestures. But don't worry about retelling the story word-for-word. Instead, be flexible. If the students really like that silly refrain you made up, insert it again. If the story is dragging, shorten it up. Strive to tell the story naturally to *this* audience rather than reciting it the same way you did in front of your mirror.

The listeners will be turned off if they think every gesture, pause, and vocal utterance is identical to the last time you told the story. They want you to tell the story to them, not to an imaginary bathroom mirror, or the memory of a previous audience. They want you to experience the story with them, sharing its warmth, spontaneity, and humor. This can be done only if you're attentive to the story as you tell it, and are continually filled with wonder and curiosity about the story. A good story is told with freshness as well as polish. Neither is absent. So focus on responding rather than reciting.

Secret Two: Concentrate Less, Relax More

My basketball coach also had us practice numerous drills in handling the ball, shooting, passing, and playing defense. He used these drills to teach us how to respond when we faced similar situations in the game. He wanted us to become so proficient at shooting that we wouldn't even have to think about it when someone threw us the ball.

I remember one game in which I became frustrated and started to concentrate on everything I was doing, *OK, Steve, keep that forty-five degree trajectory and good rotation on the ball, flick your wrist, follow through with your hand, keep your eye on the basket.* During that game I couldn't hit the broad side of a barn. And that's pretty bad—especially for a kid from Wisconsin!

What I needed to do was to play the game. I'd become proficient at the skills during practice. The moment I began to think about how I was supposed to shoot the basketball, I became too distracted to actually shoot the ball well. Rather than concentrate, I needed to relax!

When you practice basketball, you do drills and exercises to improve. But when it's time for the game, you play. You don't think about the drills during the game. Practice is practice, play is play. There comes a time to play. When you get up to tell your story, put away the watch and the notebook and your expectations and inhibitions. Let loose, and play.

When you practice a story, it's important to explore and refine body movement, voice inflection, facial expressions, gestures, etc. But when you tell the story, don't focus on the mechanics. *Experience* the story with the listeners.

Practice will give you the confidence to tell the story well. But don't get distracted by how well or how poorly you're telling the story. Relax and enjoy. If you must concentrate, concentrate on what's happening in the story, not on what could be going on, or what should be going on, or how well it went in rehearsal in front of your bathroom mirror! Pay attention to what is happening in your story right now! Attend to the moment. Abandon all your expectations, worries, and distracting thoughts and let the story flow naturally.

Secret Three: Pretend Less, Believe More

In an acting class I attended, the instructor had us approach a shoe from across the room while blindfolded. One by one my classmates shuffled across the room, bent over, and reached down. No one was even close to picking up the shoe!

Then it was my turn. I walked across the room to where I judged the shoe to be, bent over and confidently closed my hand . . . on thin air! I was shocked. I felt again. No shoe. Embarrassed at how confident I'd been, I returned to the front of the room. After the activity, the instructor asked me, "Why did you close your hand and feel the floor?"

"I was surprised I didn't have the shoe. I couldn't believe it wasn't there," I responded.

"That's right!" he said. "You were certain that something was there, even though you couldn't see it. Your hand knew what the shoe would feel like and how much it would weigh. You couldn't fake your hand's reaction. I could tell you thought the shoe was there. That's how real your story has to be when you tell it. Then you won't be pretending when you tell a story, you'll be responding to it as it happens around you."

Tony Montanaro, a well-known mime who has trained several professional storytellers, emphasized this point in his book *Mime Spoken Here:* "When I lean on a wall, I honestly *believe* that the wall is there. When I fly through the air as the legendary Icarus, I *see* the Aegean waves surging beneath me. My ability to believe these things, these images, determines the clarity of my gestures and the integrity of my sketch. My belief ignites my audience's belief, and they join me in my adventures"[1] (emphasis in the original).

In my worm monologue, I felt ridiculous acting like a worm and because of that I looked ridiculous. A lot of *pretending* was going on, but very little *believing.*

The best storytellers don't pretend. They actually imagine (picture) the story happening, and then respond naturally and realistically.

Secret Four: Explain Less, Evoke More

I heard about a dancer who was approached by an audience member after a stirring performance. "Wow!" said the lady, "your dance was incredible! But I have to say, I didn't understand it—what does it mean?"

And the dancer replied, "If I could tell you what it meant, I wouldn't have had to dance it."

I think Jesus would have liked that dancer's response. He preferred letting his listeners chew on his stories for a while. Instead of summarizing them, he let them stand alone.

In *Mystery and Manners*, novelist Flannery O'Connor wrote, "When you can state the theme of a story, when you can separate it from the story itself, then you can be sure the story is not a very good one. The meaning of a story has to be embodied in it, has to be made concrete in it. *A story is a way to say something that can't be said any other way, and it takes every word in the story to say what the meaning is"*[2] (emphasis added).

A story is always more than its explanation. It overflows its explanation in every direction. It has more depth, detail, passion, and truth than any description could ever have.

As educators, we're sometimes tempted to trust our explanations of stories rather than the stories themselves. We seem to think that the more we explain a story, the better it will be. But exactly the opposite is true! The more you explain a story, the less impact it has. Let the story impact your audience before you explain too much. And even then, don't explain too much! That doesn't mean you can't clarify a story, but try to follow Jesus' example. Jesus told dozens and dozens of stories, yet Scripture records only a few times when Jesus explained what his stories meant.

---

[1]Tony Montanaro with Karen Hurll Montanaro, *Mime Spoken Here: The Performer's Portable Workshop* (Gardiner, ME :Tilbury House, 1995), 68, 69.

[2]Flannery O'Connor (selected and edited by Sally and Robert Fitzgerald*), Mystery and Manners: Occasional Prose* (New York: Farrar, Straus & Giroux, 2000), 96.

Jesus preferred speaking truth by telling stories and letting the listeners draw out the meaning rather than explaining what he meant. Why? Because the more you explain a story, the less impact it has. So, let the story speak for itself.

Secret Five: Impress Less, Connect More

One time in college I took a friend out for ice cream. Though we'd been friends for a while, I was hoping our relationship might blossom into something a little more romantic. So, as we sat and talked, I told her about growing up and playing sports in high school. I was really getting into it, trying to impress her.

Finally, she said, "Steve, I want to tell you something."

"What's that?" I asked.

She looked me straight in the eyes. "I feel more like your audience than your friend," she said. Ouch! Do you see what had happened? I was trying to impress her and since I tend to feel more comfortable onstage, I'd started performing my life story for her rather than sharing a conversation with her!

To some extent, every told story is both a conversation and a performance. In a conversation, people talk with spontaneity and listen so they can respond to what's being said. But in a performance, one person (or a small group of people) prepares something to say and everyone else is expected to listen without interrupting.

If we were sitting in an ice cream parlor holding a conversation, it would seem natural for us to interrupt each other, talk about a variety of subjects, talk in short sentences, and pause to reflect on what we're going to talk about next.

On the other hand, if we went to see an actor perform a one-person play, we would have entirely different expectations. We'd expect to sit quietly (perhaps for an hour or more) as the performer spoke to us. We wouldn't interrupt, change the subject, or expect to get a turn. And if he paused too long we'd start to think that maybe he forgot his line.

Think of a conversation as one end of a continuum, and a performance as the other.

Conversation	Performance

Now, think back to the ice cream parlor scenario. Without realizing it, I'd been telling my story to my friend at a completely different place on the continuum than what was appropriate for our situation. I was performing, not conversing. And she'd been courageous and honest enough to let me know that!

It's vitally important to understand your audience and match the level of formality/informality with the expectations your listeners have. Once you realize where on the continuum you're more comfortable sharing your stories, you can begin to look for places to tell stories within your comfort zone. Many people are more comfortable sitting around chatting with friends than going onstage in front of a thousand people. If that's you, you'll probably do well telling stories to a small number of students in a classroom setting.

People like me, on the other hand, are intimidated by small groups. Instead, I look for opportunities to tell stories to large groups where the expectation shifts toward performance.

Summary

Practice makes permanent. Attend to the moment. Pretend less, believe more. Relax, respond, connect, and evoke.

OK, so these aren't the only secrets to storytelling. I'll admit it. But maybe, just maybe, if I had known them twenty years ago, I would be ten dollars richer today.

Chapter 13

Story Stacking

Telling Stories the Way Jesus Did

JESUS PREACHED quite differently from most teachers and preachers of today. He didn't use lesson plans, three-point sermons, or fill-in-the-blank outlines that all start with the same letter. Instead, Jesus was a master at using teachable moments and telling stories in a way that changed the lives of his listeners.

At least for a period of his public preaching ministry, Jesus taught exclusively through storytelling (Matthew 13:34). He knew that we remember best what we discover, not what we're told is important.

How Jesus Taught Truth

Jesus said that he came to proclaim the truth. And how did he do that? By using image-rich language, stories, riddles and metaphors that he rarely explained. In fact, when his followers asked him why he spoke to the crowds in parables, Jesus answered with a riddle! "This is why I speak to them in parables: 'Though seeing, they do not see; though hearing, they do not hear or understand'" (Matthew 13:13). Instead of following Jesus' example today, we tend to use *few* images, stories, riddles and metaphors and spend *most of our time* on explanations!

God doesn't want us to be comfortable analyzing, categorizing, and theorizing about him. Jesus used stories to evoke and expose rather than explain. He wasn't out to win arguments, but to win hearts.

Jesus told stories that made people uneasy, that shook them out of their comfort zones. His stories sometimes had unhappy endings. People didn't leave feeling warm and fuzzy inside. Folks walked away amazed and confused. And when Jesus' enemies heard the stories he told about them, they mocked him, tried to trick him, and even tried to arrest and kill him.

So what can we learn from Jesus' storytelling style that can help us share his story today? Here are three observations.

1. Jesus used surprising comparisons in his stories.

"The kingdom of heaven is like . . . a mustard seed . . . yeast . . . buried treasure . . . a pearl merchant . . . a net cast into the water . . . a thief in the night. . . . " See how Jesus repeatedly compared the kingdom of Heaven to different objects and situations? Some were rather shocking—how could the kingdom of Heaven be like a thief? By using these surprising images and comparisons, Jesus was able to get people thinking about the different aspects of the truth he was teaching.

2. Jesus used images to reveal the many facets of the truth.

Often, Jesus started with an image and wove that image through a series of stories:

- In Matthew 13, Jesus told seven comparison stories about the kingdom of Heaven.
- In Matthew 24, 25, Jesus told six stories about being ready for his return.
- In Luke 15, Jesus wove together three stories about lost items (a sheep, a coin, and two lost sons) into one long narrative.
- In Luke 16, Jesus told two stories about wealth, service to God, and priorities.
- In Luke 18, Jesus told two stories about prayer.

The truth that Jesus was teaching was like a diamond, and each story was another way of tilting the diamond so that the audience could see its many facets. Each story reflected the truth in a slightly different way. He allowed people to see truth from different perspectives so they could think about it in ways they'd never done before. Each additional story or comparison echoed the theme of the others, and served to interpret and enhance the point Jesus was making.

3. Jesus stacked one story on top of another.

In Luke 15, Jesus responded to a question by telling one long parable that included three short stories. Instead of taking a lot of time to explain the stories, Jesus let his listeners find the thread of meaning that ran through each story: namely, that God always celebrates when a lost sinner is restored to a right relationship with God.

Jesus stacked stories on top of each other until his listeners were impacted and moved to a response. Story stacking can be a powerful tool in your teaching as well!

How to Stack Stories in Your Lessons

How can you begin stacking stories like Jesus did? Follow these three steps:

1. Find the thread of meaning.

One day I got an e-mail from a lady who'd attended one of my workshops. It was four days before an outreach event at her church and she was desperately trying to find a story that could relate to the theme, "Running the Race with Jesus." She wrote, "I already thought about the turtle and the hare but couldn't go much further than that. Any ideas? Any help would be appreciated. The program is in four days. Yikes!"

As I sat there thinking of how I could help, I remembered a Greek myth about a race. After paging through a few collections, I found the story. It's about a woman named Atalanta who was a great runner, faster than anyone in all the world. There was a deal that any man who could beat her could marry her. But if the challenger lost the race, he would be killed!

After a whole lot of men failed, a handsome young man named Milanion (or Hippomenes, depending on the version of the myth) raced her and brought golden apples along with him. As they raced, he threw them to the side and Atalanta became distracted by chasing them. He won the race and they were married.

The story seemed like a natural application to "running the race with perseverance," with our eyes fixed on Jesus, instead of getting off course by the distractions and treasures of this world. So that's what I wrote to her. A few days later I got this reply:

> Dear Steve,
>
> I had to e-mail you one more time and let you know what a success Race Night was. I told the story of Atalanta and Hippomenes and they, kids and adults, were spellbound. I even tossed golden apples as I told/acted out the story. It was awesome. I really got into that story. It was fun to tell something besides a Bible story and still get an important Biblical truth thrown in there. At the end I gave the application of keeping your eyes fixed on Jesus and we used Hebrews 12:1b, 2a.
>
> God bless,
> Elizabeth Vaughan
> First Baptist Church, Galax, VA

The first step is to find the thread of meaning. It may not be possible to neatly summarize the specific point of a story. Instead, it may be more helpful to identify the themes and truths that run through it. For example, if you're teaching about Noah, the thread of meaning could be "obedience," since Noah obeyed God. In this case, look for other stories that teach about obedience, or show the consequences of disobedience. Or, the thread of meaning could be "faith," since Noah displayed unusual faith in God by building a giant boat in the middle of a desert. If you choose faith as your theme, you'd look for other stories that teach about faith, or lack of faith.

A virtue is amplified when we see its opposite in action. For example, if we see the opposite of truthfulness, we understand more clearly what truthfulness is. If we see unforgiveness, we can better understand forgiveness. So, our stories can either accentuate a truth, or show its opposite.

2. Look for stories with similar themes.

Where can you find stories to stack onto the story in your lesson? If you remember the acronym L.I.F.E. you'll always have a limitless well of stories to tell!

L—Literature The first place to look is in the Bible. Many New Testament stories are hinted at in the Old Testament. For example, if you were doing a lesson on Pentecost you could stack on the Old Testament story of "The Tower of Babel." At Babel, God confused the languages of the world and people were dispersed because of sin; at Pentecost God unconfused the languages of the world and people were brought together because of grace! By telling these two stories alongside each other, you add depth of meaning to them both.

Even Jesus used stories from the Old Testament. Read Isaiah 3:14 and Isaiah 5:1-7 and then read Mark 12:1-12. See how Jesus reinterpreted the parable of Isaiah and showed how it pointed specifically to him?

Don't limit your search to the Bible! Think about all of the great missionary stories, stories from church history, tales of martyrs, saints, and heroes of the faith. Think of news you've read or movies you've seen. Think of books you liked as a kid, or the ones the school librarian read to you. The whole world of literature is open to you!

I—Imagination You can make up your own stories for telling just like Jesus did! You might not think you're very creative, but when you follow these simple steps, you can make up parables and fables that will enhance your teaching and your storytelling.

1. **Limit yourself.** Think about your lesson or what the other stories in your teaching time are about. Try to focus on one truth or one way of applying truth. Or, decide on a specific Bible story that you wish to retell.

2. **Brainstorm possibilities.** Consider different ways that the truth you're teaching can be expressed. Let's say your lesson is about loving others. What does this truth look like in action? What does the opposite of love look like? Think of characters who might experience this truth in action. Let's say you decide to tell a story about a squirrel who discovers he needs to put love into action. What might lead him to make this discovery?

3. **Let yourself be surprised.** This is where wonder and imagination come in. Keep an open mind and keep your eyes peeled. God likes to surprise his children!

4. **Sharpen your focus.** Choose one specific idea and run with it! Let's say the squirrel is keeping all the nuts for himself and later finds out the other squirrels are hungry. He decides to help them by sharing. What might cause this change of attitude?

5. **Start with a struggle and then show a discovery.** Since struggles always appear in stories, start there and work your way out into the details of what happens.

F—Folklore Folklore is another source of stories. These are the stories you've heard, that have been passed down orally: folktales, fairy tales, tall tales, legends, hero tales, myths, even local history and lore. These days, people even share contemporary legends over the Internet!

Think of a fable or folktale that has a similar theme to your Bible story, or brings out the moral taught in the Bible story. Don't worry about getting the story right. Everyone who tells a folktale changes it! That's one of the wonderful things about folklore, everyone adds a part of himself to the story.

Look for a way to use that story to teach a biblical truth! For example, in the popular children's folktale of "The Three Billy Goats Gruff" the two youngest Billy goats have to rely on the strength, courage, and resourcefulness of their big brother to safely cross the bridge and eat the tasty grass on the other side.

After I tell this story to children, I ask them, "How many of you would like a big brother who was big enough and brave enough and strong enough to handle any problem that popped up in your life?" Their hands shoot up into the air. Then I tell them, "Jesus came to be just that kind of big brother for each of you. A long time ago he faced the biggest, nastiest, ugliest troublemaker of all time and dropkicked him off the bridge so we could cross over and be with God up in Heaven. It wasn't an ugly old troll. Do you know who it is that Jesus beat?"

"The devil!" they shout.

And just that quickly, before they even realize it, they've learned an important lesson about Jesus by hearing the folktale of "The Three Billy Goats Gruff"!

E—Experience Another source of stories is your own experience. Telling personal and family stories is a way to share your values with children, explain your heritage, help them understand and apply their beliefs, spend quality time with them, and deepen your relationship.

The story of "The Lost Sheep" (Luke 15:3-7)

1. Themes
   a. Being lost
   b. Being found
   c. Caring enough to seek the lost
   d. Celebration
2. Similar experiences and emotions
   a. Share about a time your pet ran away. What did you do? Did you look for your pet? Why?
   b. Share about a time you were lost. What lured you away? How did you know when you were found? (As the sheep was found.)
   c. Share about a time you endangered or attacked others. (As the wolf did.)
   d. Share about a time you searched for someone who was lost. (As the shepherd did.)
   e. Share about a time you joined a homecoming party. (As the friends did.)

The story of "The Lost Coin" (Luke 15:8-10)

1. Themes
   a. Value
   b. Diligence
   c. Celebration
2. Similar experiences and emotions
   a. Share about a time you lost your car keys. How hard did you search? Why?
   b. Share about a time you were invited to celebrate with someone. Were you jealous or genuinely joyful?

The story of "The Lost Sons" (Luke 15:11-32)

1. Themes
   a. Rebellion and restoration (younger son)
   b. Love and forgiveness (father)
   c. Bitterness and resentment (older son)
   d. Celebration
2. Similar experiences and emotions
   a. You rebelled, or were restored.
   b. You forgave, or were forgiven.
   c. You were bitter, or were the recipient of resentment.

Your story, even though it's about your life, isn't just about you! It's about what you (or someone else) learned or observed. Step out of the spotlight. Rather than being in the spotlight, you're standing behind it, directing its focus. You don't want to end up looking like the hero, taking bows on center stage. Be the mistake-maker, not the problem-solver, the recipient of grace rather than the Savior. Show the listeners your weaknesses. Emphasize not how you triumphed, but how you floundered.

Your students don't want to hear how great you are because they can't identify with that. They want to see how you faced a problem and made a discovery. Be authentic by being honest, sincere, and vulnerable. Just don't go overboard and become the victim!

To spark memories, think of your fears and dreams, your triumphs and traumas, your struggles and discoveries. And share with your students how God has impacted and affected your life. See "Appendix C" for hundreds of ideas on personal stories you can tell!

Personal stories are a way to build a bridge between the lesson and life. The box on the left contains a few examples.

3. Weave the stories together.

Finally, you'll want to bring your stories together into an integrated program. Here are a few examples of how to integrate story stacking into your lessons:

- Start with a short personal story that ties into your lesson, tell a myth or folktale, and then tell your Bible story.
- Tell an Old Testament story that includes prophecies, and then tell a New Testament story that contains their fulfillment.
- Tell an Old Testament story that has a similar theme to a New Testament story.
- Tell two stories at once by alternating between two storytellers.

Summary

Story stacking is an effective way of teaching truth. Jesus wove stories together around a common theme, and we can do the same. Choose stories from literature, imagination, folklore, and your own personal experiences. Find the thread of meaning, explore the connections, and then weave them together!

Chapter 14

Advanced Skills and Techniques

Reaching for Excellence

*L*ong ago a priest painted a picture of Christ. He was very interested in what others thought of the painting, so he asked Leo Tolstoy, the famous writer, for his opinion. He was certain that if Tolstoy liked the picture, then the other priests would admire it (and him) as well.

Tolstoy walked into the room and sat in front of the picture for an hour before nodding his head and rising.

"Well, what did you think?" asked the excited priest.

Tolstoy paused for a moment and then replied, "If you would have loved him more, you would have painted him better."

God doesn't want us to tell stories to impress others, to feel good about ourselves, or to show off. He wants us to be committed servants who will use our gifts faithfully in serving him. He wants our passionate love for him to drive us to strive for excellence.

"If you would have loved him more, you would have told his story better."

In this chapter, you'll learn ways to take your stories and your storytelling to the next level of excellence.

Make the Most of Silence and Stillness

Knowing when to be silent is just as important as knowing when to speak. And knowing when to be still is just as important as knowing when (or how) to move. Silence and stillness are essential ingredients in any story. When a storyteller "speaks" silence, it echoes through the room. A pause draws attention to the word or phrase that precedes it. It also draws attention to the word or phrase that follows it. Don't rush through your story. Take your time. Be aware of your pace, pauses, and moments of stillness.

A paradox of storytelling is that less is more. Overdramatizing or giving too much description leaves no room for the audience to imagine. What you leave unsaid is often just as eloquent as what you say. Search for the smallest way to make the longest-lasting impression. Look for ways of communicating more, by saying less.

To refine this skill, record your stories on audio or videotape and then listen to the rhythm and pace of the story. Notice how the speed at which you tell the story varies. Notice how the pace of your story is related to descriptions, suspense and action. Then listen for ways to make silence and stillness work to your advantage.

Sustain the Suspense by Postponing the Resolution

People get bored easily. If your listeners can predict where the story is going, they'll begin to tune out and think about other things. Mystery is the key. People will always be interested in what you have to say—until you say it!

Sometimes, you can give the audience a foreshadow or hint of where the story is going, but the story characters don't yet know what's going to happen. The technique of letting the audience know more about the story than the characters do is called "dramatic irony." It can be fun to let the audience in on a secret before anyone in the story catches on!

So, as you tell your story, be careful not to give too much away. Look for ways to surprise the audience and keep them interested. But don't confuse them! You don't want people to be thinking, "What is he talking about?" Instead you want them to be asking, "Where is he going with this? How is this gonna end? What's this character going to do? How will he solve this problem? What's gonna happen next?"

Use the Stage Area to Your Advantage

Whether you're telling a story in a classroom with five children, or on a platform in front of five thousand, you're using a stage! Wherever you sit or stand to tell your story is your stage. How can you use the stage area to your advantage?

First, explore ways to use more of the stage. Could you create different characters that address the audience from different places onstage? Could you move through space to tell sections of your story? Could you use different levels, by kneeling down or stretching tall for certain sections of your story? How well are you using the space onstage?

Be aware of your body movement. If you create a character, or use gestures to create the illusion of an object, don't forget where it's located onstage! Many inexperienced storytellers use gestures that aren't consistent. They may set an imaginary object down, and then later in the story, pick it up from another place! If your gestures aren't consistent, you'll confuse and annoy your listeners.

When you talk, you naturally differentiate story characters by your posture, inflection and expressions. Remember, you can portray a character by your stance, voice, costuming, or a combination of the three. Be clear in the way you portray each character so the audience can keep them apart! Consider giving each character a specific quirk or trait that's easily identifiable. Precision and simplicity of details make the characters come to life.

Remember where your characters are, and look in that direction when you address them. Watch how and when your posture changes to represent different people in the story. Be consistent so that your audience can keep everything straight.

Mean More Than What You Say

Language isn't able to communicate everything. If you try to describe a sunset, your words, although accurate, will not be complete. It's impossible to completely capture in words all that you see in a sunset! The same is true for falling in love. You can talk about it, but without the use of images you can't communicate the extent of your feelings.

Because of the limitations of language, what we describe is always less than what we've thought, felt, or experienced. So true communication must include more than words. It must include images because they fill in the gaps between words. This is what Jesus did! To communicate truth about God's kingdom, he used the image of seeds; to describe a believer's life, he used salt and light; to refer to false teachings, he talked about yeast. Solomon also did this when he used images to evoke the depth of romantic love in the Song of Songs.

Embed images in a story to communicate a truth from Scripture. Use comparisons and images to weave meaning into the stories you tell. For example, think of the meaning you might portray with the following images, then add them to appropriate stories!

storms	a withered plant	roots of a tree
seasons	a budding flower	wind
family	cocoons and butterflies	a dove
a locked door	starlight	a sailboat on a lake
an open door	a lion	a journey

Translate Words Into Sounds

Very often, when I'm done telling a story that I've created, someone will ask me where I found it.

"I made it up," I say.

"You wrote it?" they ask.

And I smile to myself and tell them, "Yeah," even though the story was never written down!

I'm not trying to deceive anybody, I just don't write down all the stories I tell. Many exist only in my imagination. I haven't written them down because I don't need to. I don't work from a script, rather the story grows as I tell it. As a result, I naturally remember it.

There's a big difference between writing a story on paper and telling a story in person. Writers are limited to using words, while storytellers use sounds and silence, movement and stillness. Gestures, facial expressions, pitch, rate of delivery, volume, sound effects, and audience response are all lost when you go from speaking to writing.

It seems strange to think about, but for a storyteller words aren't made up of letters, but of sounds! Words are the way we express thoughts on paper, for the eye to see. Sounds are the way we express thoughts in the air, for the ear to hear. So instead of thinking of your story in terms of what words to choose, think of it in terms of what sounds to use!

As you develop your story, remember that storytelling is an oral art form, not a written one. Writing and speaking are two totally different communication media.

Listen to a call-in radio show and try to guess which callers wrote out their questions before calling in. You can usually tell. How? Their sentences are longer, more detailed, and more complex. They use more adjectives and adverbs. They sound canned and rehearsed rather than spontaneous. Believe me, you can tell!

Oral language is immediate and more informal than written language. It's spontaneous and organic, growing out of the dynamic encounter between two responsive communicators (the speaker and the listener). When we communicate verbally, we don't craft sentences—we express our thoughts in sentence fragments, grunts, nods, and gestures.

If someone's speech is filled with flowery, eloquent phrases and elegant-sounding descriptions, you can tell the storyteller is either trying to impress someone, or is reciting a speech. People just don't talk that way! It's too cumbersome. It's not natural. For this reason, you can't just memorize a well-written story and make it work orally. You need to translate it into another language—the language of speech. An interpreter's job is to accurately translate meaning—not just words—from one language to another. When retelling Bible stories, your job is to be an interpreter of the written language!

When I make up stories, I don't work from a script, but when we tell Bible stories, we do! When you tell a Bible story, your goal is to show in person what's only recorded in print. You'll communicate much of what is described on the page through inflection and non-verbal communication. Try to create the same feel and mood in the oral piece. You don't do this by necessarily using the same words, but by aiming for the same reaction.

Read the story aloud to yourself. Listen for the moments that matter to you and that will move the audience. Those are the ones you need to bring out by working primarily from your heart rather than the words of the written text.

Choose Your Sounds Carefully

Sometimes storytellers get sloppy. Sometimes we inadvertently repeat certain words or phrases as we tell our stories. These repetitious words can be annoying to our listeners. Sometimes we just string a whole story together by connecting every sentence with the word "and." Sometimes we use whatever word we want, without thinking carefully about whether it's really the best word to use. While you'll want to avoid overpolishing your story, take care that the sounds (and words!) you choose are the best ones possible. And work hard to eliminate those annoying verbal habits.

Describe things in-depth. But don't describe them to death. Interesting stories contain lots of nouns and verbs, but few adjectives and adverbs.

Adjectives and adverbs are like seasoning that you sprinkle onto a story to make it juicier, richer and more succulent. But you want people to taste the steak, not be overpowered by the seasoning! So use adjectives and adverbs sparingly and specifically to create images—especially those that appeal to the senses. Nouns and verbs are still the main course. If you add too much flavoring the listener won't want to finish the meal.

Use vivid verbs and strong comparisons. Instead of saying, "The road before him was long and winding," say, "The road before him twisted like a serpent."

Don't fall in love with your first draft of telling the story! As you practice your story, smooth out transitions, try new ideas, and search for better ways of saying what you want to say. You may need to add hints that foreshadow the ending, use more vivid language, or change some dialogue.

When it comes to dialogue, make it realistic, natural, and relevant—always moving the story forward. Remember, every sound in your story has a purpose, so eliminate all unnecessary dialogue. Be careful that your story doesn't become preachy or didactic. The best stories allow the audience to learn by discovering, rather than being told what the story means. Remember, to hint is more effective than to reveal.

Remove everything from your story that doesn't belong. Add words that clarify, sharpen, or deepen the meaning of your story. Use precise language and listen for musicality and rhythm.

Believable Dialogue

- Always advances the story
- Sounds realistic and natural
- Is consistent and appropriate for each character
- Is understandable (so avoid heavy use of dialects)

Communicate Without Talking

Before you even step onstage, your listeners will be getting an impression of you as a person. From the time you enter the room people are evaluating you! Be aware of this and present yourself with poise, confidence, and composure. The clothes you choose, your appearance, the way you relate to the audience prior to telling the story, all affect the storytelling experience, as does the setting and environment, and the seating arrangement.

The first couple of minutes in your story will set the mood for the rest of the story time. Make sure that you know the beginning of your story well and that you're comfortable telling it.

Remember that whatever you do onstage will be noticed by the audience. If you put your hands in your pockets, they'll wonder why. If you pace or sway back and forth, they'll be distracted. So avoid habits that draw attention away from the story.

Create Richer and Deeper Characters

As you create characters for the stories you tell, show your listeners the personality of the characters by the way they talk, react to conflict, and treat other people. Think of the time when Jesus cleared the temple of the moneychangers. By his action in the story, you get a good impression of what Jesus was feeling!

You can show a character's personality through

- vivid description: his face looked like it'd been soaked in vinegar too long;
- expression of their thoughts: *I'm never gonna make it outta here alive!*
- dialogue with other characters: "I told you! I don't know who this Jesus guy is!"
- how they act: She prayed. Even when there was no answer in sight, she never gave up praying.

For example, you could say, "Peter was brave." Or, you could say, "Peter leaned over the edge of the boat. A vicious wind tugged at his hair and drove pellets of rain into his face. He stared down at the swirling waves beneath him, then looked up at Jesus standing near-by. *Well, here goes nothing!* he said to himself as he leaped out of the boat toward the dark and angry sea."

People in real life may wander aimlessly around and do things that are out of character or unmotivated, but characters in stories need to be motivated before they act. They need to portray their personality consistently, unless something significant and believable causes them to change.

Here are three keys to creating characters with more depth:

1. Get to know each character by identifying with his or her emotions. What would he or she be thinking or feeling in this story? Do your research and try to understand motives. Remember, Bible characters were real people just like you and I!

2. Once you identify with the emotions of the character, find something physical to do with that emotion. Pace. Make a fist. Hang your head. Find something to do other than just standing there being emotional.

3. Try to see the story through the eyes of the characters that you're portraying. And remember that every character in a story is driven by a desire for something. Actors call this "their motivation." As you develop characters ask yourself, "What does this character want and how will he or she get it?"

Summary

Make the most of silence and stillness. Sustain the suspense by postponing the resolution. Use the stage area to your advantage. Mean more than what you say by using image-rich language.

When working with Bible stories, translate words into sounds and movement. Choose your sounds carefully. Communicate without saying a word by the way you dress, and through your stage presence. And finally, create rich and believable characters by identifying with them on an emotional level.

Take care to develop your craft as expertly as you can, and paint the best pictures of Christ possible, not on canvas, but in the minds of your listeners.

Chapter 15

Making the Story Stick

Eighty Ideas for Applying any Bible Story

I N A RELAY RACE, the most important part of the race is the exchange, when one runner hands the baton to the other runner. It must be done with grace, efficiency, and precision. If a runner drops the baton or doesn't hand it off smoothly, the entire race can be lost.

Making the transition from the story into the application of the story is where many people drop the baton. Most of us explain too much. But, as I pointed out earlier, explaining stories doesn't usually help people get the point! So what can you do? How can you reinforce the message?

Often, a story lends itself naturally to other activities that will help children remember the story and enjoy the storytelling experience. This list will give you dozens and dozens of ideas for including fun, educational activities that reinforce the lesson.[1]

The ideas in this list all relate to the story of "The Prodigal Son" found in Luke 15:11-32. However, each idea can be used for dozens of other Bible stories. Just use your imagination to see how each activity could be altered to reinforce another lesson or story! Here are a few pointers on using the activities listed below:

- Let the activities grow from the story. Beware of just sticking an activity in your lesson because you've run out of other ideas that really fit!
- Don't overdo it! Obviously, you'd never try to use all of these ideas in one lesson!
- When pointing out story applications, avoid sounding preachy or authoritative. Smooth out your transitions between activities, shorten your explanations, and clarify difficult concepts by explaining them in simple terms. End on a hopeful note, or a call to action.
- Add more creative ingredients to each of your lessons. For example, use more drama, singing, puppetry, snacks, games, memory time, and (of course) STORYTELLING!
- Ask yourself if your lesson meets the "GIEIC" criteria. Every lesson should! Does this lesson

    Grab the students' attention?
    Involve them in the learning?
    Engage their imaginations?
    Inform them of God's plan?
    Challenge them spiritually?

---

[1]Dr. Flora Joy and Michael Capps, two master teachers, inspired and influenced the ideas in this chapter. My thanks goes out to them.

Creative Writing

1. Book Jackets—The younger son has just written his autobiography. Write what would appear on the back of his book jacket. Include quotes from imaginary people who've read the book.

2. Want Ads—The man who owned the pigs is taking out an ad in the paper looking for someone else to take care of his animals. What does he say? Write it out.

3. Diary Entries—The father kept a diary starting the day before his son first asked for money and continuing to the day his son came home. Write five entries in the diary showing key emotions or thoughts the father might have had.

4. Similar Theme—In Luke 15 Jesus told three stories about lost items. Have the students write a fourth story with different characters, but with the same theme, "God celebrates the return of those who are lost."

5. Letter Home—You're the son in the foreign country. You've just decided to head back home and see if your dad will hire you to work in the field. Before you leave the pig farm, you write a letter to your dad and drop it in the mail. What does it say?

6. Thank-You Note—After the welcome home party, the younger son decides to write a thank-you note to his dad expressing how grateful he is to be home. Write the note.

7. Top Ten Lists—Write a creative "Top Ten List." For example, The Top Ten Things Children Do When Their Parents Aren't Looking, The Top Ten Ways to Cook a Fat Calf, The Prodigal Son's Top Ten Ways to Ask Your Parents For Money.

8. Just the Facts—You're a police officer writing the report on the boy who ran away. Remember to include just the facts!

9. Personal Reflection—Pretend that you're a character in the story and complete the following thought-provoking sentences:

    a. If I were the father and my son just came back, I would have said . . .

    b. If I were the younger brother and I found out my older brother wouldn't come into the party, I would have thought . . .

    c. If I were the older brother and I found out they were having a party, I would have said . . .

10. Rebus—Rewrite the story in rebus; certain words are replaced by symbols or pictures.

11. Memoir—Pretend you're the younger brother, now grown into an old man. You want to write a story of what happened for your grandson to read. Write a one-page memoir.

12. Newspaper Story—You're a reporter for the younger son's hometown newspaper. You've been asked to write a story about the boy's return home. Choose an interesting headline and write the front-page story.

13. Word Search—Create a word search or a crossword puzzle based on the story. Use key words and names from the story.

14. Rhyme—Write a rhyming version of the story.

15. Acceptance Speech—The father in the story has just received the community's "Man of the Year" award for how graciously he treated his sons. Write his acceptance speech for this special event.

16. Letter to the Editor—Pretend you're a neighbor disturbed by all the noise next door where a wild party is going on. Write a letter to the editor. Then pretend that you're the father and reply to it!

17. Songwriting—Write a song about the story by changing the words to a popular tune.

18. Movie Review—A movie titled, "Son on the Run!" has just been released. You're a movie reviewer. Write a review of the movie telling what you liked and didn't like and pointing out how much (or how little) it had to do with the real story.

19. Exploring Feelings—Encourage the students to ask, "How did the characters feel? How might they retell the story today if they could? What did they tell others about their experience?" Write a poem from the point of view of one of the characters in the story, exploring how he felt at a specific moment of the story. For example, how did the father feel

- when the son asked for his money?
- when the son didn't come back for a long time?
- when he first noticed his son on the road toward home?

20. Story Sorting—Draw four pictures from the story, or write out four events from the story. Then shuffle them and have the students put them back together in the correct order. Discuss how the story would have been different if the events would have happened in another order. For a real challenge, write a new story bringing out the same point as the Bible story, but with the events in this new order.

Creative Dramatics

21. Painting to Life—Have actors freeze in the shape of a picture appearing in your curriculum. Then have them bring the picture to life and act out what might have happened right before or right after the picture was taken.

22. Talk Show Appearance—You're the host of a hit TV talk show. You have some of the characters from the story in your live TV studio. Act out what happens as you interview them about their part in the story. Get a little wild if you want!

23. Commercial—Create a commercial for a product or retail store. For example, "Fat Calf Farm—Your Party Headquarters," "Robe-o-Rama Superstore—The Best Robes Around the Globe," "Fresh Breeze Cologne: Used by Pig Farmers Everywhere!" Consider your target audience, the benefits of your store or product, and what sales tactics you'll use (celebrity endorsements, fitting in, being cool, etc.).

24. Reality Show—Have students create a reality TV show based either on the situations in this story, or the story characters. Be creative! Then act it out.

25. Mock-umentary—Create a mock version of a TV documentary about what happened in the story. Have fun highlighting things that didn't really have significance to the story— like the brand of pig-chow the son used, the places he spent his money, etc.

26. Press Conference—You're one of the news reporters at a press conference held the day after the big welcome-home party. What questions will you ask? Act out what happens at the press conference, who is there, and what they have to say.

27. Trial—Put one of the characters from the story on trial. Students act as jury, defense attorney, prosecuting attorney, and witnesses. The teacher is the judge. Come up with potential crimes or laws they might have broken. For example, the farmer could accuse the younger son of causing the death of one of his pigs by leaving before it was fed, or the older son could accuse the father of showing favoritism!

28. Movie Preview—Pretend that you're making a trailer (preview) for an upcoming movie. Have one person narrate the movie preview and pause as actors reenact the scene he is describing. They freeze as he continues. For example, "He had big plans / He yearned for romance . . . adventure . . . and freedom! / But one day, his luck ran out / And now, he's all alone in a great big world / And must decide for himself where to turn and who to trust / "The Search" opening soon at a theater near you!"

29. Improv Script—Watch a short video clip with the sound turned off. Then make up words that the characters might have said! Try to include characters from the story you're studying.

30. Charades—Act out scenes, moments, characters, or events of the story and have the other people in your group guess what you're portraying.

31. One-Person Scenes—Decide on five key events or scenes in the story. Take five students and, with the help of the other students, create them into living statues of those five key moments in the story. (The statues can be either human characters, or symbolic representations of what happened.) Then present the story by having one person at a time come onstage and freeze, until all five are lined up in a row. Present this to another class and see if they can guess what Bible story the statues represent!

32. Online Album—Have the students pose in scenes from the story and then take pictures of each scene. Scan them and make an online "Bible Story Photo Album." Write brief descriptions of who is in each picture and what's happening. Let students check them out by logging on at home!

33. Sound Effects—Give small groups of students a tape recorder and allow them to go tape ten sounds from the story. Then have them return and play the sounds, stopping after each one to tell the group what that sound represents.

34. Concert—What kind of music is playing at the party? Choose some popular music and play it in the background as you tell the story. Or, create your own new style of music. Or, find some Jewish folksongs that really might have been sung at the time and listen to them as a class.

35. Rumors—People in the boy's hometown are gossiping about him and his family. What types of things are they saying? Act out a conversation between two of the boy's old friends.

36. New Dance—After the father and his son are reunited, the father held a big dance and a party. Pretend that the father and son created a new dance at the party. What kind of dance is it? Is it wild and crazy or quiet and subdued? With a friend, create the new dance. Be ready to demonstrate it to the group!

37. Change the Style—Retell the story of "The Lost Sons" in another style. Choose from science fiction, legend, fairy tale, tall tale, myth, rap, or country preacher. Then discuss

• How was our version similar to the Bible story? How was it different?
• What things did we leave out? What did we include that weren't originally there?

38. Monologue—Retell the story from one character's point of view. Choose from the father, the younger son, the older son, the son's friend in the foreign country, the pig owner, a pig, the servant who met the older brother, someone invited to the party, or the fatted calf (uh, oh!).

39. Auditions—Pretend that you're auditioning for a musical version of the story. Read different parts in a variety of musical styles. Have fun as a group while different people audition!

40. Sculpture—Shape and mold clay, tin foil, wire, pipe cleaners, paper clips, or play dough into shapes that show feelings you experienced during the story.

41. One-Sided Phone Conversation—Act out a conversation from the story as if it were happening on the phone. But we hear only one person! Choose from the younger son asking his dad for the money, the younger son applying for a job with the pig farmer, or the older son calling home on his cell phone and hearing a party.

42. Eye Witness Account—You're a neighbor. After the son returns home and the party begins, it gets pretty loud. A police officer drives up and asks you what's going on. "I saw the whole thing, officer," you say. Tell him, in your own words, what happened.

43. Puppet Show—Write a script for a puppet show based on the story. Perform it for another class.

44. Role-play—You can role-play events that happened in the story, or that might have happened. With a partner, take turns acting out the following situations.

• You're the banker who is giving the father the money for his younger son. You're surprised that he wants to withdraw so much cash. Act out what you say to the father.
• Since he was a Jew, the son was forbidden to work with pigs by the law of Moses. Make up a conversation that he might have had with the man who hired him to feed his swine.
• You're a friend of the younger brother wondering what he did while he was gone for so long. While he's getting another plate of food at the party, you ask him. Reenact the conversation.

- After the party, the younger son is talking with his mother. She's obviously glad he is home, but finally she asks, "Why did you leave in the first place?" Act out what he says.
- You are the younger son. You've just come home and humbled yourself. You deserved nothing, but then your dad honored you with a nice ring, new clothes, and a great party! As the two of you walk back to the house, act out your conversation.

Artistic Expression

45. Mobile—Since the younger son was lost and then found, create a mobile that hangs from a compass. Think of other things that are lost and then found again and hang them (or pictures of them) from the mobile. For example, keys, crayons, pets, etc.

46. Party—In the story, there's a party where the people eat the choicest food available. What foods would you want at a welcome-home party? Plan and host your own celebration party!

47. Snack—Allow the students to make three little people out of pretzels and mini-marshmallows, representing the father and the two sons. Share a tasty snack that relates to the story! Or, eat some burgers in honor of the fatted calf (or some bacon in honor of the pigs)!

48. Missing Person Poster—Design the poster or flyer that the father puts on telephone poles and in storefronts asking if anyone has seen his son. What does it say? Is there a reward offered? If so, how much is it for?

49. Collage—Using pictures from magazines, newspapers, or other media, create a colorful collage of the story. Put it on a wall in your classroom or on a bulletin board in the hallway.

50. Web Site—Create a web site for the pig farmer's farm or the dad's business.

51. Book Covers—The older brother has just written a book about his younger brother's life. Is it complimentary or mean? Design a picture of the book cover. Write the introduction.

52. Comic Strip—Draw a comic strip version of the story including all of the adventures that the younger son had while he was away from home.

53. Greeting Card—The mother has given her son a welcome-home card. What does it say? Is it funny or heartwarming? Design the card and draw a picture on the front of it.

54. Poster—Color "Welcome Home!" signs and posters that may have been put up at the party.

55. Graffiti—Pretend that you're the younger brother in the foreign country. You decide to write some graffiti on a wall. What will you write? Write one example of the graffiti you wrote on the day you arrived, and another on the day before you left for home. (If available, set aside one classroom wall as a "Graffiti Wall." Use it throughout the year for prayer requests, answers to prayer, notes of encouragement, Scripture verses, etc. Every year, paint over it and start again!)

56. Family Shield—Create a family shield (or crest) that represents important events in the family of the father and his two sons. Use pictures to portray four different family traits or significant ideas from the story.

57. Maps—Make up an imaginary world in which the family lived. Create names for places, mountain ranges, rivers and oceans. Draw a map of the journey of the younger son. Show where he stopped and at the bottom of the map tell what he did at each place.

58. Flag—Design a flag for the country the son is from and the one he moved to. How are they different? What do the colors, shapes, and patterns represent?

59. Painting—Create a painting that explores the emotions of the people in the story. Just paint with the colors of how you feel!

60. Mural—Make life-size cutouts of the people in the story. Tape them on the wall in a frozen scene from the story or use them to act out the story!

61. Spontaneous Pictures—Draw pictures of what is happening in the story as one person retells it. Draw three scenes as the story is retold.

62. Story Completion—Read the story halfway through and then have the children draw pictures of how they think the story will end. Share the pictures with the class and have the children explain why they think the story will end like that. Then tell them the way it really ends!

Life Application

63. Agree/Disagree—Ask students to stand if they agree and to sit if they disagree with the following statements. After reading the statements and allowing the students to respond, discuss their responses as a group.

- If I were the older brother I'd be mad, too.
- The father didn't treat his younger son fairly.
- The father didn't treat the older son fairly because he didn't let him have parties with his friends.

64. Comparisons—Jesus told this story along with the story of the lost sheep and the lost coin in Luke 15. What are three ways that the stories are different? What are three ways that they're similar? How are these stories similar to life today? How are they different?

65. Field Trip—Learn about runaways in your community. Call a local shelter and see if there is anything your class can do to serve or minister to runaways. If possible, visit a shelter and talk to a homeless person about what it's like to live on the street. You could also visit a pig farm, a bank, a party store, or more!

66. Group Discussion—Allow the students to imagine that they really are the story characters. Explore the moral choices and consequences of story actions.

- Imagine that you're the younger son who ran away. Only, think of it happening today. Where would you go? What would you do? What might happen to you?
- Imagine that you're the older brother. How will you treat your younger brother now that he is home again? What kinds of things will you do together? How has your relationship changed?
- Imagine that you're the dad. Would you really forgive that son? Why is it so hard to forgive people? What are the barriers that stop us from seeking forgiveness?

67. So What?—Explore the concepts of the story and ask how they apply to life today. To create a different mood, turn off the lights and place a flashlight in the middle of the room. Pretend you're all sitting around a campfire talking!

- What would you have done? How would you have felt? What can this story teach us about life?
- How was God active in this story? How is he active in your life today?
- Think about how the younger son had to have faith and how faith in God also affects how we act each day. How did he show faith? Courage? Humility? How can we do the same?

68. Scavenger Hunt—Hand out lists of items related to the story. Have students try to find the items, or gather them by next week. As an added activity, have them try to guess the relevance of each item included on the list! For example, a two-dollar bill, a piece of bacon, a ring, a choir robe, a glass of water, a CD of dance music, a hamburger, a compass, a receipt from Wal-Mart, a seed.

69. Smell Hunt—This is a different kind of scavenger hunt! Students have to find ten smells that relate to events from the story. This activity would work great at summer camp!

70. Adopt-a-Missionary—Adopt a missionary who works in a foreign country. Learn about the culture of that country and the different types of animals the people raise, foods they eat, and parties they throw. E-mail or write the missionaries!

71. Family Stories—Collect stories from family members about a time they were lost or found, or ran away, or came back home, or celebrated the return of a family member, or refused to talk to someone in the family. All these things happened in the story!

72. What If?—Ask
- What if the younger son had never gone home? How might the story have ended?
- What if the older son had met him on the road instead of meeting his father first? What might have happened?

73. Debate—Have a debate about a moral question brought up in the story. Start by stating the issue in positive terms. For example, "Forgiveness always includes welcoming the forgiven person back into your life." Assign groups of students to agree or disagree. Give each side a chance to state their arguments and rebuttals.

74. Free Lunch—Help serve a lunch for the homeless.

75. Post Your Testimony Online—Write the story of your conversion (how you journeyed from being lost to found). Remember to emphasize God's grace and forgiveness rather than your old sinful lifestyle. For step-by-step guidelines on preparing your personal testimony check out http://www.5clicks.com.

Post your story for free at http://share.powertochange.com/story/index.html.

Creative Praying

76. Prayer Clusters—Allow students to get into groups of two to three people. Invite them to pray for the other people in their families. Encourage them to pray for anyone who is lost or who has wandered away from God.

77. One Word Prayers—Go around the group saying one thing from the story or the lesson for which each person is thankful.

78. Turn Around Prayers—One by one, have the students walk out into the hallway and pretend that it's the faraway country. Have them think of one way they've been running from God, write it down, tell God they're sorry, turn around, and come back into the room. Have a party in your room to celebrate turning back to God! Burn the papers containing sins. Use birthday candles!

79. Acronym Prayers—Create an acronym based on the story that can serve as an outline for your prayer. For example, pray for the **LOST**—those who are **L**ooking for God, **O**beying, but not loving God, **S**eparated from God, or **T**urning from God. Here are a few more examples to get you thinking:
- **CLAY**—find something to **c**onfess, **l**earn, **a**pply, and **y**ield to God.
- **PRAY**—**p**raise, **r**epent, **a**sk, and **y**ield
- **ACTS**—**a**doration, **c**onfession, **t**hanksgiving, **s**upplication

80. Echo prayers—As you pray, let the students respond by echoing back what you say, "Dear God, we pray . . . (wait for the students to repeat that short phrase) . . . for anyone who is lost . . . (again they repeat) . . . far from home . . . or looking for you. . . ."

Benefits, Resources, Story Starters, and Workshops

Go and Tell!

Thirty-five Benefits of Biblical Storytelling

STORIES ARE powerful teaching tools. Stories can educate or entertain. They can be used to deceive and mislead, or to guide and clarify. Stories can inspire, motivate, remind, and warn. They can reinforce beliefs, trigger memories, create community, and carry on traditions.

Throughout Scripture we're given both the command to tell stories, and examples of the benefits of storytelling in religious education. The Bible contains dozens of imperatives to pass on its lessons and values through the use of telling and remembering the stories of God.

Here are thirty-five scriptural reasons we use stories in Christian education today!

Stories Teach

1. Stories give us hope. The stories of the Old Testament were written to teach us and give us hope, "For everything that was written in the past was written to teach us, so that through endurance and the encouragement of the Scriptures we might have hope" (Romans 15:4).

Action points

a. Use the stories from the Old Testament to teach lessons about faith, honor, obedience, courage, grace, and love. Remind your students of all the amazing and miraculous things God has done (and is doing) for his people.

b. Remember that a primary goal of your teaching is to give hope. Pray that God's Spirit will guide you to do that in every lesson.

2. Stories give us wisdom. In the introduction to Proverbs, Solomon mentions that proverbs, parables, and riddles are ways of passing on discernment, knowledge, and discretion to the young (see Proverbs 1:4-6).

Action points

a. Follow Solomon's example and use fables, parables, imaginative proverbs and riddles in your lessons.

b. Always be on the lookout for short teaching stories that will help your children understand and apply truth in their lives.

3. Stories give us guidance. Spiritual education should be at the heart of every educational activity, not just during a separate lesson. "These commandments that I give you today are to be upon your hearts. Impress them on your children. Talk about them when you sit at home and when you walk along the road, when you lie down and when you get up" (Deuteronomy 6:6, 7).

Action points

a. Find ways to integrate spiritual truth into the educational activities you do. The best Christian educators naturally and regularly refer to Scripture and immerse their own lives in God's stories.

b. Keep an eye out for teachable moments. It's more important to take advantage of teachable moments than to cover all the material in the lesson. Use stories as examples of a biblical principle, value, or teaching.

4. Stories give us life. Bible stories actually open the way for spiritual life. In John 6:68, Peter says to Jesus, "You have the words of eternal life." Also, when Moses had finished retelling the history of God's deeds among his people, he told them to remember the words and share the stories with their children. "They are not just idle words for you—they are your life. By them you will live long in the land you are crossing the Jordan to possess" (Deuteronomy 32:47).

Action points

a. Treat God's Word with respect and teach others the power of the living Word of God.

b. Rely on God's story for your life. Don't ever underestimate the power of his Word to change the lives of your students.

5. Stories give us perspective. Some Bible stories show us how God works in the background of daily life. For example, the books of Ruth and Esther show how God works behind the scenes in everyday life. In the book of Esther, God's name is never even mentioned yet he is always present, shaping events and circumstances to carry out his plans for his people.

Action points

a. Encourage children to remember that even when they can't see God, he is present.

b. Tell stories from your own life that show how God works in the details of daily life to bring blessings to his people.

6. Stories give us understanding. Stories clarify theological issues. They can be used to illustrate or explain complex ideas or difficult biblical concepts. Jesus told lots of stories about the kingdom of God. Each story reveals a little more about God's kingdom, but no single story illuminates all the facets of the truth.

Action points

a. Rather than explaining a doctrinal teaching or theological lesson in a lengthy lecture, construct a story that reveals the truth through the use of vivid images.

b. Rather than teach from a three-point outline, weave three stories together that all talk about different aspects of the same truth. Use stories to illuminate, illustrate, and articulate biblical truths.

7. Stories give us truth. Jesus told thought-provoking stories that led to deep spiritual questioning. When the disciples didn't understand a story, he took the time to explain the imagery and symbolism to them. "When he was alone with his own disciples, he explained everything" (Mark 4:34).

Action points

a. Tell allegories and parables that are rich in meaning. Allow those who are more mature in their faith to see the parallels and analogies, but don't explain it to those who may not be ready for it.

b. Allow students to question, ponder, and reflect on God's truth. Leave time after the lesson to answer follow-up questions that students might have about the Bible story or the teaching parables you used.

Stories Inspire

8. God's story moves us. Immediately after crossing the Red Sea, Moses and the Israelites sang a song recounting God's deeds and glorifying him for rescuing them. Reflecting on God's glory naturally stirs us to creative expression. "My heart is stirred by a noble theme as I recite my verses for the king; my tongue is the pen of a skillful writer. . . . I will perpetuate your memory through all generations; therefore the nations will praise you for ever and ever" (Psalm 45:1, 17).

Action points

a. Use stories about God's great deeds to initiate praise, wonder, imagination, and creativity in your students.

b. Encourage students to express their love and devotion for God through creative storytelling, writing, drawing, painting, singing, or movement.

9. God's story gives us peace. We can turn to stories of God's greatness when we feel alone or distressed. The stories of God's miraculous power will comfort us. When the psalmist was depressed, he turned to his knowledge of God's deeds for peace: "To this I will appeal: the years of the right hand of the Most High. I will remember the deeds of the Lord; yes, I will remember your miracles of long ago. I will meditate on all your works and consider all your mighty deeds" (Psalm 77:10-12).

Action points

a. Teach your children to turn to God whenever they're lonely or afraid.

b. Meditate on God's Word by thinking about a story and turning it over in your head all day long, or even longer! Learn to live with God's Word on your mind.

10. God's story lives through us. Our lives themselves are a story written by God! "You show that you are a letter from Christ, the result of our ministry, written not with ink but with the Spirit of the living God, not on tablets of stone but on tablets of human hearts" (2 Corinthians 3:3).

Action points

a. Realize that as we live our lives, we are living out God's story! We reveal what we believe by the choices we make.

b. Take advantage of each day as an opportunity to let God express himself through your acts of compassion, love, and grace.

Stories Reveal

11. Stories reveal the will of God. God chose to reveal his prophetic Word through parables. Isaiah, Jeremiah, Ezekiel, and Zechariah all used graphic illustrations and parables to wake people out of spiritual complacency and redirect them to God. Their stories revealed God's providence, judgment, presence, and guidance. John does the same in Revelation. When God spoke thorough Hosea, he reminded the people, "I spoke to the prophets, gave them many visions and told parables through them" (Hosea 12:10).

Action points

a. Look for ways to use stories to reveal God's will for your students today. Use stories to help your students understand God's desire for their lives, and the importance of letting him guide them each day.

b. Use stories to help your students reflect on the Bible lesson and personalize the application. Prophecy had the goals of strengthening, encouraging, and comforting (1 Corinthians 14:3). Use God's story to strengthen, encourage, and comfort your students!

12. Stories reveal the Word of God. Jesus, "the Word," (John 1:1) became human and made his dwelling place among us. Jesus is a living story! God's Word is God's Story! And now, through Scripture, Jesus continues to reveal himself to others. "Consequently, faith comes from hearing the message, and the message is heard through the word of Christ" (Romans 10:17).

Action points

a. Remind students that God is the author of faith and that Jesus was both God and Man.

b. Share the Word of God openly, boldly, and clearly with your students. Faith is born and grows through hearing God's Word (Romans 10:17).

13. Stories reveal the nature of God. God chose to reveal himself through stories. Not only does the Bible contain parables, it's packed full of incredible, true stories of history, action, and adventure. Some key Old Testament storybooks are Genesis, Exodus, Joshua, Judges, Ruth, 1 and 2 Samuel, 1 and 2 Kings, Nehemiah, and Esther. In the New Testament, see Matthew, Mark, Luke, John, and Acts. "We have heard with our ears, O God; our fathers have told us what you did in their days, in days long ago" (Psalm 44:1).

Action points

a. Let your students find their favorite Bible story and act it out.

b. Over the next six months, read through the story books of the Bible to reacquaint yourself with the flow of God's story!

Stories Motivate

14. Stories warn us. The stories of the Israelites' struggles in the Old Testament serve as examples of moral choices and warnings about the consequences of sin. Why? "These things occurred as examples to keep us from setting our hearts on evil things as they did. . . . These things happened to them as examples and were written down as warnings for us" (1 Corinthians 10:6, 11).

Action points

a. Use stories to point out the consequences of negative choices and the rewards of virtuous living.

b. Warn your children through cautionary tales about what happens when God's children misbehave. Jehoash, king of Israel, even used a fable to warn his adversary about the dangers of military conflict (2 Kings 14:9-14)!

15. Stories elicit discussion. Stories can be used as discussion starters for exploring moral dilemmas or choices. Jesus very often used stories as ways of getting people to reflect about their lifestyle and to confront hypocrisy. For example, in Luke 7:36-50, Jesus used a story about forgiven debts to both comfort a sinful woman and confront a self-righteous Pharisee!

Action points

a. Use stories as discussion starters, icebreakers, and attention-getters.

b. Use stories to answer questions, like Jesus did. When people asked Jesus a question, he often answered with a story and then he used a series of questions to help them apply truth to their lives.

16. Stories show us examples. The stories of the lives of others teach us by example. Paul encourages believers to follow the godly example of other believers: "Join with others in following my example, brothers, and take note of those who live according to the pattern we gave you. . . . Whatever you have learned or received or heard from me, or seen in me—put it into practice. And the God of peace will be with you" (Philippians 3:17; 4:9). The writer of the book of Hebrews does the same: "We do not want you to become lazy, but to imitate those who through faith and patience inherit what has been promised. . . . Remember your leaders, who spoke the word of God to you. Consider the outcome of their way of life and imitate their faith" (Hebrews 6:12; 13:7).

Action points

a. Share stories from the lives of older Christians to help children know right from wrong, gain courage, and make godly choices.

b. Use true stories to bridge the gaps between knowledge and action, principle and application, head and heart.

17. Stories embolden us. We learn to withstand hardship and suffering by seeing the example of others. Hold up the life of another believer as a model of virtue, faith, or perseverance. "Brothers, as an example of patience in the face of suffering, take the prophets who spoke in the name of the Lord" (James 5:10).

Action points

a. Find stories of missionaries, martyrs, saints, and heroes of the faith to supplement your lesson. Use them to inspire boldness and courage in your students!

b. Encourage children to follow the example of faithful believers in the past. Use stories to exhort them to act in accordance with a biblical principle!

18. Stories move us to action. The example of other faithful believers can inspire us to holy living. Hebrews 11 shares glimpses of dozens of heroes of the faith. "Therefore, since we are surrounded by such a great cloud of witnesses, let us throw off everything that hinders and the sin that so easily entangles, and let us run with perseverance the race marked out for us" (Hebrews 12:1).

Action points

a. Look up the stories of the men and women listed in Hebrews 11. Have the children choose their favorite hero of the faith and learn his or her story to tell others!

b. Find other inspiring stories of faith and courage to motivate your children to trust in, and stand up for, Christ.

Stories Confront

19. Stories reveal sin. Nathan used a parable to rebuke King David after his affair with Bathsheba. Nathan told David a secular story from everyday life that the king could identify with (2 Samuel 12:1-14). More than once, God told Ezekiel to use parables or allegories to confront the sin of the Israelites (see Ezekiel 17:2 and 24:3).

Action points

a. When using non-biblical stories to confront children, use characters and situations they can identify with and easily understand.

b. Allow them to see the lesson borne out in the story before explaining the spiritual parallel contained in the Bible.

20. Stories heal relationships. At the urging of Joab, the wise woman from Tekoa used a parable to reunite King David and his estranged son Absalom (2 Samuel 14:1-24). Through this incident, David was able to reflect on his attitude and heal a family relationship that had been severed for three years.

Action points

a. Use stories of peace and justice to help students who may not get along well together to see each other in a new light.

b. Use stories to bridge gaps of understanding between children from different ethnic, financial, or religious backgrounds.

21. Stories make important points. Stories can help us sort through choices, regain perspective, and make important decisions. For example, Jotham told a fable to help the people reflect on the wisdom of their choice for a new king (Judges 9:7-15).

Action points

a. When your children face important decisions, use stories to help them differentiate between the options, consider the possibilities, and make a well-informed decision.

b. When your children have made poor decisions, use stories to help them reevaluate their choices and courageously do the right thing.

22. Stories expose hypocrisy. Jesus used stories to convict and confront the hypocrisy of his day. In Mark 12:1-12, Jesus told a story about a vineyard that the religious leaders knew was about them. In Luke 15, Jesus used a series of stories to illustrate God's love for the lost and to reveal the judgmental attitude of the religious leaders.

Action points

a. Stories are more effective than lectures because the story can sneak past the defenses of the listener and touch him in the heart, not just the head.

b. Rather than scolding children who misbehave, find a few stories that address issues they're having problems with (picking on others, listening, bullying, fighting) and—instead of scolding—tell them a story!

Stories Remind

23. Stories recall God's mighty deeds. "Only be careful, and watch yourselves closely so that you do not forget the things your eyes have seen or let them slip from your heart as long as you live. Teach them to your children and to their children after them" (Deuteronomy 4:9).

Action points

a. Personal stories can be a powerful way of sharing the truth of God's power and glory. Take an opportunity and tell how God has worked in your life.

b. Ground your students in God's powerful deeds of the past so that they put their trust in him for the future.

24. Stories connect generations. "Tell it to your children, and let your children tell it to their children, and their children to the next generation" (Joel 1:3). As we pass on God's story to the next generation we preserve the truth and pass on our faith. "Remember the days of old; consider the generations long past. Ask your father and he will tell you, your elders, and they will explain to you" (Deuteronomy 32:7).

Action points

a. Encourage parents and grandparents in your church to share their stories of faith with their children.

b. Invite a professional storyteller to your church to present a special inter-generational program. Stories often serve as a way of breaking down generational walls and act as a bridge to better understanding!

25. Stories honor the memory of faithful believers. When Mary poured expensive perfume on Jesus' feet, he was pleased and praised her in front of the grumbling disciples. "I tell you the truth, wherever the gospel is preached throughout the world, what she has done will also be told, in memory of her" (Mark 14:9).

Action points

a. Share a story about someone whose faith has greatly impacted your life. Let the children share stories about their own spiritual mentors.

b. Study Mary's life and look for other times she was faithful to Jesus. Write a monologue about Mary's relationship to Christ for yourself or for a woman at your church. Then learn it and present it in memory of Mary!

26. Stories direct us. God wanted the Israelite kings to govern wisely, so he ordered each king to copy Scripture for himself so that he would learn to revere God, follow his words, humbly obey him, and be blessed (Deuteronomy 17:18-20).

Action points

a. Take the time to memorize God's Word so God can direct you and comfort you with his promises every day.

b. Let God lead you. If you're in a leadership position, show by example how important Christ is to your life.

Stories Proclaim

27. Stories reveal the kingdom of God. The teaching method of choice for Jesus was storytelling. In almost all of Jesus' teaching, he used stories to share God's Word. Notice in this passage how Jesus spoke the Word: "With many similar parables Jesus spoke the word to them, as much as they could understand. He did not say anything to them without using a parable" (Mark 4:33, 34). See? Jesus spoke God's Word by telling stories that he made up!

Action points

a. Learn from Jesus and speak God's Word through stories that you make up!

b. Tell stories to get your students thinking about a familiar concept in a new way. Try retelling a familiar Bible story with a fresh twist.

28. Stories convince. People can come to faith by hearing us share what God has done for us. When Jesus met the woman at the well, she returned to her town and shared her story of what had happened when she met Jesus. And the people responded! "They came out of the town and made their way toward him. . . . Many of the Samaritans from that town believed in him because of the woman's testimony, 'He told me everything I ever did'" (John 4:30, 39).

Action points

a. Teach your children to share their faith with others. They don't need to be eloquent—just honest and caring.

b. Keep it brief! Even simple stories can impact others. The man Jesus healed of blindness had one of the world's shortest testimonies: "Whether he is a sinner or not, I don't know. One thing I do know. I was blind but now I see!" (John 9:25). What a powerful witness for Christ!

29. Stories strengthen. Stories confirm the faith of other believers as they hear how God has worked in our lives. Paul shared stories of how God had worked through him: "I will not venture to speak of anything except what Christ has accomplished through me in leading the Gentiles to obey God by what I have said and done" (Romans 15:18). The entire book of Nehemiah shows how God worked through Nehemiah!

Action points

a. Stories can be used as a testimony to God's providence and grace.

b. Feel free to share the stories of what God has done through you. It's one of the most powerful ways of encouraging others to be used by God!

30. Stories protect. It's important to remind ourselves of God's stories so that we'll submit to him. "When our fathers were in Egypt, they gave no thought to your miracles; they did not remember your many kindnesses, and they rebelled by the sea, the Red Sea. . . . But they soon forgot what he had done and did not wait for his counsel" (Psalm 106:7, 13). See how forgetting God's story led to rebellion? After Joshua's faithful generation died off, a generation grew up that didn't know what God had done—because they hadn't been told what God had done! "After that whole generation had been gathered to their fathers, another generation grew up, who knew neither the Lord nor what he had done for Israel. Then the Israelites did evil in the eyes of the Lord and served the Baals" (Judges 2:10, 11).

Action points

a. Let God's story move you. When God speaks to you through one of his stories, let him shape and change the way you approach life. Hearing God shouldn't be just an intellectual exercise—hearing and heeding should be the controlling focus of your life!

b. Pass on the stories! If the next generation never hears the stories of God, it isn't their fault—it's ours.

31. Stories persuade. Paul repeatedly told the story of his conversion when he shared the gospel (see Acts 22:3-21 and Acts 26:2-27). Personal stories are some of the most effective ways of sharing our faith. A testimony (or conversion narrative) is a personal story in which the storyteller explains how he or she was once lost (without God) and then came to be at peace with God. The implication is that if you, the listener, are not at peace with God, you can be, too!

Action points

a. Teach children to bring others to Jesus by saying, "God did this for me and he can do it for you, too." Teach them to be bold in sharing their story, just like Stephen, the first Christian martyr, was!

b. Each time Paul retold his story, he synthesized and summarized some of the information in his presentation. Teach children to feel free to share their testimony in different ways for different people and situations.

32. Stories prove. Stories provide subjective evidence that a biblical value or teaching is true. The reason God performed the plagues in Egypt was to give his people a story that would prove his identity as their God! Look at what he told Moses: "Then the Lord said to Moses, 'Go to Pharaoh, for I have hardened his heart and the hearts of his officials so that I may perform these miraculous signs of mine among them that you may tell your children and grandchildren how I dealt harshly with the Egyptians and how I performed my signs among them, and that you may know that I am the Lord'" (Exodus 10:1, 2).

Action points

a. Use your changed life as evidence of God's grace. Paul pointed to examples from his life to support the truth of the Christian message (1 Corinthians 15:32).

b. Lean on God's promises and the stories of Scripture for proof of God's power and plan!

33. Stories influence. When we tell what God has done for us, we can eternally impact the lives of our family and friends. Jesus ordered a man who had been demon-possessed, "Go home to your family and tell them how much the Lord has done for you, and how he has had mercy on you" (Mark 5:19).

Action points

a. Take the message of Christ's transforming love to your family. Let them know what he has done for you and how his mercy has changed your life.

b. Pray that God's story, lived out in your life, will reach into the lives of those who live and work closest to you.

34. Stories solidify. Luke told the story of the risen Christ to his friend so that he might know with certainty that the things he'd heard about Jesus were true. "Since I myself have carefully investigated everything from the beginning, it seemed good also to me to write an orderly account for you, most excellent Theophilus, so that you may know the certainty of the things you have been taught" (Luke 1:3, 4).

Action points

a. Turn to God's Word in times of doubt or uncertainty.

b. Use Scripture to encourage and convince others when they have questions about Christ.

35. Stories spread the gospel. The most important story you can tell is about Christ's death and resurrection. Paul points this out in his letter to the church at Corinth, "For what I received I passed on to you as of first importance: that Christ died for our sins according to the Scriptures" (1 Corinthians 15:3).

Action points

a. Remember to include the gospel story regularly in your lessons. Don't lose sight of it!

b. Remember the greatest storytelling command of all time, "Go into all the world and preach the good news to all creation" (Mark 16:15)!

Resources and Storytelling Organizations

Y OU CAN QUICKLY become overwhelmed by the number of storytelling sites and resources on the web! Here are a few of the best links:

www.nobs.org—The Network of Biblical Storytellers provides resources, plans events, and trains teachers on retelling sacred stories from Scripture.
  Contact Information:
  1810 Harvard Blvd.
  Dayton, OH 45406
  Telephone: 1-800-355-NOBS or 937-278-5127
  Fax: 937-279-0848
  E-mail: nobsint@nobs.org

www.storynet.org—This is the official web site for the National Storytelling Network. This network offers excellent conferences, festivals, resources, and events for storytellers.
  Contact information:
  National Storytelling Network
  101 Courthouse Square
  Jonesborough, TN 37659
  1-800-525-4514 or 423-913-8201
  Fax: 423-753-9331
  E-Mail: nsn@naxs.net

www.storyarts.org—Author and storyteller Heather Forest offers articles, resources, lesson plans, ideas, and links.

www.storyteller.net—This site includes articles related to storytelling, audio stories, links, and free web pages for storytellers.

www.tiac.net/users/papajoe/ring/ring.htm— "The Storytelling Ring" is a series of hundreds of storytelling web sites and links. This is a great place to start looking for storytelling ideas online!

www.storyconnection.net—This web site of storyteller Dianne de Las Casas has great links and resources, and is easy to navigate.

http://falcon.jmu.edu/~ramseyil/drama.htm— This site includes links, articles, and resources on storytelling, creative dramatics, puppetry, readers theater, and more.

385 Story Starters

"WHAT IS HARD to bear becomes sweet to remember."
—a Portuguese proverb

Stories about the events that shape our lives can be powerful teaching tools. Use your personal story as a way of introducing your lesson, as a bridge into the lives of the listeners, or as an example or illustration of the biblical principle being taught.

How to Use Story Starters

Think about the people, places, and events that have shaped your life. Consider milestones, turning points and times of transition.

adoptions	environments	meals
anniversaries	funerals	money
arrivals	going back to school	moving
baptisms	going back to work	new family members
births or birthdays	graduations	new homes
body image	grandchildren	new jobs
building projects	health issues	priority shifts
camping trips	heroes	pursuits
confirmations	holidays	retirements
decisions	honeymoons	reunions
divorce	hospitalizations	rivalries
dreams	houses	separations
emotions	injustices	vacations
empty nests	jail convictions	weddings

Look at significant objects from your life . . .

childhood toys	heirlooms	memorable places
diaries	letters	photo albums
documents	memorabilia	school records

Finally, think about a time when you struggled with something or discovered something new. The following list of 385 story starters will help you draw stories from the experiences of your life!

Use the story starter as a springboard to think of related biblical *issues:*

1. You showed **mercy** to another person. *When was mercy extended in the Bible? What happened as the result? Why is it often harder to receive mercy than to give it?*

2. You wished you didn't have to **grow up**. *What did Jesus say about growing up? Does he want us to be more grown-up or more childlike? Why? What's the difference between childlike faith and childish faith?*

3. You questioned **authority**. *When shouldn't authority be questioned? When should it? What happens when you question authority? Did Jesus ever question authority?*

4. You **forgave** someone who didn't deserve it. *How do you feel when you truly forgive someone? Can you forgive someone and not respect him? Who in the Bible found it hard to forgive? What happened?*

Or, think of related biblical *images:*

5. You lost the **race**. *Think of races. What kinds of races are there? When is losing a good thing? What races are mentioned in the Bible? What kinds of races do we run?*

6. You saw your **family** in a new way. *Think of families in the Bible. When did someone see her family in a new way? What did Jesus have to say about his family?*

7. You wondered about **love**. *Think of love. What love stories are recorded in the Bible? What types of love are there? Why is love so hard to find?*

8. You **cried** and were not ashamed. *Think of tears. In the Bible, David, Jeremiah, Peter, and Jesus all cried. Why did each of them cry? Were they ever ashamed of their tears? What can that teach us?*

Or, think of related biblical *incidents:*

9. You **watched history change** forever. *Pharaoh standing in his palace watching the Israelites leave Egypt . . . Joseph in the stable witnessing the birth of Jesus . . . the centurion who watched Jesus die.*

10. You were **full of hope and wonder**. *The shepherds at Jesus' birth . . . the Israelites seeing the Promised Land . . . anyone witnessing a miracle . . . Adam and Eve looking around the Garden of Eden for the first time . . . the disciples when they met the risen Jesus!*

11. You **experienced forgiveness**. *Joseph forgave his brothers . . . Jesus forgave his executioners . . . Samson refused to forgive anyone!*

12. You **ignored someone in trouble**. *The visitors to Sodom had trouble finding a place to stay . . . the priest and the Levite walked past the hurting man . . . the disciples deserted Christ, and then Peter denied knowing him.*

Additional Story Starters

13. You saw a bridge emerge between two things, ideas, or people.
14. You looked into someone's eyes and realized something.
15. You felt pain over the loss of a loved one.
16. You experienced joy over seeing a loved one.
17. You witnessed a teacher bring about peace.
18. You were afraid of dying.
19. You felt rejection.
20. You peeled off a mask you were wearing.
21. You tried to forgive, but couldn't.
22. You stood up for someone else.

23. You abandoned the rat race.
24. You redefined your view of success.
25. You were lost.
26. You were found.
27. You were almost killed.
28. You witnessed new life.
29. You flirted with death/disaster.
30. You were given a second chance.
31. You weren't caught doing something wrong.
32. You experienced discrimination.
33. You had butterflies in your stomach.
34. You knew you were going to panic.
35. You felt paralyzed.
36. You were uptight.
37. You were angry at injustice.
38. You witnessed hypocrisy.
39. You realized people don't spend time on important things.
40. You fit in when you should have stood out.
41. You stood out when you should have fit in.
42. You longed to make up for a wrong you'd done.
43. You wished there was somewhere to turn.
44. You found out it was too late to help someone.
45. You wished you were someone else.
46. You felt rejected by God.
47. You felt loved by God.
48. You felt alone in the midst of many people.
49. You were proud of an accomplishment.
50. You saw inspiration flash into someone's eyes.
51. You felt helpless.
52. You were thankful to be alive.
53. You did something completely spontaneous.
54. You realized that you are unique.
55. You were in the right place at the wrong time.
56. You were embarrassed for someone else.
57. You didn't care when you should have.
58. You were the recipient of a gift you didn't deserve.
59. You went on an incredible trip.
60. You were followed by a strange person.
61. You fell in love.
62. You wished for something magnificent.
63. You dreamed an impossible dream.
64. You sought adventure.
65. You were falsely accused of wrongdoing.
66. You met someone very famous and weren't impressed.
67. You met someone unknown and were astonished.
68. You saw compassion in action.
69. You stopped to smell the roses.
70. You heard a funny joke, but couldn't remember it.
71. You experienced a broken heart.
72. You were healed of your hatred or anger.
73. You let go of bitterness.

Making Sense of Experience

We make sense of our experience by combining our memories (both the facts and the feelings) with meaning (the lessons or truths we attribute to that experience). Ask yourself these questions to get started:

- What is it about this memory that grabs my attention or is significant?
- What happened and what was my role?
- What question or crisis did I face? How was I hurt or what did I struggle with?
- What did I learn, discover, understand, or how did I mature as a result of this experience?
- How has this lesson changed the way I live?
- How would my life have been different had I not experienced this event?
- Can others identify with this struggle as well?

74. You resisted an urge.
75. You discovered the meaning of life.
76. You saw the most beautiful thing in the world.
77. You struggled with temptation.
78. You learned an important lesson.
79. You were wounded, but grew as a result.
80. You strove for something you couldn't attain.
81. You lost your innocence.
82. You were overcome with emotion.
83. You discovered a new way of looking at life.
84. You were afraid for someone you loved.
85. You struggled with yourself.
86. You wrestled with God.
87. You gave in to pride.
88. You wanted to fight.
89. You asked God, "Why?" and he didn't reply.
90. You saw someone give up on life.
91. You had the power to harm someone.
92. You were lured by power.
93. You had to humble yourself and admit your mistake.
94. You asked for mercy.
95. You sawed off the branch you were sitting on.
96. You changed your mind.
97. You began to respect someone you didn't like.
98. You wanted to hide but there was no place to go.
99. You were helpless and needed to be rescued.
100. You realized there was no excuse and no escape.
101. You accepted credit for something you didn't do.
102. You were deceived into believing a lie.
103. You approved of wrongdoing.
104. You had a brush with disaster.
105. You struggled with rejection.
106. You let go of a loved one.
107. You were hurt and it was hard to trust again.
108. You grew roots and they were hard to pull up.
109. You walked to the edge of the cliff to see how close you could get.
110. You went along with the crowd.
111. You turned your back on someone in need.
112. You found out what it feels like to be genuine and sincere.
113. You laughed at something God would weep over.
114. You didn't feel like being good any longer.
115. You desired something you shouldn't have.
116. You didn't fall, but rather drifted into sin.
117. You ached for someone you didn't know.
118. You discovered you couldn't make up for a wrong.
119. You were provoked.
120. You awakened to a new day.
121. You agonized over the problem of pain.
122. You couldn't help but be discouraged.
123. You realized the evil you are capable of.
124. You learned how vulnerable you are.
125. You betrayed a trust.

126. You were overcome with frustration.
127. You were refreshed.
128. You met someone you'll never forget.
129. You found an unusual treasure.
130. You saved something no one else would have saved.
131. You changed your attitude.
132. You didn't care when you should have.
133. You realized you hadn't been worshiping God.
134. You didn't take time for yourself.
135. You gave thanks.
136. You were charmed into believing a lie.
137. You tried your hardest, and failed.
138. You redefined success.
139. You passed a test you'd previously failed.
140. You searched, but never found.
141. You went off to seek your fortune.
142. You were prepared for battle.
143. You became a captive to your desires.
144. You finally obtained what was rightfully yours.
145. You tried to run from God, but he wouldn't let you.
146. You turned over a new leaf.
147. You recovered something (or someone) precious.
148. You kept a secret too long.
149. You thanked God life isn't fair.
150. You were the bearer of bad news.
151. You faced the hardest decision of all.
152. You chose the path of healing.
153. You made a fatal mistake.
154. You believed the unbelievable.
155. You did things God's way for once.
156. You let anger tell you what to do.
157. You got into trouble.
158. You needed to be punished.
159. You didn't care what happened.
160. You were glad you got caught.
161. You should have been more bold.
162. You admitted you were weak.
163. You loved and lost.
164. You were in the eye of someone else's storm.
165. You were no longer content.
166. You went from rags to riches.
167. You had faith in the wrong thing.
168. You didn't take responsibility for your actions.
169. You had inner peace.
170. You learned something about holiness.
171. You turned your back on your old life.
172. You experienced inner poverty.
173. You forgave but you didn't forget.
174. You hurt the one you loved. Again.
175. You took action before it was too late.
176. You became a victim of your own desire.
177. You tricked your way out of a blessing.

178. You opened your big mouth.
179. You prayed for your enemy.
180. You learned by example.
181. You felt abandoned.
182. You were ignored. And it was OK.
183. You gave advice instead of listening.
184. You faced the consequences of your actions.
185. You went on a quest to discover yourself.
186. You dared to go someplace new.
187. You knew you were boxed-in.
188. Your job became a calling.
189. Your feelings were hurt.
190. Your dreams turned to dust.
191. Your loved ones turned their backs on you.
192. Your friends betrayed you.
193. Your curiosity had brutal consequences.
194. Someone helped you withstand the pressure.
195. Life overwhelmed you.
196. A burden was lifted.
197. Worry made you tremble.
198. The strong flower wilted.
199. Rumors destroyed a friendship.
200. One person became a majority.
201. Stormy seas were finally calmed.
202. The outcast was accepted.
203. Unexpected news stunned you.
204. God sent you an awkward blessing.
205. Restlessness stirred your soul.
206. Suffering and sadness gripped you.
207. Vengeance seemed more important than love.
208. Mourning turned to dancing.
209. Joy came in the morning.
210. Ambition blinded you.
211. Favoritism hurt you.
212. Seduction came knocking at your door.
213. Encouragement came from nowhere.
214. You were finally free.
215. Reinforcements arrived.
216. Life didn't make sense.
217. A ghost from the past pursued you.
218. Everyone laughed at you.
219. A promise was kept.
220. A promise was broken.
221. A prayer seemed to go unanswered.
222. Something you said was taken the wrong way.
223. The pain of regret was healed.
224. An old wound was reopened.
225. An injustice occurred in front of you and you were helpless to change it.
226. A child reminded you of something special.
227. The good guy didn't win.
228. The underdog had a big finish.
229. The person you looked up to let you down.

230. Life became boring and routine.
231. Life became adventurous and wild.
232. Your house became a home.
233. The dark cloud lifted.
234. A simple thought changed your life.
235. Love replaced infatuation.
236. Zeal consumed you.
237. Joy bubbled out of your soul.
238. Relief finally came.
239. Everything you believed in crumbled.
240. Time seemed to stand still.
241. Courage seemed impossible.
242. Disaster seemed imminent.
243. Everyone accepted you.
244. No one seemed to care.
245. Someone overlooked the past.
246. Feelings dictated your actions.
247. The joke was on you.
248. Inspiration came at last.
249. Amusement made up for disappointment.
250. Church became an excuse.
251. Quitting seemed like the only option, but you persisted.
252. No one seemed to notice your effort.
253. Opportunity knocked.
254. Wisdom outshone knowledge.
255. A small deed changed your life.
256. The fat lady sang . . . but the opera continued.
257. Both of the options were acceptable.
258. Everything fell into place.
259. A friend brightened your day.
260. A stranger appeared at just the right moment.
261. Good news finally arrived.
262. Things went better than expected.
263. Clouds parted enough to reveal a rainbow.
264. It felt good to go home.
265. The secret was finally revealed.
266. The confession was finally made.
267. Even your friends seemed far away.
268. Hope came knocking at your door.
269. A new pathway suddenly appeared.
270. Saying goodbye was the hardest thing to do.
271. Faith was a source of strength.
272. Laughter exploded out of you.
273. The letter you'd been waiting for arrived.
274. Something unpredictable happened.
275. Hope reappeared.
276. Tragedy struck.
277. The look in a child's eye made life seem OK.
278. Simple wisdom emerged from an unexpected place.
279. A prediction came true.
280. A person from your past re-entered your life.
281. A family heirloom was passed down.

282. The brevity of life became apparent.
283. An accident happened and you were there to help.
284. Truth became crystal clear.
285. Neither option seemed acceptable.
286. A big move caused you to reevaluate your life.
287. The urgent overshadowed the important.
288. Only one thing mattered.
289. Embarrassment opened a door.
290. Your response surprised you.
291. A regret that you've lived with resurfaced.
292. Shame clouded your reasoning.
293. Innocence was betrayed.
294. Guilt became overpowering.
295. Opportunity knocked, but you weren't home.
296. Peace surpassed understanding.
297. Because of foresight, a crisis was narrowly avoided.
298. Wisdom came from an unexpected source.
299. A new challenge arose.
300. Wounds were healed.
301. The future seemed bright.
302. The past became significant.
303. Seeing wasn't believing.
304. God became real.
305. Peace flooded your life.
306. Wonder and awe filled your heart.
307. Desperate measures were called for.
308. Grief made joy impossible.
309. Love made grief bearable.
310. A heart was broken.
311. Shame caught up with you.
312. The world seemed cold and uncaring.
313. Darkness moved in.
314. A little white lie grew into a betrayal.
315. A misunderstanding led to hatred.
316. Lust took root in your mind.
317. It was hard to break free of a habit.
318. Memories of good times caused you to cry.
319. Forgiveness was the only option.
320. God answered prayer in an unexpected way.
321. Two roads diverged and you had to choose.
322. Jealousy became easier and easier.
323. Something insignificant became valuable.
324. A gift changed everything.
325. Someone touched you with a kind word.
326. A long struggle finally ended.
327. The mystery was suddenly solved.
328. Temptation lured you in.
329. You doubted and were reassured.
330. Greed blinded you.
331. When wronged, you chose to be quiet and let God defend you.
332. Someone took your place.
333. The ladder you were climbing was leaning against the wrong building.

334. Selfishness became a way of life.
335. Evil seemed to have the upper hand.
336. Someone else's success made you envious.
337. Life didn't seem fair.
338. Strife in your family made life difficult.
339. A rival was successful at your expense.
340. An obstacle was overcome.
341. The guilty person walked away unpunished.
342. Quiet joy replaced giddy happiness.
343. The world seemed like a cruel place to raise a child.
344. The story had a happy ending.
345. Pleasure was ruined by passion.
346. Purity was lost or regained.
347. A warning came from an unusual place.
348. The champion gave up on his cause.
349. A disguise came off and you saw the real person.
350. Two enemies were reconciled.
351. The effects of past choices became evident.
352. A debt was paid.
353. Everything was turned upside down.
354. A hero emerged.
355. An honorable sacrifice was made.
356. A warning was not heeded.
357. A curse became a blessing.
358. A blessing became a curse.
359. Something familiar became an idol.
360. You discovered something you wish you hadn't.
361. The forbidden seemed safe.
362. Obligation drained your enjoyment.
363. A quarrel broke out.
364. Controversy erupted.
365. A rivalry separated good friends.
366. The victim sought revenge.
367. You were powerless to prevent something awful.
368. A dark desire sprang up inside your soul.
369. Duty called.
370. Suspicion arose.
371. Insult was added to injury.
372. The punishment didn't fit the crime.
373. Life imitated art.
374. The imitation seemed like the real thing.
375. Danger complicated matters.
376. Respect deteriorated.
377. Hard work didn't pay off.
378. Perseverance did pay off.
379. Hope sustained you.
380. Love was more than a feeling.
381. Someone else's success brought you discontent.
382. Devotion prevented disaster.
383. Sorrow overwhelmed you.
384. Wisdom saved the day.
385. A wish came true.

Preparing Yourself

**Overcoming Five Myths About
Becoming a Storyteller**

Tips and Suggestions
- Feel free to adapt the ideas to fit the needs of the people at your workshop.
- Take into account the experience and expertise of your audience as you lead this workshop.

What You'll Need
- Photocopies of pages 134, 135 for each student.

What to Do Before You Begin
- Review chapter one and make sure you understand the concepts being taught.
- Read the workshop material and practice saying the suggested comments. Decide how you'll make the transition from one activity to the next.
- Familiarize yourself with the student handouts. Wait to distribute the handouts until after the introductory activity.

Introductory Activity
Say, **To get this workshop started, I'd like you each to find a partner. To start your introduction, tell each other your favorite type of dessert. Go ahead.**

After they have finished introducing themselves, choose *one* of the following activities and read it to your workshop participants.

"Think of your favorite teacher you've ever had. Tell your partner why he or she was so memorable."

"Share a story with your partner about a struggle that you or a friend had when you were in high school."

"Tell your partner about a goal or dream you had growing up. Then explain how you did, or why you did not, see it come true."

After the activity, point out that each of us is unique and will therefore differ in the way we teach and tell stories, and that each of us is already a storyteller with interesting and memorable stories to tell.

Say, **Think about what the world would be like with no stories. There would be no jokes, no news, no plays, no theater, no folktales, no legends, no movies, no novels, no memories, no dreams, and no Bible as we know it. For we are storytelling creatures. That's how God made each one of us. And our God is a storytelling God.**

Explain that human beings remember events through stories, communicate ideas through stories, and think about the world around them through stories.

Say, **You and I are already storytellers by the time we speak our first words! Our goal today isn't *to become* storytellers, but *to become better* storytellers so that we can tell**

God's story more effectively. Today, we're going to talk about five common misconceptions, or myths, about being a storyteller. You'll learn practical steps you can take to gain confidence in the storytelling abilities God has already given you. So, turn to your partner and tell him or her, "You are a storyteller!" Go ahead, it'll feel good to say it and to hear it!

Myth One—"I'm not a storyteller!"

As you distribute the handouts, explain that the first myth many educators believe is that they are not storytellers, but the truth is *We are all storytellers.*"

Myth Two—"I'm not a good enough speaker to be a storyteller!"

Say, **Jesus' disciples were the very first Christian educators. They were the very first Christian storytellers.**

Take time to discuss the qualifications Jesus looked for when he was choosing his disciples. Either in groups of two, or in a large group, try to come up with three to five qualities the disciples shared.

Then say, **When Jesus chose his disciples, did he choose the most gifted speakers of his day? No! He chose people with very little expertise and experience in public speaking. As someone has said, "God doesn't call the equipped, he equips the called." And look at what the disciples did with God's help!**

Explain that there are hints on the handouts for learning to take confidence in God rather than ourselves. Say, **The second myth many educators believe is that they have to be gifted speakers to be storytellers, but the truth is,** *God is more interested in your availability than your ability.*

Myth Three—
"I'm too nervous speaking in front of people to be a storyteller!"

Point out that studies have shown that many people are more afraid of public speaking than of dying! But what are people afraid of? As a group, brainstorm five or six things people fear when speaking to groups. Then decide which of these are real dangers and which are not. Discuss ways of overcoming the fears.

Say something like, **It's natural to feel nervous in certain situations. None of us wants to look silly, embarrass ourselves, or make fools of ourselves. But millions of other Christians have learned ways of handling their fears in this area and you can, too!**

Draw attention to the hints at overcoming storytelling anxiety included in the handouts. Have someone read 1 Corinthians 2:3-5 aloud. Then ask, **Was Paul nervous when he preached to the Corinthians? How can you tell? How did he deal with his anxiety? Perhaps one of the most encouraging things of all is that even though we may be nervous, God can still use us. According to Paul, weakness, fear, and trembling are assets, not liabilities, because they make us rely on God's power for results. Truth number three is,** *When sharing God's story, weakness, fear, and trembling are assets, not liabilities.*

Myth Four—"I don't know any stories!"

You may wish to do this as a large group, or divide into groups of four or five people, each group working on a different category of stories.

Say something like, **Let's list some different types of stories that we know or have heard. When I mention a category, let's see if we can think of six stories that fit into that category.**

Choose from this list:
- Old Testament stories
- New Testament stories
- Fables
- Fairy tales
- Legends
- Greek myths

Point out that this group already knows many stories. Then conclude by saying something like, **We've all heard, read, and experienced hundreds of stories. The truth is, our lives are immersed in stories. The secret is finding a way to review them and connect them to the one story we've all been asked to share—the gospel story!**

Explain that even though it sometimes seems like you can't remember any stories, *you already know enough stories to last a lifetime!*

Myth Five—"No one will listen to the stories I tell!"

Explain that stories appeal to our sense of wonder, curiosity, and imagination. Stories capture the attention of the students, help them remember the lesson, and allow them the chance to more easily apply truth to their lives. That's why Jesus was a storyteller!

Children love stories. Our job is simply to share God's story so that it connects with their lives. Close by pointing out that children really will want to listen to you, because *telling stories is the natural way to teach!*

Closing Prayer

Say, **Please join me in a closing prayer.** *"God, we are your servants. Prepare us to tell your story, your way. Help us not to worry so much about our inadequacies or weaknesses, but instead help us rely on your power and strength. We submit ourselves to you. Fill us with your Spirit and reach out to the lives of the children we teach through the stories we tell. Amen."*

Preparing Yourself
Overcoming Five Myths About Becoming a Storyteller

Myth One

"I'm not a storyteller!"

Truth One— _____

Jesus said, *"What I tell you in the dark, speak in the daylight; what is whispered in your ear, proclaim from the roofs"* (Matthew 10:27). God wants us to take the message of hope that we know and share it with others. Remember

- God has called us each to tell his story to others;
- we can improve our storytelling through prayer, practice, and patience.

Myth Two

"I'm not a good enough speaker to be a storyteller!"

Truth Two— _____

Paul, referring to the confidence believers had in sharing the gospel story, wrote, *"Such confidence as this is ours through Christ before God. Not that we are competent in ourselves to claim anything for ourselves, but our competence comes from God"* (2 Corinthians 3:4, 5). Remember, your confidence comes from God! So, rely on the Spirit rather than yourself for confidence.

Measure success by how faithful you have been in honoring God with your gifts rather than in how entertained the students seem to be.

To improve your speaking skills, listen—really listen—to inspirational speakers, actors, comedians, storytellers, and others. Listen to the way they use sounds to shape mental images. Notice the good habits they have—the delicate pause, the rapport with the audience, the natural flow of movement, and the gestures they use. Notice also the bad habits—the distracting mannerisms, the annoying verbal habits, and the awkward transitions. Learn from them!

Listen to the way the story sounds as you practice it. Some storytellers string every sentence together with the word "and." It's really annoying! Listen for words that you repeat over and over such as "um," "uh," or "well." Then weed them out.

Think about the language you chose for retelling this story. Is it appropriate for your audience? Are the words too big? Are the ideas too complex? Listen to the audience (by watching and observing them) as you tell your story.

Myth Three

"I'm too nervous speaking in front of people to be a storyteller!"

Truth Three— _____

When Paul went to preach to the people in Corinth, he was focused on his objective. He wasn't interested in impressing them with his wisdom or wowing them with his eloquence. Instead, he wrote, *"I came to you in weakness and fear, and with much trembling. My message and my preaching were not with wise and persuasive words, but with a demonstration of the Spirit's power, so that your faith might not rest on men's wisdom, but on God's power"* (1 Corinthians 2:3-5). God doesn't want you to rely on yourself, but on his power working through you when you tell his story! Strive for excellence rather than perfection. The goal is not to tell the story right but to tell the story well.

Myth Four

"I don't know any stories!"

Truth Four _____

"Come and listen, all you who fear God; let me tell you what he has done for me" (Psalm 66:16). We all have at least one story to share! As believers in Christ, we are called to share the gospel—the good news about what God has done for *us!* Look for personal parallels to the Bible stories you know. Then look for specific ways to apply the story today.

The stories we know tend to fall into four categories:

Stories from my experiences

Stories from my imagination

Stories I've heard

Stories I've read

Myth Five

"Nobody will listen to the stories I tell!"

Truth Five _____

"Jesus spoke all these things to the crowd in parables; he did not say anything to them without using a parable" (Matthew 13:34). Jesus knew his listeners would rather hear a story than a lecture. Our listeners do, too! As you look for ways to connect with your listeners remember to

- Watch the audience as you tell your story. Be prepared to change and adapt the story to fit the needs and responses of the audience.
- Add details to the stories you tell. Use strong nouns and vivid verbs to create memorable images in your stories
- Picture the story as you tell it. Use your imagination to help the story and its images come alive in your mind and in the minds of your listeners. If you can "see" the story happening before you, so will your audience!

Six tips to help you relax when telling your stories:

1. Work on learning your *story*, not just the *words* that make up the story. It's more important to know the story well than to try to learn it word-perfect. Instead of learning a story word-for-word, learn your story image-for-image.

2. When you practice, don't just practice the words, practice actually moving through the story—stories are told with our bodies as well as our voices.

3. Take your time of personal Bible study seriously. Discover what the story is really about and then think about how it applies to the lives of your listeners.

4. Practice your story in a variety of ways until you become comfortable with the way it sounds and feels. Get to know the story so well that you're comfortable changing, deleting, or repeating sections based on reactions from your listeners. Readiness means not only preparing your story, but also being prepared to respond to the audience while you're telling the story.

5. Practice walking up, introducing yourself, and beginning your story with no one else present. Take it slowly!

6. Relax right before beginning your story. Don't worry about what people think! Your students want you to be comfortable, successful, and at ease when speaking to them. They don't want you to be scared or embarrassed or afraid. So, face the audience, use good posture, and smile at them. Then take a few deep breaths to compose yourself. Remember, when you relax, the story spills out!

Preparing Your Listeners

How to Prepare Your Audience and Room

Tips and Suggestions

- Feel free to adapt the ideas to fit the needs of the people at your workshop.

What You'll Need

- Four sheets of paper (or blank overhead transparencies).
- Photocopies of pages 138, 139 for each student.

What to Do Before You Begin

- Write the audience descriptions (found in the "Understanding Your Audience" section of this workshop) on the sheets of paper (or overheads).
- Review chapter two and make sure you understand the concepts being taught.
- Read this section and practice saying the suggested comments. Decide how you'll make the transition from one activity to the next.
- Familiarize yourself with the student handouts. Distribute the handouts as the participants arrive.

Understanding Your Audience

Say, **Get a partner who is seated nearby. See who has a larger hand. That person will be partner "A." The other person will be partner "B." Position yourselves so that partner A can see up front, but partner B cannot. In a moment, partner B will begin telling the story of "The Three Little Pigs" to partner A. As the story is being told, I'll hold up a sheet of paper with a description on it, and partner A will act like whatever person or group is described on the sheet of paper!**

Explain that you'll hold up two different sheets of paper for partner A, and then the partners will switch roles and you'll repeat.

Here are the descriptions. Choose four of these six for your workshop, or use three with the first partner, and three with the second partner.

- You are restless two-year-olds.
- You are hungry kindergartners.
- You are second graders who are scared of the storyteller.
- You are bored fifth graders.
- You are a teenage volunteer helping with the class.
- You are a tired Sunday school teacher at a workshop!

See if the partners can guess who their audience is supposed to be. Discuss differences in audiences.

After the activity, say, **One of the keys to being an effective storyteller is to understand your audience. You need to be able to relate to them, connect with them, respond to them, and understand them. Think about the expectations they have of the storytelling time— do they think it will be boring, or exciting? Consider the physical conditions of the room—is the room temperature too hot, too cold, or is it comfortable?**

Discuss other aspects of understanding your audience. Then say, **Once you've taken the time to understand your audience, it's time to prepare them for your story!**

Preparing Your Audience

Say, **Many educators fail to take time to prepare their students to listen. That means making sure they feel safe, welcomed, and ready to listen. From your own experience, what are some practical steps you can take to make sure your children are ready to hear your story?**

Discuss. Then explain that there are three steps to preparing your audience:

1. The set-up: You introduce, or make the transition into the story. During this time you communicate how much participation you desire, and how many interruptions you will allow. You may put on a storytelling vest, hat, or costume, or chant a specific song to let the children know that now it's story time and not playtime.

2. The story: You tell the story.

3. The send-off: You prepare your students for the next activity.

Say, **Once your audience is prepared, tell your story in a way that they can relate to. Jesus' stories were rich with connections between the lives of his listeners and the spiritual truth he was conveying. One of the keys to effective storytelling is adapting your story and the style of your storytelling to your audience.**

Point out that this can be done by asking questions relating to the five areas listed on the handout under the second point.

Preparing Your Room

Lead a group discussion on the reasons it's important to prepare your room. Say, **In your notes there is a list of five actions to take to prepare your room for the storytelling event. Let's look at each of them in turn and discuss why it's an important step for a storyteller to take.**

- **Why is it helpful to have a neutral background? What happens if you don't? How does the background affect how well the children can pay attention? What types of distractions can there be in the background?**
- **How can lighting affect the storytelling event? What would happen if you stood in front of a window? Would the children be able to see you? Why not?**
- **Obviously, you can't remove all distractions. How can you deal with those that you can't remove? What are some that you can remove?**
- **How does seating affect the attention span and expectations of the audience? Look around this room. What things do you see in this room that help facilitate a good atmosphere for storytelling? What things detract from it? How could we improve the seating arrangement in this room for our workshop right now?**
- **What are some of the reasons children can't hear stories? How can these distractions be removed?**
- **Are there any other specific ideas you can think of that would be helpful in preparing a room for storytelling?**

Closing Comments

Review the importance of understanding your audience, preparing them for the story, and arranging your room for storytelling. Say, **These simple steps happen before a single word of the story is spoken, yet they can have a huge impact on the storytelling event. Let's close with prayer and ask God to be with us as we prepare to be better storytellers for him.** Pray.

Preparing Your Listeners

Understanding Your Audience

Different factors affect the audience's expectations—past experiences in Sunday school, previous knowledge of this Bible story, how long they expect the story to be.

If they expect the story to be boring, you'll want to communicate to them early on that this story is exciting and worth paying attention to!

Notes:

Preparing Your Audience

1. Three ways to prepare the audience

- **The set-up**—Welcome the children and help them feel safe. Make clear what is expected of them; are they supposed to sit quietly and listen, or are they allowed to wiggle and participate? Are they supposed to carry on a conversation with you (or others) during the story, or are they supposed to be quiet and not interrupt? Introduce the story. Spark their interest, and clarify the level of involvement you want. Encourage your listeners to listen, not just sit still.

- **The story**—Respond to your children as you tell your story. Not only does a storyteller prepare his material with the audience in mind, he also responds to them while he is telling the story. Use discernment and good judgment both in choosing your material and in presenting it.

- **The send-off**—Make the transition into an application, a brief explanation, another story, a prayer, or another related activity. If you were doing wild audience participation during the story, you may wish to do a cool-down activity or song.

2. Develop trust and intimacy with the audience. When the audience and the teller feel comfortable with each other, creativity can express itself without fear. Ask yourself, Where is my audience in each of the following areas?

- **Physically**—Are they hungry, tired, or seated in a comfortable position? Can they see me without distraction? Are they ready to listen?

- **Developmentally**—Are they able to understand the vocabulary I'm using? Can they grasp the concepts? Will the illustrations make sense to them?

- **Spiritually**—Are they ready for the issues, themes, and content of this story? If not, how do I need to change the story for them?

- **Emotionally**—Do they trust me with this story and with their time? If not, what do I need to do to earn their trust?

- **Mentally**—Are they alert and ready to listen, or do they need a mental break?

Notes:

Preparing Your Room

- Find a neutral background.

- Stand in the light.

- Remove distractions.

- Arrange the seating to your advantage.

- Make sure you can be heard.

Notes:

Room Checklist
- Am I standing in a well-lit area of the room?
- Is the space behind me free from distractions?
- Are all other distracting sounds turned off?
- Can the children easily see me and my props?
- Is the temperature comfortable?
- Is the seating arrangement conducive for this storytelling event?
- Can the students easily hear me?

Workshop Presenter Notes for

Understanding Your Story

The Seven Parts of a Story

Tips and Suggestions

- Feel free to adapt the ideas to fit the needs of the people at your workshop.

What You'll Need

- Photocopies of page 142 for each student.
- An overhead projector or dry erase board and markers.

What to Do Before You Begin

- Review chapter three and make sure you understand the concepts being taught. Make sure you're familiar with the seven components of a story (character, struggle, discovery, change, emotion, action, and choices).
- Read this section and practice saying the suggested comments. Decide how you'll make the transition from one activity to the next.
- Familiarize yourself with the student handout. Distribute the handout as the participants arrive.
- Make transparencies of the illustration on page 25. (Photocopy the page, cut apart the elements, make separate transparencies that you can lay down as you speak.) Or, if you are comfortable with drawing simple figures, you can draw this illustration on the board or on an overhead transparency. Use a stick figure to represent the character, a lightening bolt to represent struggle, a light bulb to represent discovery, and a butterfly to represent change. Write the words, "emotion, action, and choices" in the pictures.

Introductory Activity

Read the poem on page 22 aloud and remind participants that we are telling the greatest story of all time! Say, **This workshop will help you understand how to find out who a Bible story is really about, and how to remember Bible stories more easily. Once you understand story structure, you'll be able to construct better-told, more engaging, and more biblically accurate stories for your students.**

What Is a Story?

Ask, **Is this a story: "Preset the oven to 400 degrees"? How about this: "That chair had four legs"? How about this: "Last summer I went to the beach, then I came home, then I ate a hamburger, then I sat in my chair, then I watched TV, then I went to bed, then I woke up, then I got dressed"? Some people might call this last example a story, but nothing goes wrong and the character doesn't change. Author and speaker Steven James defines a story as "transformation unveiled." In a story, there is always a transformation of a person or a situation.**

As you introduce each of the seven story components, draw its corresponding picture on the overhead projector or the dry erase board, or use the transparencies you have prepared. Brief notes are given to help you explain each concept.

Character

A story always has characters. The character might be an object, creature, angel, demon, God, or a person.

Struggle

In a story, something must go wrong. The main character struggles with something. Often there will be an outer struggle, and an inner struggle.

Discovery

As a result of facing the struggle, the character discovers or learns something about herself or her situation. Often, something from the outer struggle will reveal something about the inner struggle.

Change

The character is never the same at the end of the story as she was at the beginning. There is a change in her life. Sometimes this change is only hinted at in the story.

Where character and struggle meet, there is **emotion**. Whenever a character has a struggle, there is emotion.

Where struggle and discovery meet, there is **action**. Action is what moves the story from the struggle to the character's discovery.

Where discovery and change meet, there are **choices**. In a story, characters make choices that result in changed lives or situations.

Say, **Don't worry about finding the plot of a story. Plot is simply the pathway the character in the story takes through the emotion, struggle, discovery, action, and choices to a change in her life. Instead of trying to figure out the plot, simply look for someone who faces a problem and learns a lesson!**

How Will This Help Me?

Divide the participants into discussion groups of two to four people. Assign them the story of "Jesus and Peter Walking on the Water" (Matthew 14:22-33), or, if you desire, choose another story. Have the participants ask the seven questions on their worksheet. As a group, compare and contrast answers.

You may wish to point out that this story is an excellent example of transformation unveiled. As the story progresses and builds to a climax, the disciples go from being alone in the boat, to seeing Jesus at a distance, to having Jesus close by in the boat. When the storm first blows in, the disciples are terrified, when they see Jesus they are uncertain, and when he gets in the boat they bow to worship him as Lord. At the end of the story, the storm (outer struggle) is calmed, and their terror (inner struggle) is transformed into worship! Point out that action runs throughout the story and doesn't just happen at a specific place or moment in the story.

Closing Comments

Say, **Use these questions as you study stories. May God bless you as you seek to tell his story more faithfully!**

Understanding Your Story

The Seven Parts of a Story

How Will This Help Me?

See the story of "Jesus and Peter Walking on the Water" (Matthew 14:22-33).

- Who is the **main character**?

- What is the **struggle**?

- What does he **discover**?

- How does he **change**?

- What **emotions** run through the story?

- What is the **action** sequence of the story?

- What **choice** does the main character make that results in a changed life?

Workshop Presenter Notes for

Studying Your Story

How to Understand, Interpret, and Apply Bible Stories

Tips and Suggestions

- Feel free to adapt the ideas to fit the needs of the people at your workshop.
- Take into account the experience and expertise of your audience as you lead this workshop. You may wish to talk through each section in-depth, or simply provide the handouts as reference material for your teachers.

What You'll Need

- Photocopies of pages 146, 147 for each student.
- A Bible.

What to Do Before You Begin

- Photocopy two copies of the dramatic reading, "Let There Be a Story" (page 144).
- Review chapter four and make sure you understand the concepts being taught.
- Read this section and practice saying the suggested comments. Decide how you'll make the transition from one activity to the next.
- Familiarize yourself with the student handouts. Distribute the handouts as the participants arrive.

Introductory Activity

Invite two volunteers to the front. Give each of them a copy of the dramatic reading on page 144. Allow them a chance to read over the script and familiarize themselves with it. Then have them read it aloud to the group. Encourage them to read with feeling.

After the reading say, **Let's give our volunteers a hand for reading that to us today! This workshop is all about looking at that story—the greatest and grandest account of all—and understanding, interpreting, and applying it in our lives. As you study the stories you're going to tell, you'll need to think about nine different concepts. Don't be intimidated! You probably think about them already! Let's talk through them and then try to apply them to a story we're preparing to tell.**

Point out that the first five areas of exploration deal with story *content* and the last four areas of exploration deal with storyteller *technique*.

Talk through each point in as much or as little detail as you like. Notes and ideas have been provided for you.

1) Story Message

Explain that the first thing to ask when studying a story is, "What is this story really about?" Point out that it may take a little digging to unearth the main point, but it's always worth the time and effort!

• Let There Be a Story •

Reader #1: And God said,

Reader #2: Let there be . . . a story.

Reader #1: And in this story, let there be love, mystery, adventure, and romance.

Reader #2: And for this story, let there be a stage. And lights up above! And lots of scenery! Let there be animals and fish and birds and men and women.

Reader #1: Let there be a promise, whispered through the ages.

Reader #2: Let there be a stable and kings and shepherds. Let there be a young man and his bride.

Reader #1: Let the bride be beautiful and holy and pure.

Reader #2: In my story, let there be healing and hope and life!

Reader #1: Let there be pain and a cross and a grave.

Reader #2: But then, after death . . .

Reader #1: Let there be LIFE!

Reader #2: Let there be a happy ending to my story!

Reader #1: Let there be a happily ever after and a sunrise in eternity!

Reader #2: A feast! Let there be a feast! A party to which all are invited!

Reader #1: Let there be a story—

Reader #2: A love story—

Reader #1: The final and greatest and grandest tale of all!

Reader #2: A story to be told forever and ever!

Together: Amen!

2) Story Context

Different authors of Scripture wrote for different audiences and for different reasons. Look at what happens before and after the story to get the context in which it is told. Identify the storyteller and the audience. See if there is an explanation of the story in the Bible. Ask yourself, "What is the context of this story?"

3) Story Structure

Point out that finding repetition and refrains (or patterns such as reversals, ruin to redemption, and rags to riches) can help you understand and remember the story. Ask yourself, "What is the structure of this story?"

4) Characters

Look for the character who struggles, discovers, or changes as a result of the action of the story. Ask yourself, "To whom does this story happen?"

5) Scenes

Look at the backdrop of the story. Identify the changes in scenery or time during the story. This will help you remember the story and see how the story progresses. Ask yourself, "Where does this story take place?"

Say, **Let's look at an example. In Acts 8:26-40, Philip meets a man from Ethiopia, a country in Africa. This man is the first recorded African convert to Christianity. Let's have someone who has a Bible here today read through the story aloud, and then let's ask these first five questions. Ready? Let's try it!**

1. What is this story really about? Write down what you think the story is about, and after we've answered the other questions, see if you still think that's the main point.

2. What is the context of this story? Look at what's happening in the book of Acts at this time. Why do you think this story is recorded? What is the significance of its context? (Hint: see Acts 8:4-8.)

3. What is the structure of this story? Philip listens to God each time God speaks to him. There is also an example of ruin to redemption since the Ethiopian trusts in Christ.

4. Whom does this story happen to? Is the main character Philip or the Ethiopian man? How can you tell? Usually, you'll begin telling a story with the character who changes. Look for characteristics of the characters. What makes them different? In this story, Philip is portrayed as responsive to the Holy Spirit. The Ethiopian is shown to be inquisitive and unafraid to take action. So, as you tell the story, keep in mind their different characteristics and the picture Scripture paints of them.

5. Where does this story take place? Philip begins the story away from the desert, he travels to the desert, and then he leaves it again at the end of the story.

Note: If you're planning to lead other workshops from this book, explain that these last four areas of exploration will be discussed at another time. Otherwise, you may wish to apply them to the story of Philip and Ethiopian, or to a story you're currently preparing to tell.

6) Changes

Explain that you may need to condense time, limit the number of characters, leave out objectionable content, and explain difficult or foreign ideas or concepts as you tell the story. Ask yourself, "How do I need to change this story?"

7) Technique

Look for creative and memorable ways to retell this story. Bring your own personality to the story and retell it in your own way. Ask yourself, "How can I best tell this story?"

8) Introduction

Think through the transitions to and from the story. Ask yourself, "How shall I introduce and wrap up this story?"

9) Application

Once you've discovered what the story is about, and who the story is about, you can apply the story to life today. Ask yourself, "How shall I apply this story?"

Closing Comments

Say, **You don't need to study every story in this much detail. But asking these questions will help you to better understand and prepare your stories.** Close with prayer.

Studying Your Story
How to Understand, Interpret, and Apply Bible Stories

These first five questions deal with story content:

1) Story Message
- a) What is this story really about? What is the message, moral, truth, or principle being taught? Is this truth different from the one my Bible curriculum emphasizes?
- b) Is there a key verse, question, thought, or summary word that tells what this story is about? What thoughts are repeated? Where does this story begin and end?
- c) How can I naturally bring out the true meaning of the text in the way I retell the story?

2) Story Context
- a) Who is telling this story?
- b) Who is the audience?
- c) Why was the story told?

3) Story Structure
- a) Is this story told in detail, or is it summarized? Is it mostly dialogue or mostly narration? What is the feel of this story, and how can I bring that out when I retell it?
- b) What patterns occur in this story? Does the story include rhythms or rhymes I can use?
- c) Is there a refrain I can use or write that shows the change in the life of the characters, or the application of the story to the lives of my listeners?

4) Characters
- a) Who are the characters in this story? Who struggles, changes, or grows?
- b) How is he at the beginning of the story? How is he different at the end of the story?
- c) How does the main character change as a result of facing the struggles in the story? What does he discover?

5) Scenes
- a) Where does this story take place? What are the scenes of the story?
- b) Can I incorporate these scenes into the retelling of the story?
- c) Can these scenes help me remember the sequence of story events?

These last four questions deal with storyteller technique:

6) Changes
a) As I retell this story, what changes do I need to make to make the story come alive to my listeners?
b) What changes in wording will make the story easier to understand?
c) Is the content appropriate for my students? If not, what will I leave out and how will that affect the way this story is told?

7) Technique
a) What storytelling techniques naturally lend themselves to this story? (Music, movement, creative dramatics, etc.)
b) How can I make this story more memorable or engaging?
c) What specific talents or techniques has God given me that can be best utilized in telling this story?

8) Introduction
a) How will I introduce this story to my listeners? What background information do they need in order to understand the story?
b) What questions will children have about this story? Is it better for me to explain this information, or provide a learning activity that prepares them for the story?
c) What transitions will I use to flow into this story? How will I make the transition from this story into the next part of my lesson?

9) Application
a) What can I learn from this story? What application or lesson does this story have for my life and the lives of my students?
b) How can I naturally bring out the truths of this story by the way I retell it?
c) What draws me into this story? What part of this story rings true in my life? What character can I readily identify with?

Growing Your Own Tale

**Hints on Rehearsing and
Learning Your Stories**

Tips and Suggestions
- Feel free to adapt the ideas to fit the needs of the people at your workshop.
- Think of a short story you can learn as a group. For example, "The Parable of the Net" (Matthew 13:47-50).

What You'll Need
- A wedding ring, a toy car, a glass of water, an orange highway cone (safety cones can be purchased at school supply stores and toy stores), a packet of seeds, and a cookbook.
- Photocopies of pages 151, 152 and the chart from 150 for each student.
- A Bible.

What to Do Before You Begin
- Review chapter five and make sure you understand the concepts being taught.
- Read this section and practice saying the suggested comments. Decide how you'll make the transition from one activity to the next.
- Familiarize yourself with the student handouts. Distribute the handouts as the participants arrive.
- Prepare your props for the various object lessons.

Introductory Activity
Invite a participant to read Mark 4:26-29 aloud. Explain that Jesus said the kingdom of God is like a growing seed, and so is the storytelling process! It's not a mathematical process like 1 + 1 + 1 = 3, or do this and this and this and you'll be the world's greatest storyteller. Say, **In fact, I can't even tell you the right way to tell a story. No one can! Why not? Because there is no one right way to tell a story! Each time you tell a story is a unique experience with different people, expectations, and goals. I can give you examples of how I might tell a story, ideas on learning new stories, and suggestions on how to improve the stories you already tell—but that doesn't mean that my words or techniques will work for you or connect with your students. What will work for you is developing stories that make the most of your God-given talents as you reach the students in your class. These ideas will show you how.**

Note: There's a suggested object lesson for each of the six phases. For each phase, point out suggestions and observations from the chapter. If desired, choose a scriptural story (such as "The Parable of the Net") and work through these six phases in groups of two people, learning and then beginning to shape the story for telling!

Phase One: Getting to know your story.
Hold up a ring—Explain that before you get engaged to someone, you take the time to

really get to know him or her. You become friends first. Friendships take time, just as it takes time to really get to know a story. Say, **Before you ever try to practice your story, you need to get to know your story—not just meet it, but really get acquainted! The first phase of growing your story is** *getting to know* **your story.**

Discuss what this phase involves and how to implement it.

Phase Two: Test-driving your story.

Hold up a toy car—Observe that before you buy a car, you test-drive it. Before you can make a story your own, test-drive it. Hop inside and take it for a spin! Say, **The second phase you'll move through is** *test-driving* **your story. This is where you actually try it out!**

Discuss what this phase involves and how to implement it.

Phase Three: Paying attention to your story.

Hold up a glass of water—Explain that a river flowing through the countryside can be easily diverted into many channels until it has lost its force and slows to a trickle. Our attention spans are like that—they can be easily diverted. Say, **Both as you practice your story and as you tell your story, step into it and notice what's happening in the story.** *Paying attention to* **your story is phase number three!**

Discuss what this phase involves and how to implement it.

Phase Four: Navigating through your story.

Hold up an orange highway cone—Explain that if a road is closed and you don't know any alternate routes, you're stuck. Point out that there are many routes through a story, but when you memorize words, you only learn one road. If you forget the next word, you're stuck!

Then ask, **How many of you have ever told a joke or story and it was funny the first time around, but when you told it again it flopped? Me, too! Usually, when a joke flops, it's because we haven't adapted the story to the new situation and new audience.**

Discuss why it's important to be able to adapt a story to meet the expectations of your listeners. Point out that this is the reason most storytellers don't memorize their stories. Say, **Never tell the same story twice. Do I mean never repeat a story? After you spend all that time learning it, you can't tell it to another class someday? Well, yes . . . and no. Each time you tell a story, you're telling it at a different point in your life, to a different group of listeners with a different set of expectations. All of these factors will change (sometimes in very subtle ways) the manner in which you tell the story. Because of that, every time you tell a story is the first time you tell** *that* **story. The fourth phase is** *navigating through* **your story.**

Discuss what this phase involves and how to implement it. Use the handout, "Tips on Remembering Your Story."

Phase Five: Growing your story.

Hold up a packet of seeds—Explain that when you plant seeds, they grow naturally, and a bit mysteriously. Explain that as you work on developing a way to deliver a story, you grow it from the way it appears in the Bible. Say, **Phase five is the process of** *growing* **your story from your own personality and from the Scripture text itself.**

Give the examples from pages 34 and 35. Have someone suggest a Bible story and then discuss how to apply this phase to that story.

Phase Six: Developing your story.

Hold up a cookbook—Explain that when a chef begins mixing ingredients together, it's always with a specific goal in mind—the finished dish! In the same way, as you work on developing your story and mixing all the ingredients of gestures, voice, and movement together, you'll also keep your audience in mind and look for ways to help them connect with this story. Say, **The last phase is** *developing* **your story by keeping your listeners in mind as you learn the story. Find the best ways to connect your listeners to this story.**

Talk about the "Story Summary Worksheet" and point out the different ways to remember stories.

Closing Comments

Review and summarize these six phases. Then say, **Begin with prayer. Then let your story grow and develop. A key to good storytelling is orchestration, or putting all the pieces together so that the whole is greater than the sum of its parts. Rely on God and let him produce fruit in the lives of your listeners!**

Close with prayer.

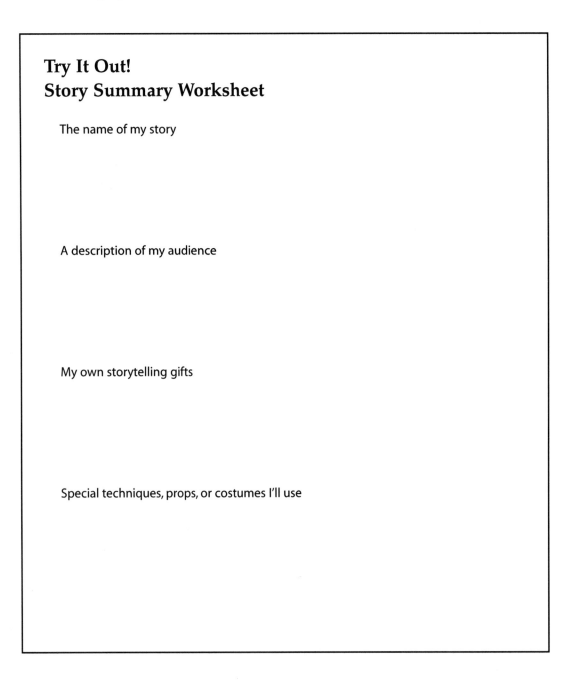

Try It Out!
Story Summary Worksheet

The name of my story

A description of my audience

My own storytelling gifts

Special techniques, props, or costumes I'll use

Hints on Rehearsing and Learning Your Stories

Phase One: _____ your story.
- Take the time to get acquainted with the story.
- Think about and talk about the story, but don't worry about perfecting it.
- Notes:

Phase Two: _____ your story.
- Try out the story. Explore the possibilities for retelling it.
- Read it aloud or talk through the story the best you can, but stay open to possible changes in the way you might tell it.
- Notes:

Phase Three: _____ your story.
- Focus your attention on the story. Picture its images. Be aware of what's happening in your story as you tell it. See the story as you tell it. Forget about performing it, just share it genuinely, moment by moment, from your heart.
- Each time you practice, remember and notice different aspects of the story. Pay particular attention to beginnings and endings. You really want to make sure the story starts and ends strong!
- Notes:

Phase Four: _____ your story.
- Practice the story, not the words. Tell the story with your whole body, not just your mouth.
- Never tell the same story twice. Avoid the temptation to memorize your story.
- Notes:

Phase Five: _____ your story.
- Let the way you tell the story grow from the way it's told in the Bible.
- Find a personal connection with the images or emotions of the story. What moments in the story draw you in or speak to you personally? Connect with those moments first, and then build the rest of the story around those sections.
- Notes:

Phase Six: _____ your story.
- Practice your story with the audience in mind.
- Include audience participation when appropriate. And have fun! If you're not having fun, neither are your listeners!
- Notes:

Tips on Remembering Your Stories

One of the best ways of remembering a story is to have more than one mental association with it. Each of these techniques will help you remember a story, but when you combine several together, they will make remembering your stories even easier!

1. **Episodes**—Remember a story by events, or episodes. Limit yourself to seven major events or it'll be too tough to keep them straight.

2. **Movement**—Movement triggers memory. The more gestures and movements you have, the easier the story will be to remember.

3. **Storyboarding**—Some people find that they can remember the story better if they draw a series of pictures that represent the scenes of the story. Each scene shows the progression of the action in the story. Don't worry about drawing masterpieces; just use simple pictures to help ignite your memory!

4. **Objects**—Objects, costumes, and props will help spark your memory. As you pick up each object, it'll help you remember the next section of the story.

5. **Images**—Some people imagine the story in their minds and watch it as though it were a film. Watch the story in fast forward to get the big picture, and then in slow motion to notice the details!

6. **Action**—Stories naturally progress to a climax. Just think about what has to happen next to move the story forward!

7. **Repetition**—If you can find events or phrases that are repeated throughout the story, it'll make it easier to remember.

8. **Practice**—You guessed it. Tell your story! Practice it different ways—while seated, walking around, with no gestures, or with no words! Tell your story whenever you can, over and over. By hearing your voice you'll learn what needs to change in the story.

9. **Encouragement**—Practice with a partner. Find someone who'll encourage you as you begin learning your story, and then give you constructive feedback as you develop and improve the way you tell it.

10. **Listening**—Video or audio tape your story and then listen to the way you tell it. If you do this, listen to the story several times and listen for (or look for) different things. First, listen for the overall impact. Second, listen for timing, pauses, and flow. Finally, listen for words or phrases that aren't as clear or concise as you'd like. Change them and improve!

11. **Outlining**—Outlining a story, summarizing it, or even writing down a version of it is helpful for some story learners.

12. **Questions**—Remember the story by the questions that are asked. In the story about the conversion of the Ethiopian official (see Acts 8:26-40), each time the Ethiopian spoke to Philip, he asked Philip a question. Each question resulted in a specific action. As you tell the story, you can use the natural progression of the questions to remember the order of events.

Question one—"How can I understand God's Word unless someone explains it to me?"
Resulting action—Philip got into the chariot.

Question two—"Is the prophet (Isaiah) writing about himself or someone else?"
Resulting action—Philip explained the gospel.

Question three—"Here is some water. Why shouldn't I be baptized?"
Resulting action—Philip and the man got out of the chariot and stepped into the water.

Workshop Presenter Notes for

Sing It Out!

How to Tell Stories with Music, Chants, Rhymes, and Refrains

Tips and Suggestions
- Feel free to adapt the ideas to fit the needs of the people at your workshop.

What You'll Need
- Photocopies of pages 156-158 for each student.
- If desired, gather musical instruments and CDs of sound effects.

What to Do Before You Begin
- Review chapter six and make sure you understand the concepts being taught.
- Read this section and practice saying the suggested comments. Decide how you'll make the transition from one activity to the next.
- Familiarize yourself with the student handouts. Distribute the handouts as the participants arrive.

Introductory Activity
Say, **Listen to what Paul writes in Ephesians 5:19, "Speak to one another with psalms, hymns, and spiritual songs. Sing and make music in your heart to the Lord." Did you notice the *two* audiences mentioned in that verse? Let me read it again.... Now, do you see them? The two audiences are God, and one another! An important way to share God's story with our students is through song and music!**

How to Develop and Include Chants and Refrains in the Stories You Tell
Point out that repetition appears throughout the Bible. God called repeatedly to Samuel in the Old Testament; each day of creation ended with the refrain, "And God looked at what he'd made, and it was good!"; and the story of "The Ten Plagues" contains many similar scenes as Moses confronts Pharaoh. Say, **Repetition helps people remember words and ideas. Repetition helps people remember words and ideas. Repetition helps people remember words and ideas. Repetition helps people remember words and ideas. What does repetition do?** (Encourage audience to respond.) **Right! So look for repetition in the stories you tell and then find ways of inviting the children to participate by saying, singing, or doing something each time the repetition occurs. For example, as Jesus feeds the crowd of more than five thousand people, the listeners could say, "We like it! We love it! We want more of it! We like it! We love it! We want more of it!"**

If time permits, tell the version of "The Good Samaritan" found in chapter six.

Say, **Let's practice! Get into groups of three or four people. I'm going to assign each group a different Bible story. I want each group to identify an idea, phrase, or thought that is carried through the story, and then come up with a refrain that expresses that idea or phrase. As you create your refrain, keep your audience in mind and choose whatever age group you like. You don't have to make your refrain rhyme. OK? Let's go!**

Go throughout the room and assign the following stories to different groups:

- The story of "Creation" (Genesis 1)
- The story of "The Prodigal Son" (Luke 15)
- The story of "The Grumbling Israelites" (Exodus 16, 17)
- The story of "The Three Guys in the Fiery Furnace" (Daniel 3)
- The story of "Daniel in the Lion's Den" (Daniel 6)

After a few minutes, have each group share their refrain. Draw their attention to the story entitled, "Keep First Things First!" Point out that it has a singable refrain the storyteller can use as she tells the story. Show how the refrain naturally makes the transition into the application of the story.

If time permits, explain that there is a story recorded in Jeremiah 37, 38 that is rarely included in Bible curricula. It's a story full of courage, intrigue, and adventure. Say, **Open your Bible and let's take a look at this story and how we might include "Call and Response Storytelling" or "Group Refrain Storytelling" techniques in a creative retelling of "The Adventures of Jeremiah!"**

Explain that in this story, Jeremiah was told by the Lord to tell the king that he should not resist the enemy. The king, however, is scared of what will happen and doesn't listen to Jeremiah. As a result, he is captured and imprisoned, just like Jeremiah warned.

There are three scenes in the story and each ends with a refrain already recorded in the Bible: "And Jeremiah remained in the courtyard of the guard" (this refrain appears in Jeremiah 37:21; 38:13; and 38:28).

Scene one: Jeremiah is thrown into prison.

Scene two: Jeremiah is thrown into a deep pit.

Scene three: Jeremiah meets secretly with the king.

With this repetition and refrain, you could easily tell a "Call and Response" story, in which the audience repeats the refrain when you cue them. Decide as a group if you would use this refrain or create a new one.

There are three main characters in the story:

1. Jeremiah, the bold prophet
2. Zedekiah, the wimpy king
3. Nasty city officials, out to get the prophet

Since all these characters appear in each scene, you could do a group refrain story! You could divide the audience into three groups and assign a phrase for each group to say every time you cue their group. For example,

Jeremiah: *(boldly, clearing his throat)* "I'll speak for the Lord no matter what!"

The King: *(wimpy, wringing his hands)* "But what's gonna happen to me?"

Officials: *(cruelly, pointing a mean finger)* "We'll get you yet, Jeremiah! We'll get you yet!"

As a group, write a "Group Refrain" version of this story and then have someone tell it.

Adding Music to the Stories You Tell

Discuss the seven ideas and as a group try to come up with an example of a Bible story for which you could use each technique. Examples are provided for you if your group has a hard time coming up with ideas:

- Make music with instruments—The story of Miriam leading dancing with her tambourine.

- Make music with your body—Pat your legs to represent walking as the Israelites wandered through the desert.

- Make music by singing—Write a short song about "The Parable of the Lost Sheep" to the tune of "Away in a Manger."

- Make music with a cheer, chant, or rap—Create a cheer that Mary Magdalene might have said (if she were a cheerleader) when she found out Jesus was alive!

- Make music by adding a choral response—When telling the story of "Daniel and the Lion's Den," have all the girls say, "You're lookin' really yummy! Come jump into my tummy!" and have the boys respond (pretending to pray), "Please, don't let those cats attack! I'd rather not become a snack!"

- Add mood music—When telling the story of Jesus' betrayal in the Garden of Gethsemane, play a tape of somber or scary music.

- Add sound effects—Use your mouths to create sound effects for the storm during the story of Jesus calming the waters.

Direct attention to the page titled "Examples of Music and Singing from the Bible." Point out the many ways to include music and singing in stories.

Closing Activity

End by encouraging all your teachers to take the time to study their stories and then work at finding creative, musical, participatory connections.

Say, **Remember when I read Ephesians 5:19 to start our workshop? Well, let me read it again, and this time include the next verse. "Speak to one another with psalms, hymns and spiritual songs. Sing and make music in your heart to the Lord, always giving thanks to God the Father for everything, in the name of our Lord Jesus Christ." Let's make these our goals as we teach: to communicate with each other, to praise God, and to always give thanks for everything. In fact, let's do it right now.**

Close with prayer.

How to Tell Stories with Music, Chants, Rhymes, and Refrains

How to Develop and Include Chants and Refrains

Use music, singing, or repetition to include your students in the story. Refrains should grow naturally from the story. Whenever you add music, chants, rhymes, or refrains to your stories, they should add to the story, not detract or distract from it.

Creating and using catchy refrains
- Look in the story for a recurring theme, a repetitious idea, or a refrain.

- Create a catchy chant, refrain, or chorus. Make the refrain something funny and appropriate. Add your own flavor, style, and personality to the story!

- Include a fun action or gesture to do while the refrain is being said.

- Teach the refrain to your students. (Be sure to cue the audience when to do their part!)

- Invite them to join you as you tell the story!

Two Techniques

In "Call And Response Storytelling," the audience says, sings, or acts out a part at specific times throughout the story.

In "Group Refrain Storytelling," different groups from the audience say, sing, or act out their parts when the storyteller cues them to do so.

As you look for ways to include these two creative storytelling techniques, follow these 6 steps:

1. Read all the way through the story.

2. Look for changes of scenery.

3. Look for repetition.

4. Ask, "What is this story about?"

5. Ask, "Who is the story about?"

6. Ask, "Do the main characters appear in each scene?"

• Keep First Things First! •

(based on Luke 10:38-42)

Once, long ago, in the town of Bethany, two sisters were preparing for Jesus to visit.

Mary peered out the window and watched the road so she could see him the moment he arrived.

Martha tried to quickly clean the house and get things ready.

"Aren't you gonna give me a hand? Just look at this mess! There's dirt all over the floor . . ."

"But Martha, there's supposed to be. We have a dirt floor!"

"My point exactly! And what about those pots? They look like they're covered with mud!"

"Martha, they're made of clay!"

"Oh."

Mary finally sighed and said . . .

Martha, Martha, why are you so worried?
Why are you so worried about these things?
Jesus is coming! Jesus is coming!
And he's more important than anything!

"That's my whole point! Jesus is coming and the house is a mess!"

"Oh, Martha."

Now, what do you think they were gonna have for supper? Pork? Chicken? Hamburgers? No, they ate a lot of lamb. Yup, they were gonna have lamb-burgers.

Suddenly, Martha gasped. "Oh my goodness! I'm all out of mayo and ketchup! What's Jesus gonna put on his lamb-burger?"

"Look Martha! He's here! Jesus is here!"

"He's here! But I haven't even set the table! The lamb-burgers aren't done!" And Mary turned to her and smiled and said:

Martha, Martha, why are you so worried?
Why are you so worried about these things?
Jesus is here! Jesus is here!
And he's more important than anything!

When Jesus came in, he sat down and started to talk to Mary. He told her a few of his favorite stories, and she sat spellbound, listening to every word. She sat beside Jesus' feet and listened and laughed and looked into his eyes.

But Martha was getting upset!

Finally, she went over to Jesus and said, "Jesus! Doesn't it even bother you that my sister is just sitting here doing nothing while I slave away over a hot stove—oh, wait, stoves haven't been invented yet—over a hot fire, roasting lamb-burgers? I'm doing all the work by myself! Tell Mary to give me a hand!"

But Jesus just turned to her and smiled and said:

Martha, Martha, why are you so worried?
Why are you so worried about these things?
Mary has chosen, Mary has chosen,
What is more important than anything.

And even today, we sometimes get more worried about the urgent things than the important ones. That's why God wants us to remember:

Children, children, why are you so worried?
Why are you so worried about these things?
Jesus is coming! Jesus is coming!
And he's more important than anything.

Adding Music to the Stories You Tell

- Make music with instruments
- Make music with your body
- Make music by singing
- Make music with a cheer, chant, or rap
- Make music by adding a choral response
- Add mood music
- Add sound effects

Examples of Music and Singing from the Bible

What Happened	Where It's Found	How to Apply This to Your Storytelling
When God delivered the Israelites, Miriam led a dance of song and praise!	Exodus 15:19-21	When telling this story, hand out banners or ribbons for the children to swirl and twirl! Use tambourines just like Miriam did to add music to your story! Make up your own praise dance!
When God provided water to the thirsty Israelites, they wrote a song to commemorate it!	Numbers 21:16-18	Think of a time when God has done something great in your life, or the life of your church. Then, write a short song about it to the tune of a popular song such as "Jingle Bells" or "Twinkle Little Star."
After Deborah and Barak conquered the Canaanite king, Jabin, they sang a victory song!	Judges 4, 5	Make up a victory chant or cheer (like you might hear at a basketball game) telling how great God is and how thankful you are that he is your God!
When Hannah's baby was born, she praised God with a joyful prayer.	1 Samuel 2:1-10	Write a lullaby that expresses joy, praise for God, and thanks for baby brothers, sisters, or babies in general. Write it to the tune of "Rock-a-Bye Baby."
When the ark was returned to Jerusalem, David sang and danced before the Lord to celebrate.	1 Chronicles 15:16–16:6	Think of a way we could celebrate God's goodness through music and movement! Pray to God by the way you creatively move around the room.
Often when David was in trouble, he wrote a song about it.	Psalms 3, 7, 18, 34, 51, 52, 54, 56, 57, 59, 60, 63, 142	Write a song based on something that has happened in your life. Or, have the class write a song that summarizes the Bible story you're studying.
Jehoshaphat conquered the armies of Ammon, Moab, and Mount Seir with a praise band!	2 Chronicles 20:1-30	What a great example of the power of praise! Retell this story with instruments and all the energy, enthusiasm, and praise to God that a spiritual war would require!
When Jehoiada was crowned king, there was a great concert with trumpets and song leaders and lots of musical instruments.	2 Chronicles 23:11-16	Use musical instruments to celebrate a special day in the life of your community, nation, or church. Let every child make his own simple instrument, or have enough on hand for each child to participate!
When the walls around Jerusalem were completed, Nehemiah celebrated with singing and choruses!	Nehemiah 12:27-43	Write two choruses or refrains for the story that you're telling. Divide the students into two groups. Assign each group a part. Then, retell the story with a choral response!
When Jesus' mother, Mary, visited Elizabeth, she burst into a song of praise to God.	Luke 1:46-55	Make up a song or poem about Jesus' birth as did the angels (Luke 2:13, 14) and Simeon (Luke 2:25-35). Zechariah also praised God for Jesus, and for his own son John (Luke 1:68-79).
Before Jesus and his friends left the Last Supper, they sang hymns to celebrate the Passover.	Mark 14:26	Find and learn Jewish folksongs or hymns. Or, have a snack of juice and crackers and remind yourself of Jesus' Last Supper. Sing songs before and after snack, or have background music playing during the snack.
When Paul and Silas were imprisoned, they sang songs through the night.	Acts 16:25	As you tell the story, sing a few favorite songs. Then say, "OK, kids! Let's get back to the story to see how Paul and Silas get out of jail!" Or, have a late-night sing-a-long in honor of Paul and Silas!

Workshop Presenter Notes for

Act It Out!

How to Tell Stories with Movement and Creative Dramatics

Tips and Suggestions
- Feel free to adapt the ideas to fit the needs of the people at your workshop.
- This is the longest workshop in the book. You'll probably need an hour if you demonstrate examples of all ten techniques!

What You'll Need
- Photocopies of pages 162, 163 for each student.
- Two copies of "Big Bad Naaman's Big Bad Bath" (pages 52, 53).
- A water pistol or spray bottle.

What to Do Before You Begin
- Review chapter seven and make sure you understand the concepts being taught.
- Read this section and practice saying the suggested comments. Decide how you'll make the transition from one activity to the next.
- Familiarize yourself with the student handouts. Distribute the handouts as the participants arrive.
- Prepare specific notes and activities for each of the ten techniques.

Opening Comments
Say, **This workshop is all about telling stories with movement and creative dramatics. So guess what we're gonna do in the workshop? Yup! We're gonna move, we're gonna be creative, and we're gonna be dramatic! So let's get started. Everybody stand up!**

1) Imaginary Journey
Lead the group on an "Imaginary Journey" to the stormy lake that Jesus calmed. Use your own words. Here is an example of what you might say:

"OK, let's pretend that we're no longer in this room, but that we're in the middle of a lake on a gently swaying boat. Sway with me. Good! OK, now pretend that the boat is REALLY swaying! The wind is picking up! It's blowing in your face! Grab onto something so you don't fall off the boat! Oh, no! Here comes the rain! (*If it's appropriate for your group, break out a water pistol or spray bottle and start squirting everyone!*)

"Wait, look over there! Some of the people on the boat are waking up a guy who was sleeping! It's Jesus! (*Keep swaying violently and then stop suddenly.*) He calmed the storm! Let's all sit down and find out what he has to say."

Explain to your group that they have just participated in an *"Imaginary Journey."* Point out reasons why this is a useful attention-getting drama activity.

2) Organic Storytelling

Say, **Our next technique is called** *"Organic Storytelling."* **With this technique, we'll grow a story based on audience suggestions! I'll show you how it works.**

Demonstrate an organic story based on the shepherd searching for his lost sheep. For example, begin by saying, **Once there was a shepherd who lost his sheep. Where do you think he looked first? A cave? Right! He looked in the cave. But there were no sheep. Where else might he have looked?** ...

3) Masks

Explain that real or imaginary *masks* can be used effectively for creative dramatics. Practice putting on imaginary masks, then invite a volunteer up front and have her look over the sample "Partner Masks" story below.

As you tell the story in your own words, let your volunteer respond to what you say.

Once upon a time, there was a giant named Goliath. *(Your partner stands on a chair and puts on a mean-looking mask.)* He was so frightening that the Israelite soldiers were terrified of him! *(Your partner steps down and puts on a frightened mask.)*

But there was a young shepherd boy named David who wasn't afraid. *(Partner puts on a brave mask.)* David knew that God was strong enough to protect him from the mean giant *(chair/Goliath mask)*. He walked right past the scared Israelites *(scared mask)* and faced the giant.

Since he trusted in God, he was very brave *(brave mask)*. Goliath just laughed at him *(mean, sneering face)* but David didn't care. He ran toward the giant and struck him in the forehead with a rock *(Goliath mask, and rub your head)*. With God's help, David killed the giant! *(Goliath mask, and stick out your tongue like a dead animal.)*

And everyone praised God! *(Partner puts on a reverent praise mask.)*

4) Pantomime

Say, *Pantomime,* **or mime, is the process of using your body to communicate.**

Explain "Human Sculpture" and "Narrative Pantomime." Direct the attention of the class to the information about "Using Narrative Pantomime" found on their handout. If desired, demonstrate a "Human Sculpture" or a "Narrative Pantomime."

5) Gestures and Finger Plays

Explain that using simple hand *gestures* is a great way to include children in a story. Discuss the best ways of doing this. Ask if anyone has already tried using gestures or *finger plays*. Discuss what types of stories they work best in, and, if time permits, share some examples with the group.

6) Audience Echo-Mime

Say, **The sixth creative drama technique is called** *"Audience Echo-Mime!"* Demonstrate this technique by doing a short example of "Big Bad Naaman's Big Bad Bath." Explain that this technique works best when you have a partner to do the actions while you read or tell the story.

7) Devotion in Motion (Creative Movement and Dance)

Explain that some stories lend themselves to creative movement or *"Devotion in Motion"* as a way of praising God! Encourage your teachers to look for ways to allow children to creatively express themselves with movement and with objects such as scarves or ribbons.

Discuss how you could use creative movement and toilet tissue to make children into mummies for a creative retelling of the story, "Jesus Raising Lazarus from the Dead" (John 11:1-44). If time permits, demonstrate!

8) Add-On Storytelling

Explain the process of *"Add-On Storytelling."* Then, as a group, tell an add-on story of the "The Prodigal Son" (see Luke 15:11-32). When you're done, say, **As you can see, this process works well as a way of reminding us we don't know as much as we think we do. It might be a good activity for those of you teaching preteens!**

9) Improvisation

Invite three volunteers forward and explain that you're going to give them a situation that relates to the story you just reviewed ("The Prodigal Son"). Have them decide who will play the part of the younger brother, who will be the older brother, and who will be the mother. Then give them this situation:

Reenact what happens when the older brother finally walks into the party and starts talking with his brother. What might have happened? What do you think he says? What happens next? What happens when their mother comes into the room? Make it up and act it out!

When they are finished, invite everyone else to give them wild and heartfelt applause for being brave enough to try this activity.

Say, **This is called** *improvisation,* **or improv. It is a great review activity and discussion starter, especially among older children!** Explain that when you use audience participation, if you say "no" to the actors, it'll drain energy out of your presentation. Strive to say, "Yes! And. . . ." Use whatever they give you and build on it. This is one of the keys to improvisation.

10) Guessing Games

Invite two volunteers up front. Assign one of them the role of being a statue, and the other the role of being a sculptor. Say, **Using just one finger, shape the statue's body into a character from the Old Testament doing something memorable! Go!**

After the sculpture is complete, have the audience try to guess who is being portrayed and what he or she is doing. Then have them switch roles and do it again, only this time portraying a New Testament character doing something he or she shouldn't have been doing!

Explain that when this type of *guessing game* is done with an individual, it's called "Frozen Poses."

Then explain "Scripture Snapshots." If desired, have a small group come forward and create a Scripture snapshot from the book of Daniel. See if the rest of the group can guess what scene is being portrayed!

Closing Comments

Say, **As you can tell, not all of these activities will work with every class. However, let's be on the lookout for ways of creatively incorporating more drama and movement into the stories we share. Let's close with a pop-up prayer of thanksgiving. All you need to do is pop up out of your seat and say something from this workshop or this day that you're thankful for. When we're all standing, we'll say "Amen!" together to end our prayer and our workshop. I'll go first.**

How to Tell Stories with Movement and Creative Dramatics

1) _____ Journey
- Can be told before the story, to set the stage for the storytelling event.
- Can be woven through the story, interspersed with narration.
- Can be interspersed with monologues by other teachers.
- Can be continued through the telling of the whole story.

2) _____ Storytelling
- Start with the framework of the story, and add details.
- Use whatever the audience suggests, no matter how bizarre!

Using Narrative Pantomime

1. With older children, don't tell the story first. Let them be surprised by the action as you read it and they act it out. With younger children, tell the story first and then say, "Let's have some fun and act out this story!" That way, they'll have an idea of what's happening while they act it out.
2. Encourage the actors to be a little silly and have fun. Choose volunteers who'll ham it up for the audience—if they're too shy and intimidated, the story won't work.
3. Accept whatever happens onstage and respond to it. If people say or do something unexpected, weave it into the story. Don't get upset about it, just accept it and use it!
4. Prompt the players. Give them instructions, look at them, and smile as you read the parts of the story in which they're involved. When necessary, prompt them on what to do.
5. You may wish to check out different Bible translations to find the one that sounds most natural when told or read aloud.
6. Limit the number of volunteers. If you have too many people, you may have a difficult time involving them all in the story. This storytelling technique is fun to watch, so be sure you have enough people in the audience to enjoy what's happening onstage!
7. Sit in the audience when you read the story. The actors will naturally look at you as you read the story. By sitting in the audience, you can assure that the actors will face the audience as they act out the story.
8. When the drama is over, lead the audience in applauding for the actors and then have them sit back down.

3) _____
- Imaginary
- Real

4) _____
- Human Sculpture
- Narrative Pantomime

5) _____
- Can be done with fingers!
- Can be done with arms!
- Can be done with feet!

6) _____ Echo-Mime
- Keep the stories short, but action packed.
- Make sure your partner is familiar with the movements of the story before you begin telling it.

7) Devotion in _____ (Creative Movement and Dance)
- Consider handing out dowel rods, streamers, banners, ribbons, or scarves and letting the children explore creative movement during part or all of your story.
- Look for ways to incorporate more creative movement and expression in your lessons.

8) _____ Storytelling
- Use this technique when children think they already know the story really well.
- Tell the story a line at a time as a large group, then compare your version with the version found in Scripture!

9) _____
- Create situation cards that you can hand out to small groups of your students.
- Explore issues related to the lessons of your story through role playing.

10) Guessing _____
- Frozen Poses
- Scripture Snapshots

Fifteen Sure-fire Ways to Mess Up any Audience Participation Story

1. Demand that everyone join in. If the children don't feel comfortable or safe joining in, make them do it anyway! Be sure to embarrass those who don't.

2. Don't bother to teach the students what to do, when to do it, or when to stop. They should be able to figure it out on their own if they'd just pay closer attention!

3. Plan plenty of embarrassing actions that will be offensive to members of your class.

4. Expect the students to do everything perfectly the first time through. Cringe, scream, beat your chest, and throw a tantrum if they don't.

5. When you're done, never do a cool-down activity. Leave the children wild and rowdy. Parents will love you for it!

6. Use class participation techniques in lieu of story preparation. As long as you have lots of stuff to do during the story, you don't need to do a quality job of telling the story!

7. If children have settled in comfortably, be sure to ask them to stand up and sit down repeatedly throughout your performance. It won't be distracting!

8. Never cue the students by nodding your head to them, pausing, or signaling in some way for them to join you. They should be able to read your mind and know precisely when you want them to participate.

9. If you make a mistake or forget a section of your story, break into tears, apologize profusely, run from the room, and never tell another story again.

10. Make certain that all story refrains are difficult, long, and confusing. This way the students will be forced to pay better attention.

11. If you hand out props, become angry if they get damaged, lost, or become a distraction during the story.

12. When you call volunteers up front, never introduce them to the class, make them stand for a long time with nothing to do, and then tell them to sit down because they weren't needed!

13. Use plenty of finger plays, felt-board stories, nursery rhymes, and picture books with preteens. They love acting like kindergartners in front of their friends!

14. When receiving suggestions from the class, point out the stupidest ideas and invite everyone to laugh at the person who offered them.

15. Most important of all, keep in mind that you want the students to remember your gimmicks, rather than your story!

Workshop Presenter Notes for

Costumes and Props

How to Use Stuff to Tell Stories

Tips and Suggestions
- Feel free to adapt the ideas to fit the needs of the people at your workshop.
- Get as elaborate or as simple as you like with this workshop. The more props and costume pieces you bring, the more ideas you'll generate!

What You'll Need
- Photocopies of pages 166, 167 for each student.
- Two large sheets of paper (posters). One that says, "That was good!" And another that says, "That was bad!"
- Gather the following costume pieces and props: sunglasses, scarves, hats, overcoats, paper, scissors, dowel rods or chop sticks, clay, and balloons.
- A treat for the winning cluster (see introductory activity), if desired.

What to Do Before You Begin
- Review chapter eight and make sure you understand the concepts being taught.
- Read this section and practice saying the suggested comments. Decide how you'll make the transition from one activity to the next.
- Familiarize yourself with the student handouts. Distribute the handouts as the participants arrive.
- Arrange your costume pieces and props for easy access during the workshop.

Introductory Activity
Say, **Divide into groups of people with the same eye color as you have. Ready? Go!** After the groups have formed, move people wherever you need to in order to create groups of four to five people.

Explain that for today's workshop, each group will be a separate Creativity Cluster. Say, **In a moment we're going to play a game. I'll give each cluster a hundred points for every idea they come up with, and a thousand points for every idea they come up with that no other cluster thinks of! You'll have thirty seconds. Jesus often used objects in his teaching. In each Creativity Cluster, see how many objects you can think of that Jesus used to teach spiritual truth. Ready? Go!**

Share ideas as a large group. Total the number of points. If desired, give the winning cluster a treat.

Tell the participants that in today's workshop, they'll be looking for ways of doing the same thing Jesus did—making our lessons stick by using stuff to tell stories!

Making the Connection

Explain that the first step in creating ways to use objects and costumes in storytelling is to limit yourself. Say, **You need to start somewhere. Let's practice each of the three steps listed on your handout to see how this process works. First, let's decide on a Bible story. Pretend we're telling the story of baby Moses being placed in a basket in the Nile River. What types of props or costumes could we use to help us creatively retell that story?**

Allow them to work in their clusters. After a few minutes, encourage them to think outside the box and come up with some really unusual objects that would work for the story. Share as a large group.

Then say, **OK, great! Now, let's decide on an object first** (*point to a chair*). **Let's start with this chair. Who can think of a Bible story that we could use this chair to help us tell? Let's see if we can come up with ten different uses or Bible stories for which we could use this chair as a prop!**

After gathering ideas for the chair, say, **OK. This time I want one person in the room to name a Bible story, and someone else to name a simple prop. We'll see if there are any ways we can use that prop to tell that specific story. What Bible story should we use? And what is our prop going to be? OK, here we go.**

Point out that selecting your objects isn't a complex process! You simply make a decision, brainstorm connections, and then evaluate your options!

Using Costumes

Share the example found on page 57 on retelling the Old Testament story of Joseph with costume changes. Say, **We don't know for sure if this technique was used, but it sure would have been a helpful way of remembering the story!**

Hand out a variety of costume pieces (such as sunglasses, scarves, hats, overcoats, etc.) to each cluster. Allow each cluster to decide which Bible story they think that costume piece would work best in, and then share ideas as a large group!

Using Props

Invite two volunteers to come forward. With their help, tell the story, "That Was Good! That Was Bad!" found on page 61. You'll need two signal cards for this activity.

Draw attention to the specific props listed on the handout and explain that you'll be exploring a few other props in the remaining minutes of the workshop.

Say, **As a cluster, decide which Bible story you would like to retell. Then send one person from your group up here and I'll give him or her a prop. You'll have five minutes to come up with a creative way of using that prop to tell that story. Go ahead and decide on your story. When you're ready, send a volunteer up front and I'll give you your prop. Go!**

As volunteers come forward, hand them props such as paper and scissors, dowel rods or chop sticks, clay, balloons, or whatever else you come up with.

Closing Comments

Say, **Let's review the process for creatively integrating props and costumes into your storytelling. First, make a decision based on the three choices at the top of your handout. Second, brainstorm connections. And third, evaluate your options and get started!**

Invite a volunteer to close the session in prayer.

Costumes and Props
How to Use Stuff to Tell Stories

Introduction—Find the Connection

1) Decide on a Bible story and then brainstorm what types of props you might use as you tell it.

2) OR, decide on an object and then brainstorm possible Bible stories to use it with.

3) OR, decide on a Bible story AND an object and then brainstorm possible ways you can use that object to tell that story!

After brainstorming ideas, decide which ideas are possible, practical, and will work with your students. Look for costumes and props that are simple to use and have a natural connection with the story. Practice the story a few times to see if it'll really work, make the necessary changes, and—presto! You're ready to go!

Notes on Using Costumes

Notes on Using Props
1. Signal Cards

a) Cue the audience to say a short phrase at specific points in the story.

b) Make the cards large enough for everyone to see. You could also use overhead transparencies.

2. Manipulatives

a) Curl, cut, shape, twist, or mold objects to help you tell a story. This usually works best with smaller classes.

b) Look for stories with specific objects, shapes, or transformations. These types of stories work best, because you can show the changes in the story by the way you manipulate the object.

3. Puppets

a) If your puppet has a mouth, open and close the mouth as you would your own mouth, on each syllable! Don't make the puppet look like a badly dubbed movie!

b) Keep your puppet moving all the time. Movement provides the illusion that the puppet is alive. As soon as it stops moving, it stops looking real!

c) Turn your puppet's head to face the person (or group of people) she is talking to.

4. Felt Boards

a) Remember that the felt figures are there to help you tell the story; don't let them become distracting. If they fall down or curl over or don't stick right, the children will be distracted and lose their focus on the story.

b) When you tell a story with a felt board, you lose eye contact with the children. They'll be focused on the felt figures. Some storytellers use a felt apron or vest. If you do that, you can tell the story on yourself! That way, you become the stage and as you pull the figures off yourself, all of the attention goes back to you as you continue telling the story!

Wiggles and Giggles

**How to Creatively Tell Stories
to Young Children**

Tips and Suggestions

- Feel free to adapt the ideas to fit the needs of the people at your workshop.

What You'll Need

- Photocopies of pages 170, 171 for each student.

What to Do Before You Begin

- Review chapter nine and make sure you understand the concepts being taught.
- Read this section and practice saying the suggested comments. Decide how you'll make the transition from one activity to the next.
- Choose one story from the four sample stories included in the chapter. Practice telling it and prepare to use it as an example during the workshop.
- Familiarize yourself with the student handouts. Distribute the handouts as the participants arrive.

Introductory Activity

Say, **Before we look at specific ways of telling stories to young children, let's remind ourselves what young children are really like. I'm going to yell out an age, and I want you to begin acting like people who are that old! OK? Everyone stand up, and start walking around a little bit.**

As you do this activity, give them enough time to act like each age group. Have fun and encourage them to ham it up a little!

Say, **Here we go. . . . Act like you're forty-five . . . hmm . . . not bad. . . . Alright . . . Act like you're thirty. . . . OK, now fifteen. . . . Ten. . . . Five. . . . Three. . . . One. . . . Zero. . . . Good job!**

After the activity is finished, have the group share insights into what young children are like. By the time you're finished, be sure you've mentioned the following:

- Young children love to move, play, and wiggle—it's how they pay attention!
- Young children love to pretend.
- Young children can't sit still for long.
- Young children would rather hear a story told than explained.
- Young children can't understand abstract concepts.
- Young children are easily distracted.

Say, **As we look at how to tell stories to young children, remember these concepts and look for ways to use them to communicate with your class.**

Step One: Study the story.

Explain that before a pilot taxis down the runway to take off, he knows where he's going to land. He begins with his destination in mind. Say, **Storytellers do the same thing! We** always begin with the end in mind. We start by looking at the end of the story first! The first step is always to *study the story*. The beginning of a story is more than just the first thing that happens. The beginning is the originating action, the one that sets in motion all that will follow. And the end is the resolution. So look closely at the story as a whole. Ask what's going on, what's being taught, and who the story is really about.

Encourage your teachers to choose appropriate stories for telling. You may want to use King David as an example. His adventures were often bloody, brutal, and very graphic. His sins (murder, adultery, and pride) resulted in the deaths of tens of thousands of people! Yet, David is a favorite for curriculum authors of stories for young children! You'll find his showdown with Goliath in nearly every Bible curriculum for young children. Be careful to include only appropriate content!

Say, **The younger the children you're speaking to, the shorter you'll want to make the stories you're telling.**

Step Two: Involve your audience.

Say, **Look for ways of including the children in the story as you tell it.** Tell the sample story that you've prepared from chapter nine.

Tell your teachers to prepare their stories with their students in mind. Say, **The first thing to look for in a story is *action*. Anytime you can find action in a story, you can find a way to include your students.**

Use the story of "Jesus Feeds More than Five Thousand" as an example (see Mark 6:30-44). Review the story if necessary. Then say, **Let's think about this story. What actions happen in this story that we could act out with our students?** Gather ideas. Remind your teachers that actions can include wiggling fingers, using gestures, and even moving your whole body!

Repeat this process looking for *sounds, repetition,* and *objects.* Say, **You may wish to use a surprise bag when you tell stories. As you tell the story, pull out objects for the students to see, smell, touch, or taste! They'll pay close attention because they'll wonder what you're going to pull out next!**

Remind your teachers that you won't necessarily include all of these ideas in a single story. But encourage them to include at least one of the four involvement ideas, and use it throughout the story. Review by saying, **After you've studied the content of the story, look for ways to include *action, sounds, repetition,* or *objects* to involve the students in your storytelling time.**

If time permits, break into groups of four or five and have the different groups share how they would use one of the four ideas (action, sounds, repetition or objects) to tell a specific story to children. Allow each group to retell the story to the rest of the teachers at the workshop.

Step Three: Put it all together.

Remind your teachers to let the way they tell the story grow out of their own personality, gifts, and interests. Say, **It's more important for you to connect with the students than for you to read the story as it's found in your Bible curriculum. The lesson plan may have some good ideas in it, but you know your students best. Feel free to change the story to relate better to your students!**

Draw attention to the tips on their handouts. Remind your teachers not to ask too many questions because questions can distract children from the story. Also, remind them to end the lesson with a clear application.

Closing Activity

Spend time praying for each other and for your students.

Wiggles and Giggles
How to Creatively Tell Stories to Young Children

Introduction: Some Observations About Young Children

Step One: _____ the _____ by asking yourself:

- What is going on here?

- What is this story really about?

- Who is the main character of this story?

- What might I need to change in this story to tell it to young children?

Step Two: Look for ways of involving the children in the story as you tell it.

- Involvement idea 1—Look for _____

- Involvement idea 2—Look for _____

- Involvement idea 3—Look for _____

- Involvement idea 4—Look for _____

Step Three: Put it all together.

- Practice your story, but don't try to memorize it.

- Feel free to change the story and adapt it (even while you're telling it)!

- Trust that God will use you to impact young lives when you're faithful in serving him.

Ten Tips for Telling Stories to Young Children

1 Speak with Respect

A strange thing happens to many otherwise normal adults when they start to tell stories to young children. They begin talking in a sappy, singsongy voice that doesn't sound real or genuine! Don't talk down to your students. Instead, talk to them in a natural, energetic, and lively way that doesn't belittle them.

2 Choose Appropriate Stories

Some stories in Scripture deal with themes and issues that young children aren't ready to understand or even hear about. Parents disagree about what their children should be exposed to at a young age. So, be honest, but not always forthcoming about what information appears in the stories you're teaching young children. Avoid dealing with sex, violence, adult themes, and adult language in your stories. Leave out graphic details that young kids aren't ready to hear.

3 Start at the End

Before beginning to work on your story, read through the story in the Bible. Look at what comes before and after the story to see the context in which it was told. Take the time to really study and get to the heart of the story. Then look for the main point of the story and see who it's really about. Avoid stories with too many characters or too much symbolism. Ask yourself, "Will my students really understand this story?" Especially with younger children, ask what changes in wording, content, or order you may need to make to the story.

4 Create Simple Refrains

Look for repetition, simple plots, and simple resolutions. Nail down the main idea and then add a chant, movement, or instrument.

5 Stay Focused on the Story

Rather than asking lots of questions before or during the story (which can distract the children), stay focused on the action and emotion of the story. As you tell the story, look at your children. Look at their faces to see if they understand and enjoy the story. You can usually tell if you're making a story too long or too frightening by the size of your students' eyes! Keep the stories short, simple, and action-packed!

6 Look for Connections

As you study and prepare your story, look for sounds, actions, and refrains in the story. If you can find ways to connect the story to music, creative dramatics, or movement, you'll be able to include audience involvement.

7 Tell the Story Your Own Way

Tell the story in your own words; don't try to remember the "right" words. Use natural gestures. Some people talk with their hands. If that's natural for you, great! If not, don't try to imitate someone else. Do what's most natural for you. Funny faces, funny voices, and silly costumes will work well for this age group!

8 Move Through the Story

Let your body help you tell the story. If a character in your story is large and scary, stand big and lower your voice. If the character is tiny, scrunch up small and raise your voice. As you practice the story, practice your movement and gestures.

9 Tell the Story First

Many lesson plans include good ideas for audience participation, but before inviting young children to act out a story, always tell the whole story so that the children understand what's going on and can remember the sequence of events. After telling the whole story say, "OK, everyone! Now, let's have some fun with this story! Let's act it out!"

10 Relax and Enjoy

Smile and have fun as you tell your stories. Value this time of connection with your students! Tell the story with lots of expression and don't be afraid to look silly. Rely on God and let him work through you!

Workshop Presenter Notes for

"Been There, Done That!"

**How to Connect with
Older Elementary Students**

Tips and Suggestions
- Feel free to adapt the ideas to fit the needs of the people at your workshop.

What You'll Need
- Two copies of "No Iguanas Allowed" (pages 70, 71).
- One copy of "The One That Didn't Get Away" (page 72).
- Five copies of "The Bravest Beauty Queen" (pages 74, 75).
- Photocopies of pages 174, 175 for each participant.

What to Do Before You Begin
- Review chapter ten and make sure you understand the concepts being taught.
- Read this section and practice saying the suggested comments. Decide how you'll make the transition from one activity to the next.
- Familiarize yourself with the student handouts. Distribute the handouts as the participants arrive.

Introductory Activity
Say, **Imagine that you're fifth and sixth grade students who've heard the same Bible stories every year for the last eight years. Your teacher walks up front and starts telling the story of Jonah. What are you thinking? Write down your reaction in the space provided on your handout.**

Give them time to respond. Then discuss characteristics and expectations of preteens. Say, **In today's workshop, you'll learn ways to grab and keep the attention of preteens by using seven creative storytelling techniques that they'll enjoy.**

Technique One: Tandem Storytelling
Demonstrate this technique by inviting two volunteers to read "No Iguanas Allowed." Say, **The first technique is called *"Tandem Storytelling."*** Point out that with this technique, you need two storytellers who are willing to spend the time practicing a story together.

Technique Two: Fill-in Storytelling
Demonstrate this technique by telling the fill-in story found on page 72, "The One that Didn't Get Away." Then say, **The second technique for preteens is called *"Fill-in Storytelling."***

Technique Three: Contemporary Retelling

Say, **The third technique is called** *"Contemporary Retelling."* **Let's do this with one of the stories Jesus told!**

Explain that in Matthew 25:1-13, Jesus told "The Parable of the Ten Virgins." Review, read, or tell the story to make sure people are familiar with it.

Say, **The secret to telling a story in a contemporary way is to find connections between the Bible story and the world of your students. Think of the life of a twelve-year-old today, and let's brainstorm some ways to complete the sentences on your handout.**

- Instead of going out to meet the bridegroom, the girls could be . . .
- Instead of forgetting to buy oil, they could have forgotten to . . .
- Instead of being locked out of the wedding, they could be denied . . .

Draw attention to the section "What Is This Story Similar To?" included on the handout.

Technique Four: Reader's Theater

Invite five people up front (if possible—three men and two women), and hand them each a copy of the script for "The Bravest Beauty Queen" (page 74). Allow them a moment to look over the scripts, and then demonstrate this technique.

Explain that this technique is called *"Reader's Theater."*

Technique Five: What If? Storytelling

Explain this technique and read the story on page 76 if time permits. Say, **The fifth technique is called** *"What If? Storytelling."*

Technique Six: Monologues

Point out that *monologues* can be told from the perspective of any of the characters in the story, but they're most effective when the lesson the character learns can be easily transferred to the lives of your students.

Technique Seven: Spontaneous Melodrama

If time permits, demonstrate the spontaneous melodrama found on page 80. Then say, **The last creative storytelling technique for preteens is** *"Spontaneous Melodrama."*

Closing Comments

Say, **By using these seven techniques, you can create humorous, inviting, and active ways of retelling Bible stories that your preteens will identify with and enjoy!**

End with prayer.

How to Connect with Older Elementary Students

Introduction

Technique One: _____ Storytelling
- Two people tell a story together, alternating speaking parts. They take turns playing the part of different story characters while the story is told.
- This technique takes a little extra time and effort, but the results are worth it!
- Variation—Two people act out a discussion. For example, two actors could play the two disciples walking on the road to Emmaus (Luke 24:13-34), or the two spies in Jericho (Joshua 2). They carry on their conversation in a dialogue that the audience gets to witness!

Technique Two: _____ Storytelling
- Write down the story, leaving out some key words.
- Fill-in the blanks with suggestions from the audience.

Technique Three: _____ Retelling (Matthew 25:1-13)
- Find connections between the biblical story and the lives of your listeners.
- Retell the Bible story by changing the place, events, or characters to make the story more contemporary.
- Instead of going out to meet the bridegroom, the girls could be . . .
- Instead of forgetting to buy oil, they could have forgotten to . . .
- Instead of being locked out of the wedding, they could be denied . . .

What Is This Story Similar To?
"The Four Soils" (Luke 8:4-15)
• Story Summary—Ask, "What is this story about?" In this story, a farmer scatters seeds along the path. Only a small percentage of the seeds take root and produce fruit. The other seeds are eaten, trampled, or choked out.

• Story Similarity—Ask, "What (in today's world) is this story like?" This is similar to . . . sending out an e-mail message with a link to a great new web site. Some of your friends delete the message, others ignore it, still others save it but never read it. Only those who take the time to read it and apply it (by logging on) will benefit.

• Story Starter—Once upon a time, there was a kid who discovered a great new web site where he could download some of the coolest games on the web for free. He decided to let his friends know about this new site by e-mailing each of them the link to the site. . . .

"The Good Samaritan" (Luke 10:25-37)
• Story Summary—Ask, "What is this story about?" In this story, a hurting man is ignored by two religious leaders and then helped by someone who would typically be his enemy.

• Story Similarity—Ask, "What (in today's world) is this story like?" This is similar to . . .

• Story Starter—

Tell a Story from an Object's Point of View

- **Elijah's cloak** tells of his adventures with the famous prophet and his young apprentice; "I still remember the day he slipped me on…."
- The **book of the law** that had been lost and forgotten tells what it was like to be found and read once again; "It was dark and lonely. I didn't think anyone would ever read me again. But then one day, the lights went on…."
- The **sandals that didn't wear out** share their version of the Israelite's trek through the wilderness; "Whew! You wouldn't believe the smell of some of those feet!…"
- **David's slingshot** recalls what it was like to be used to slay the giant; "Yeah, Dave was my owner, alright. And we had lots of adventures…."
- **Moses' staff** shares about the plagues and miracles; "Ol' Mo and I, we go way back! We first met when he started working as a shepherd out there in the hills…."

Technique Four: Reader's _____

- This technique is easy, fun, and engaging for students.
- Choose volunteers who are comfortable and confident being onstage.
- Variation—Read part of the story and then tell part of the story.

Technique Five: _____ Storytelling

- Ask yourself how a story might have ended. Look for ways to use this technique to spark interest and discussion.
- Take children by surprise when you tell this type of story. Let them start thinking, "That's not the way that story is supposed to go . . . is it?"
- Variation—Pretend you're a TV reporter. Pull out your imaginary microphone and briefly interview students. You can poke fun at your own story, create interactive sections to the story, or provide an interlude between stories. You can even have one person pretend to be a Bible character and interview her!

Technique Six: _____

- Tell the story from the point of view of one of the characters in the story.
- Don't limit yourself to people! You can also tell a story from the perspective of God, Satan, angels, demons, animals, and even objects!
- Variation—As you tell a story, one person from the audience calls out a different character or emotion. You immediately take on that character's personality (or the new emotion) and continue telling the story. It can be a little tricky, but it's lots of fun!

Technique Seven: Spontaneous _____

- Volunteers act out the story as it is told (or read).
- Notice how each character has a specific time to be onstage, and something active to do. When they're done with their part, they leave the stage until they're brought back onstage by the continuing action of the story.

Workshop Presenter Notes for

Seconds, Anyone?

How to Cook Up a Tasty Delivery

Tips and Suggestions

- Feel free to adapt the ideas to fit the needs of the people at your workshop. You may wish to skip some activities and simply explain the next ingredient.
- You may need to remind students that this workshop is not about the ingredients of a story, but rather the ingredients (or skills) of a storyteller. (See chapter three for a better understanding of story structure.)

What You'll Need

- A dry erase board and markers (or another means of recording the ideas in the introductory activity). Remember to write the words large enough so that everyone in the workshop can see them.
- Photocopies of page 179 for each student.
- A handkerchief, stick, or chalkboard eraser for ingredient seven.

What to Do Before You Begin

- Review chapter eleven and make sure you understand the concepts being taught.
- Read this section and practice saying the suggested comments. Decide how you'll make the transition from one activity to the next.
- Familiarize yourself with the student handout. Distribute the handout as the participants arrive.

Introductory Activity

Explain the cake analogy found on page 83. Then say, **Let's brainstorm the ingredients to telling a good story. What are some of the things a storyteller uses to create the world of the story in the minds of her listeners?**

As the participants provide suggestions, record them on the dry erase board. Draw attention to any extra ideas they come up with. Then teach the eight ingredients found in this chapter.

Ingredient One: Voice

Ask, **Can any of you make a strange sound with your voice? Let's practice some weird sounds.** As people volunteer, have everyone else imitate the sounds the volunteers make. If participants are hesitant to volunteer at first, suggest sounds such as a creaky door, wind blowing through the trees, an owl, seagulls, crickets, the giant Goliath, little tiny Zacchaeus, etc. After this activity, explain a few of the suggestions for caring for your voice. Then say, **The first ingredient the storyteller uses is his or her *voice*.**

Ingredient Two: Face

Say, **Reach under your chair and grab the box of imaginary masks that I put under there. Everyone ready? I'm going to put on a mask and I want you to put on the same** mask. **Let's practice.** Practice putting on happy, sad, angry, fearful, confused, and surprised masks. Explain the importance of using your face to express emotions and characterizations in stories. Then say, **The second ingredient the storyteller uses is his or her** *face.* Discuss how your face communicates what's going on in your heart, and how it can be used to express the emotions of the story.

Ingredient Three: Eyes

Invite the people in the workshop to get a partner. Then say, **I want you to recite the nursery rhyme "Mary Had a Little Lamb" to your partner without looking away from his or her eyes. The shortest person may go first. You may begin.** Allow each partner to take a turn. Then have them say it without making any eye contact at all. Discuss how eye contact affects communication and how and when it is most effective. Then say, **The third ingredient the storyteller uses is his or her** *eyes.* Explain principles of effective eye contact.

Ingredient Four: Posture

Say, **We've talked about four ingredients so far. Let's start seeing how three of them work together! With the same partner you had before, try to communicate the emotion I will write on the board using only your facial expression, eye contact, and posture. Your partner will try to guess what emotion you're expressing. Actors, turn to face me; guessers, face the back of the room. The first emotion is:** (write on the board, "You are shy.") **Begin.** Try angry, deceptive, intimidating, embarrassed, distracted, devious, or romantic. Do one emotion, then switch roles. Repeat as many times as desired. Then say, **The fourth ingredient the storyteller uses is his or her** *posture.*

Ingredient Five: Movement

Invite everyone to stand and begin milling around the room greeting each other and shaking hands as if they're attending a party. Then say, **As I yell out a Bible character, I want you all to start not only standing, but walking around as you imagine that person would have. Ready? The first is Moses—begin.** Remind them to keep in mind the size, age, and personality of the character. Try other characters such as Absalom, Methuselah (the oldest guy in the Bible), Goliath, Zacchaeus, John the Baptist, and Mary, the mother of Jesus. Experiment with characters of different ages, carrying different items, or thinking about different things. Then say, **The fifth ingredient the storyteller uses is** *movement.*

Ingredient Six: Gestures

Say, **Movement leads us naturally to the next ingredient—***gestures.* **Pretend that you're Jonah telling your fish story to the people of Nineveh—but you've lost your voice! Share your story with a partner using only gestures, movement, and expressions. Go ahead!** When you're finished, discuss how no one practiced their gestures before telling the story, they just did what seemed natural. The same is true for telling stories when we actually do practice them; natural-looking gestures are a must!

Ingredient Seven: Imagination

Hand out an object such as a handkerchief, stick, or chalkboard eraser to the group. Then say, **Let's see if we can come up with twenty different uses for this object that are not what people would normally use this object for. If you have an idea, raise your hand and we'll pass the object to you. Ready? Let's begin!** After doing the first object, explain that with the next object you want to limit the ideas to telling Bible stories. See if you can come up with ten different uses or ten specific Bible stories for each object. Point out that props or costumes can be useful for telling stories as long as they don't distract from the story.

Then say, **The seventh ingredient is** *imagination.* Explain that imagination is at the heart of our faith. How can we believe in the unseen without imagination? God is an imaginative and creative God who made us in his image. And when we tell stories, we use our imaginations to construct the images that we communicate to our listeners. Say, **You've been using your imaginations all afternoon (morning) especially coming up with all those ideas for using props! OK, let's move on to the last ingredient for today—the secret ingredient.**

Secret Ingredient Eight: Yourself

Explain that when a great cook bakes a cake, she often adds that special ingredient that makes the cake indescribably delicious. Say**, As storytellers who share God's story, we have a secret ingredient, too—ourselves. Turn to the person sitting next to you and stick out your tongue. Go ahead! Scientists tell us that just like a fingerprint, every one of us has a unique tongue print! There's no one else in the world with the same tongue print (or fingerprint) as you. You are unique. And the secret ingredient to add is** *yourself!* **When you tell stories, don't try to imitate how someone else would do it. Instead, use the gifts, talents, personality, and abilities God's Spirit has equipped you with. Tell the story with your own style, flair, and personality. That's the way God intended it!** You may wish to point out that God has always used people telling his story in their own unique way:
- Solomon used proverbs, parables, sayings, and riddles (Proverbs 1:6).
- Paul reasoned through public debate, logic, and argumentation (Acts 17:2, 3).
- The man Jesus healed of blindness simply shared his own story (John 9:9-11, 25).
- Luke carefully investigated everything and wrote Jesus' detailed biography (Luke 1:3, 4).

Closing Comments

Summarize by referring back to the cake analogy. Say, **Remember, the key is to bake up a story that tastes great! The more you develop expertise in these eight areas, the more tasty your stories will become—as long as you add just the right amount of each ingredient to each story!**

Allow time for questions and answers. If time permits, work on a particular story, using some of the activities described in this chapter.

Seconds, Anyone?
How to Cook Up a Tasty Delivery

Ingredient One: _____

Activity—Weird mouth sounds

Ingredient Two: _____

Activity—Masks

Ingredient Three: _____

Activity—Look deep into my eyes!

Ingredient Four: _____

Activity—Guess the emotion

Ingredient Five: _____

Activity—Biblical party

Ingredient Six: _____

Activity—The fish story

Ingredient Seven: _____

Activity—Twenty ideas

The Secret Ingredient Eight: _____

Activity—Tongue prints

The more you explore these storytelling ingredients, the more natural and comfortable you'll feel using them. It's like learning a foreign language; you need to expand your vocabulary and then you can begin to feel comfortable talking in more and more elaborate sentences!

Practice takes time, but the more you expand the vocabulary of your vocal range, facial expressions, body movement, and gestures, the more intricate and wonderful your stories will be!

Five Storytelling Secrets

**Foolproof Ways to Improve
Your Delivery**

Tips and Suggestions
- Feel free to adapt the ideas to fit the needs of the people at your workshop.

What You'll Need
- Photocopies of page 182 for each student.
- A one-dollar or five-dollar bill.
- A dry erase board and markers.
- A rope that's just long enough for each person in your group to hold onto it with two hands, standing shoulder to shoulder.

What to Do Before You Begin
- Review chapter twelve and make sure you understand the concepts being taught.
- Read this section and practice saying the suggested comments. Decide how you'll make the transition from one activity to the next.
- Before anyone arrives, hide the money somewhere in the room.
- Familiarize yourself with the student handout. Distribute the handout as the participants arrive.

Secret One: Recite less, respond more.

Say, **A good way to summarize this first storytelling secret is to say, "Practice makes . . ."** (Don't finish the sentence, instead let the participants call out "perfect!") Then say, **No, practice doesn't make perfect. Practice makes** *permanent.* **If you practice something the wrong way, you're not ever going to do it perfectly; you'll keep doing it wrong, every time. Forever!**

Discuss helpful ways to practice a story. Explain that style of story delivery should always depend on the *story,* the *storyteller,* and the *audience.* Point out that storytellers strive to respond to the audience rather than recite their story.

Secret Two: Concentrate less, relax more.

For this activity, you'll need a long rope—preferably just long enough for all the people in your workshop to hold onto it with both hands and be a little crowded as they do. Invite them to all take a place along the rope, then say, **I want you to pretend that all of you have super strong glue on your hands! From now on you can't slide them or remove them from the rope! Now—without sliding or removing your hands—I want you to see if you can, as a group, tie an overhand knot in the center of that rope. You'll have to move and work together! Let's begin!** If they don't know what an overhand knot is, tell them it's the knot you start with when you tie your shoes.

As the group begins, they'll think the job is easy, but it's not! Give your group about five to ten minutes to see how well they do. Then say, **Simple jobs that we do every day, like tying an overhand knot, are tough when you have to think about how you actually do them! We do them best naturally—when we concentrate too much we get confused!**

Explain that the same thing is true about storytelling. Rather than worrying about how your story should be going, relax, and focus on imagining the story.

Secret Three: Pretend less, believe more.

Tell everyone that somewhere, hidden in the room, is a one- (or five-) dollar bill. Say, **You have one minute to find the money. If you find it, you get to keep it. Ready? Go!** (To increase the excitement, count down the time. You could also increase the money to ten or twenty dollars!)

End when someone finds the money or your minute has elapsed. Then say, **Now, here is my question. How many of you were looking for that money?** (Allow them to respond.) **And how many of you were pretending to look for the money?** (Allow them to respond.) Then ask, **What's the difference?**

Discuss the difference between acting and doing. Is there a difference? What would give away that a person was only pretending rather than doing?

How does this apply to storytelling? Well, the more you believe the story you're sharing, the more real it'll become for the listener. It takes imagination to step into the story and picture the scenes in your mind. Say, **The moment you start pretending to be someone or something you're not, people can tell. The secret to making your stories powerful is to** *believe* **that they're happening. Pretend less and believe more!**

Secret Four: Explain less, evoke more.

Tell the story about the dancer found on page 91. Discuss how it applies to storytelling.

Say, **How many of you have ever heard a pastor tell a really gripping story as an illustration, and then spend the next twenty minutes draining all the impact out of it by explaining it? Very often, stories stand on their own. We do them a disservice by thinking we can add to them by explaining them. Draw a simple application from the story and move on. The students probably understand the point of the story better than you think. Don't overexplain it. Let the story do its job.**

Secret Five: Impress less, connect more.

Invite two volunteers forward. Explain that they're going to act out two little skits. Give them scenario number one:

Person one: You're trying to convince this police officer you weren't speeding.

Person two: You're a police officer who has heard all these excuses before.

The second scenario is:

Persons one and two are best friends talking on the phone trying to decide which video to rent.

Tell them just to make up the conversation and keep it going for about a minute. After they're finished, thank them and say, **We talk to people in different ways because we have different goals in different situations. Sometimes we converse, other times we perform.**

On the dry erase board, draw the continuum found on page 92 and describe the difference between performance and conversation. Explain how important it is to find the place on the continuum you're most comfortable with, and then to find storytelling situations that match your comfort level.

Closing Comments

Review the five secrets and then say, **As you implement these ideas and weave them into your storytelling, you'll find that your stories have more impact, resonance, and power than ever before.** Close with prayer.

Five Storytelling Secrets
Foolproof Ways to Improve Your Delivery

Secret One: Recite less, respond more.
- Practice makes _____ !
- _____ (content, truth, emotion) + _____ (goals, attitude, personality, style) + _____ (response, expectations, mood) = delivery.
- Notes:

Secret Two: Concentrate less, relax more.
- Let the story flow naturally.
- Spend more effort imagining and less effort worrying!
- Notes:

Secret Three: Pretend less, believe more.
- Believe the story is happening and respond to it.
- Let your gestures flow out of responding to the story rather than planning them and then rehearsing them.
- Notes:

Secret Four: Explain less, evoke more.
- Avoid the temptation to summarize and explain everything. There's always more to a story than its explanation.
- Focus more on telling the story well than on getting the point across. Trust the story and let the story speak for itself.
- Notes:

Secret Five: Impress less, connect more.
- Match the level of formality or informality in your storytelling to the level expected by your listeners.
- Understand the difference between conversation and performance.
- Notes:

Workshop Presenter Notes for

Story Stacking

Telling Stories the Way Jesus Did

Tips and Suggestions
- Feel free to adapt the ideas to fit the needs of the people at your workshop.

What You'll Need
- Photocopies of page 186 for each student.
- Photocopies of "Appendix C, 385 Story Starters" for each student.

What to Do Before You Begin
- Review chapter thirteen and make sure you understand the concepts being taught.
- Read this section and practice saying the suggested comments. Decide how you'll make the transition from one activity to the next.
- Familiarize yourself with the student handout. Distribute the handout as the participants arrive.

Introductory Activity

Practice reading the story below and pausing at the appropriate times. Assign parts to different groups of workshop participants. If you have a small group, just have three sections and leave out the "Fakes" group.

• The Princess and the Pea •
(A group refrain version of a story by Hans Christian Anderson)

Prince: *(pouting)* But I want a bride with sensitive skin! Humph!
Princess: *(yawning)* I need a good night's sleep.
Fakes: *(slyly)* Hey, cutie pie, wanna marry me?
Pea: *(singing)* All we are saying . . . is give peas a chance!

Once upon a time, there was a very picky *prince*. He wanted to get married, but not just to anyone. Oh no, his bride had to be a REAL *princess*, not an imposter, or a *fake*.

He searched and searched, but couldn't find the right woman. All the women he met who claimed to be of royal blood were *fakes*. He found *fake* after *fake* after *fake*!

Now, at that time in history, the ladies with the most tender skin of all were real *princesses*. Folks said they could even notice a single *pea* placed under their mattresses.

Well, one night, there was a terrible storm. And suddenly, someone was knocking on the castle door! She didn't look very impressive. She was dressed in rags and dripping wet. But she claimed to be a real *princess*!

The young man was thrilled! "But how can I know she's not a *fake?*" wondered the *prince.*

He decided on a test! Under twenty mattresses he placed a single *pea.* When the *prince* said goodnight to the *princess,* he went up to his room and she climbed to the top of the tower of mattresses. But all night long she tossed and turned and didn't get a single moment's rest—because even on all of those mattresses she was getting bruised by that tiny *pea!*

So, the next morning, they were married! And that *prince* and that *princess* lived happily ever after. Just like two *peas* in a pod.

And remember, that's a true story, not a *fake!*

Say, **Hey, great job! Now here's the question—can you think of a way we could use this story to teach a biblical truth?**

Allow them to respond. Then say, **What about the story of David's calling? Remember what Nathan said in 1 Samuel 16:7, "The Lord does not look at the things man looks at. Man looks at the outward appearance, but the Lord looks at the heart." You could tell the story of "The Princess and the Pea" and then the story of David's calling and weave them together since they both have a similar message! To tell a variety of stories that all have the same theme or imagery is called "Story Stacking." In this workshop, you'll learn to stack stories for more impact in your storytelling and your teaching.**

Step One: Find the thread of meaning.

Point out that Jesus often taught by piling one image on top of another. Give examples from your own observations or from the chapter. Then say, **We can use this technique in our storytelling as well. The first step is to find the thread of meaning in the story you're planning to tell. You might start with a Bible story and look for other stories with a similar theme; or you might have another story in mind that you'd like to tell, but don't have a biblical application for it yet. Either way is OK! Let's pretend we want to tell the story of "The Sleeping Beauty."**

As you highlight the steps listed below, feel free to use the example provided or, if you prefer, simply explain the process in your own words.

1. Explore the story. For example, if you were summarizing the story of "The Sleeping Beauty" you might say, **In this story, the careless princess pricks her finger and falls asleep until the prince awakens her by his kiss.**

2. Explore the parallels. Search for similarities between the story you're working on and Scripture. Then clarify the parallels in your own words. For example, in "The Sleeping Beauty"

- A wicked witch casts a spell on the princess. Like the princess, we've been cursed by sin.
- Thorns surround and imprison the princess. Thorns were the result of the fall into sin, and they were also used to wound Jesus. We are surrounded by thorny temptations, and are often pricked or gouged by sin.
- The people sleep one hundred years, unable to wake themselves. Like those people, we're spiritually asleep and unable to save ourselves.
- Many princes tried to get through the thorns, but failed. Like the princes, many good people have tried to rescue humanity apart from God, but have failed.
- After the prince's kiss, the spell is finally lifted. Because of Christ's love, the curse has been lifted and we can live happily ever after!

3. Craft your story. Restructure the folktale to highlight the changes you've made!

Step Two: Look for stories with similar themes.

Say, **Where can you find stories with themes that relate to the Bible stories you're teaching and telling? It's easier than you think! The secret is to search all of LIFE—that's L-I-F-E—to find them. LIFE contains a limitless well of stories to tell!**

As you explain the acronym, give examples of your own, or use some of those found in chapter thirteen.

L—Literature

I—Imagination

F—Folklore

E—Experience

As an example of folklore, tell or read the following story:

Once upon a time, a dog named Rover became friends with a wolf named Tim (short for Timber). Every day, Tim would visit Rover and they'd talk and play and romp in the yard. One day, Tim said, "Hey, why don't you come over to my house in the woods? We can play there!" But Rover replied, "Um . . . I can't come, I'm chained to a tree! But why don't you stay here with me?"

For the first time, Tim noticed the shiny chain that was attached to the dog's collar.

"Wow!" said Tim. "You can't leave the yard!"

"But it's worth it!" Rover said. "My owner brings me food and takes care of me. If you stick around maybe he'll give you a chain, too!"

"No thanks," Tim replied, trotting toward his forest home. "I'd rather be free and hungry than well fed and enslaved."

Then ask, **What images or biblical truths come to mind when you hear that version of one of Aesop's fables? What Bible stories do you think of?**

As an example of experience, explain that Jesus used examples from his personal life in his teaching and storytelling. Remember, Jesus was a carpenter! He told stories about unfinished building projects (Luke 14:28-30), the importance of finding a strong foundation for home construction (Matthew 7:24-27), and he even used the example of getting sawdust in your eye (Matthew 7:3-5)!

We can draw from personal experience in our storytelling as well. Hand out the copies of Appendix C and briefly discuss the ideas.

Step Three: Weave stories together into your lesson.

Explain that as you plan your teaching time, you can weave the stories together by adding brief comments or transitional thoughts between each story.

Discuss the advantages and drawbacks of using secular stories in your teaching. Is it wrong? Is it wise? When is it appropriate?

Closing Comments

Close by saying, **Today we've been studying "Story Stacking." Let's close by prayer stacking—each of us will add a short prayer for God's guidance and help in changing us into storytellers who are more and more like Jesus. I'll begin. Let's stand and hold hands.**

Story Stacking
Telling Stories the Way Jesus Did

You can use ancient and contemporary folklore, fables, myths, and legends in your lessons. Learn how to look beneath the surface to find applications to scriptural principles. Identify and solve the problems of using secular stories in your presentation.

Step One: Find the thread of meaning.

1. Explore the story. Ask yourself
   - What happens in this story?
   - What images or emotions are central to the story?
   - How would I summarize the action?
2. Explore the biblical parallels. Then clarify the parallels in your own words.
3. Craft your story. Restructure the folktale to highlight the changes you've made.

Step Two: Look for stories with similar themes.

L _____

I _____

F _____

E _____

For example, if your thread of meaning is faith, ask yourself
- What Bible stories deal with faith? How could I use them to help teach this truth?
- Are there other stories from literature that relate to this lesson?
- Could I create my own story to teach this lesson?
- What fables, folklore, myths, or legends deal with faith?
- What experiences from my own life teach lessons about faith (or lack of faith)?

Step Three: Weave stories together into your lesson.

As you plan your teaching time, remember that you want the audience to be focused and attentive until the very end. Generally, if you're including a series of stories, have the Bible story be the last one you tell. That way, the other stories point in the direction of the lesson and you can end with the biblical application.

Advanced Skills and Techniques

Reaching for Excellence

Tips and Suggestions
- Feel free to adapt the ideas to fit the needs of the people at your workshop.
- Be sure your participants know this is an advanced workshop for experienced story-tellers. Take this time to really challenge people to grow and pursue excellence in their work!

What You'll Need
- Photocopies of pages 190, 191 for each student.

What to Do Before You Begin
- Review chapter fourteen and make sure you understand the concepts being taught.
- Read this section and practice saying the suggested comments. Decide how you'll make the transition from one activity to the next.
- Familiarize yourself with the student handouts. Distribute the handouts at the end of the workshop.

Introductory Activity
Share the painting story found on page 98 and emphasize how we should use our gifts to God's glory rather than our own. Say, **We should give God our best, without holding anything back or making excuses. In this workshop, you'll be challenged to grow as a storyteller by studying eight skill areas for advanced storytellers.**

Skill One: Make the most of silence and stillness.
Divide into pairs. Explain that, in a moment, one of the people in each group will tell her partner a story but will have to pause whenever her partner raises her finger! Tell people to raise their fingers at weird times! Try it out and have fun. Then switch roles and repeat. Have each storyteller share the story about how she met (or didn't meet) the love of her life.

Say, **Knowing when to pause and where to pause are important skills for a storyteller to acquire. Can you think of a time when a storyteller should pause? What happens if you pause too long? How can a storyteller predict how long to pause?**

Explore and explain other points brought out in chapter fourteen related to silence and stillness.

Skill Two: Sustain the suspense by postponing the resolution.
Discuss how unenjoyable a mystery novel would be if someone told you "who-dun-it" before you started reading, or how unexciting a pre-recorded ballgame would be if someone told you who won before you could watch it. Say, **Don't give away the ending until the end. Sustain the suspense!**

Discuss how to sustain the suspense and increase the interest of your listeners.

You may wish to add, **By the way, if you ever choose to tell scary stories (and a good number of stories in Scripture are scary!) don't leave your students frightened or fearful. Rather, show them resolution and closure.**

Skill Three: Use the stage area to your advantage.

Invite people to stand up and mirror your actions. If you stretch your hands high, so do they. Explore levels (high, low, and medium), movement styles, etc. Then choose a new leader and have that person lead different movements.

Mention that storytellers sometimes don't use their space as well as actors do. Say, **As you explore your story, try to really explore how you can use space to your advantage.**

Then pretend to be shopping. Tell everyone to push an imaginary shopping cart and look for their favorite food along the imaginary aisles. Say, **Be careful not to run into anyone else with your cart!** After people have found their favorite food, have them take it off the shelf, put it in their carts, push their carts around, and then return and put the food back in the exact same place on the shelf!

Say, **When you create an imaginary world for your audience, it's important to remember where everything is! Be consistent or you'll confuse your audience.**

Skill Four: Mean more than what you say.

Point out that in the Song of Songs, Solomon used lots of imagery to deepen the romantic undertones of the song. Ask for examples of imagery he used to hint at and express the beauty of sexual intimacy.

Say, **When you use images, you can mean more than what you say. Enjoy and celebrate the language, but experience the images. See the story as it is told. Be drawn to the images, not the words.**

If desired, discuss humor: What makes a story funny? Are people funny when they try to be funny? Why or why not? React to the statement, "You understand a culture when you understand what makes it laugh." Explain that often, humor is truth exaggerated, with all of its possibilities and absurdities explored.

Have a volunteer tell a personal story or joke and then ask, **What were some of the events in the story that were true? Which events were probably exaggerated? Were they humorous? Why or why not?**

Skill Five: Translate words into sounds.

Ask if anyone in the room knows a foreign language. If so, ask her to explain some of the problems of translating from one language to another. Then explain that changing a written story into a told story is really a process of translating from the language of print to the language of voice.

Take the sentence, "I didn't say you are ugly." Have six different people say it, each one emphasizing a different word in the sentence. Point out that the sentence can mean six different things as each of the different words is emphasized!

Skill Six: Choose your sounds carefully.

Talk about the difference between using lots of adjectives and adverbs, or using nouns and verbs. Which style sounds more natural? Which sounds more performed?

Discuss how to create believable and realistic-sounding dialogue. Discuss how dialogue between characters in a literary (written story) nearly always involves words like "he said," and "she said." Ask, **Is this necessary in a told story? Why or why not? What are the other ways that the storyteller identifies who is speaking?**

Skill Seven: Communicate without talking.

Discuss the impression you would give by wearing a three-piece polyester suit, having lots of body piercings, or wearing sandals and a tie-dyed shirt.

Discuss how clothing, appearance, movement, proximity to audience, and the use of the stage area affect the impressions of your listeners. Point out that unconscious gestures (playing with your hair, putting your hands in your pockets, rolling up your sleeves) all communicate something to the audience.

Skill Eight: Create richer and deeper characters.

Explore how you could express these characteristics through action, dialogue, and vivid description: "Goliath was mean," "Jesus cared for others," and "Judas was dishonest."

Have everyone stand up, create a character with their bodies (the way they stand, move, and look) and then say, **In character, pretend that you've lost something, go looking for it, and then find it.**

Practice as a group, and then have volunteers perform this search individually. Observe and learn by watching people transform themselves into characters!

Closing Activity

If time permits, discuss the handouts. Or, have each partner tell a story and then encourage the storytellers to go through the handouts together and discuss how each person could improve. Close with prayer.

Advanced Skills and Techniques
Reaching for Excellence

Skill One: Make the most of silence and stillness.
- When do my pauses and silences seem awkward? Where should I add more silence or stillness?
- Does the pace contradict what's going on in the story? In other words, am I speaking quickly and slowly at the right times?
- Does the rate, rhythm, speed, and timing of my story help build excitement at the right times in the story? If not, what changes do I need to make?

Skill Two:
Sustain the suspense by postponing the resolution.
- Have I given too much away too early? If so, how can I change what I say or do to sustain the suspense?
- Does the story take too long to set up? How can I grab the attention of the listeners by introducing the struggle earlier in the story? Is the ending strong and clear?
- If I were listening to this story for the first time, would I get bored? If so, why? What needs to change to grab and keep the listeners' attention?

Skill Three: Use the stage area to your advantage.
- Am I using all of my stage area? If not, does this story provide natural opportunities to use more movement or gestures? How can I use more of my space onstage?
- Am I consistent in the way I represent characters and in how I relate to the imaginary world I create onstage? If not, what do I need to change?
- Am I standing in the best place onstage for people to see me? Is the lighting good? Is the attention of the audience directed toward me? If not, what do I need to change to make the most of the lighting and stage placement?

Skill Four: Mean more than what you say.
- Do I use strong images in my stories? If not, can I include more image-rich language? What images come to mind when I think of this story? Is there a way to naturally weave these images into the way I tell this story?
- How well did I use inflection to communicate meaning? How could I improve and clarify the meaning I wish to portray by subtly changing my inflection?
- What can I learn from Jesus about using images in my stories and my teaching? How can I begin to see more parallels between biblical truth and everyday objects?

Skill Five: Translate words into sounds.

- Have I done a good job of translating this story from words to sounds?
- Does my story sound canned, or spontaneous? How can I better express spontaneity in this story?
- Does it sound like I'm reading a script, or telling a story? What do I need to change to make the story sound more natural and less rehearsed?

Skill Six: Choose your sounds carefully.

- Have I used strong nouns and verbs in my story? Have I chosen the right words to use? Have I prepared my introduction to the story? How will I make it clear when the introduction is over and my story begins?
- Is the message of my story clear? Have I produced the effect I was aiming for? If not, why not? What do I need to add, change, or delete from my story to produce the effect I'm aiming for? Was this story appropriate for my audience?
- If I used foreshadowing, have I related back to that image or idea at the end of the story? It not, how can I bring that idea back into focus?

Skill Seven: Communicate without talking.

- What impression will my clothes and appearance give to the audience? Is that the impression I want to give?
- How will the proximity of the stage and the amount of lighting affect the audience's expectations of my story? Is this what I want? If not, what will I do?
- Do I appear confident and prepared? Am I nervous or relaxed? Do I rock back and forth, or am I still and composed? Do I have any annoying habits that distract from the story? How can I eliminate those? What will I do instead when I'm nervous?

Skill Eight: Create richer and deeper characters.

- Are my characters believable? If I use different voices or posture to portray different characters, are they consistent? If I use dialect, am I slipping out of dialect or keeping it going through the whole story?
- How am I expressing emotions—through my body, face, or voice? Am I physically eloquent?
- Do I tell people what the characters were like, or do I show them? How can I improve the way I create and portray my characters?

Workshop Presenter Notes for

Making the Story Stick

Eighty Ideas for Applying any Bible Story

How to Lead This Unique Workshop

1) Choose eight creative activities from chapter fifteen and gather the necessary objects.
2) Photocopy the entire chapter and give it to your workshop participants.
3) Mention that many of these ideas will work best with older students. (They were written with third through sixth grade students in mind.)
4) Discuss ways to transfer these ideas to other lessons or stories.
5) Demonstrate the eight activities you've selected.
6) Close with prayer.